Financial Literacy in Europe

Are people ready to make pivotal financial decisions like choosing a mortgage, saving for retirement, or investing their savings? How does the degree of knowledge about financial products and services affect the quality of their choices? Can financial fraud be prevented by increasing consumer financial knowledge?

Financial Literacy in Europe addresses these important questions and more. In the first part, the author investigates the concept of financial literacy by analyzing its components and comparing different definitions from previous studies. This then forms a comprehensive measure of financial literacy to be applied in empirical studies that analyze the role of financial literacy in explaining consumers' financial behaviors. In the second part of the study, the author uses brand new data collected by the Consumer Finance Research Center (CFRC) from several European countries (the UK, Germany, France, Italy, Sweden, and Spain) to assess financial literacy in Europe and highlight similarities and differences across countries.

Filling an important gap in previous research, the author develops a rigorous approach in the measurement of financial literacy in order to examine European financial literacy issues in great detail. This book, therefore, is a useful resource for assessing the effectiveness of single financial education programs or planning national strategies on financial education. It can also support policy makers in developing financial regulation and consumer protection strategies, considering the consumer perspective and their ability to deal with financial markets and institutions.

Gianni Nicolini is Associate Professor of Finance at the University of Rome "Tor Vergata" (Department of Management and Law). His main research interest is Consumer Finance, with a special interest in Financial Literacy and Financial Education. In 2016 he established, with other researchers, the Consumer Finance Research Center (CFRC) with the aim to develop high quality research on consumer issues.

Routledge International Studies in Money and Banking

For more information about this series, please visit: www.routledge.com/
series/SE0403

Financial Literacy in Europe

Assessment Methodologies and Evidence from European Countries

Gianni Nicolini

Routledge
Taylor & Francis Group

LONDON AND NEW YORK

First published 2019
by Routledge
2 Park Square, Milton Park, Abingdon, Oxon OX14 4RN

and by Routledge
52 Vanderbilt Avenue, New York, NY 10017

First issued in paperback 2020

Routledge is an imprint of the Taylor & Francis Group, an informa business

British Library Cataloguing-in-Publication Data
A catalogue record for this book is available from the British Library

Library of Congress Cataloging-in-Publication Data
Names: Nicolini, Gianni, 1976– author.
Title: Financial literacy in Europe : assessment methodologies and evidence
   from European countries / Gianni Nicolini.
Description: Abingdon, Oxon; New York, NY : Routledge, 2019. | Series:
   Routledge international studies in money and banking | Includes
   bibliographical references.
Identifiers: LCCN 2018049164 | ISBN 9781138362611 (hardback) |
   ISBN 9780429431968 (ebook)
Subjects: LCSH: Financial literacy—Europe. | Finance, Personal—Europe.
Classification: LCC HG179 .N5335 2019 | DDC 332.0240094—dc23
LC record available at https://lccn.loc.gov/2018049164

ISBN 13: 978-0-367-66228-8 (pbk)
ISBN 13: 978-1-138-36261-1 (hbk)

Typeset in Bembo
by Apex CoVantage, LLC

To all those who do research caring about the consumer's perspective.

Contents

Foreword

This book provides a comprehensive overview of financial literacy in Europe. It starts with an in-depth analysis of the definition and measurement of financial literacy, providing an excellent overview of the methodologies that have been used to measure financial literacy and the strengths and weaknesses of current measures. It next examines the links between financial literacy and financial behavior, implicitly going after the very important question of whether financial literacy matters in explaining financial decision making and how much. In the second part, the book provides an analysis of financial literacy in Europe. This part starts with an overview of the findings from two important projects, the Programme for International Student Assessment (PISA) and the OECD-International Network for Financial Education (INFE) study. It then provides an analysis of financial literacy in six countries, the UK, Germany, France, Italy, Spain, and Sweden. Using data from the Consumer Finance Research Center, the book reports a thorough analysis of the characteristics and determinants of financial literacy for each country.

This is one of my favorite books about financial literacy for three main reasons. First, the attention to measurement issues about financial literacy is enormously important. We cannot study financial literacy without a deep understanding of how financial literacy is measured and how it should be measured. Any serious analysis should start with measurement. Having spent a large part of my research dealing with measuring financial literacy for both young and old people, I highly appreciate the attention and care devoted to measurement issues. This topic is even more important when dealing with financial literacy across countries; the measurement should refer to a definition that is applicable to different contexts. This is the second reason for why there is a lot to like about this book. The analysis of financial literacy across countries is not only important but very informative. The information about financial literacy is very rich – it is measured using a set of 50 questions on ten different financial topics. It is from this analysis, for example, that one discovers that findings about financial literacy are surprisingly similar across countries. It is also possible to understand a lot more about the findings for a specific country. For example, the gender difference in financial literacy documented in the book becomes a lot more salient when one sees that differences in financial literacy between women and men are not only large but also present in all countries. A third reason I enjoyed very much reading this book is the attention devoted to the PISA data and the OECD-INFE International Survey of Adult Financial Literacy Competencies. PISA is a truly visionary project. The addition of the financial literacy assessment in 2012 to the information that PISA normally collects about the skills that 15-year-olds need to be able to participate in society is enormously important. The data that the OECD-INFE has promoted to measure financial literacy among adults across countries are also a very important addition to the data that exist so far. However, these data are still underutilized, and it is my hope that this book will help promote the use of these data.

Most importantly, this book can provide important information to practitioners, policy makers, the financial and pension industry, and everyone interested in promoting financial literacy. It is clear from the rich evidence provided in each chapter that individuals are not well equipped with the skills that are needed to be able to thrive in today's complex economic environment. This is particularly true for some demographic groups whose financial literacy is particularly low, such as women, the young, and those with low educational attainment. The findings provided in the book offer suggestions on ways we can improve financial literacy and the groups we should target to be effective.

I would like to conclude with a mention of Italy, which is one of the six countries covered in the book. The information provided in Chapter 7 is not only very useful but also timely. A new Financial Education Committee has been created in Italy with the objective to increase both financial literacy and financial capability among Italians. As Director of the Committee, I will use this important work to inform the programs that we plan to implement in Italy.

In summary, this is an important book covering the most important topics related to financial literacy, from measurement issues to the evidence in six major countries in Europe. It is a must read for those who are interested in a comprehensive analysis of financial literacy using micro data, and those interested in understanding how we can promote financial literacy across countries. I have learned a lot by reading this work, and I plan to apply that learning in my own research and field work as well.

As we say in Italy *"buona lettura"*.

Annamaria Lusardi
Denit Trust Chair of Economics and Accountancy, the
George Washington University School of Business
Director, Italian Financial Education Committee

Acknowledgements

This book is the result of interaction and the sharing of ideas with many researchers from different universities and research institutes. I thank all of them for their comments and suggestions and for the time they have spent in our conversations during conferences, face to face meeting, and by emails.

First of all, thanks to the anonymous reviewers for their precious contribution to the final release of this book.

A special thank you to the members of the American Council on Consumer Interest (ACCI) for being an amazing research community and for the opportunity to keep in touch with awesome consumer finance researchers during the ACCI annual conferences. Thanks to the Kompetenzzentrum Verbraucherforschung Nordrhein-Westfalen for organizing the 2014 and 2016 International Conference on Consumer Research (ICCR), where the seminal idea of this research comes from.

Thanks to the Unione Nazionale Consumatori (UNC), and particularly to its President Avv. Massimiliano Dona, for the support in the preliminary tests of the questionnaire used to collect the data of this study. Thanks to the IEF – Instituto de Estudios Financieros – of Barcelona (Spain) for the support in the data collection in Spain. In this case a special thank you goes to Josep Soler Alberti (Director of IEF), Jordi Martínez Llorente (Director of the Financial Education programs at IEF), and Laura Rincón Pérez (SCR program coordinator).

A fundamental contribution came from all the colleagues of the Consumer Finance Research Center (CFRC) without which support the data analyzed in this study would never have been collected. So, thanks to Tommy Gärling, Jeanette Hauff, and Anders Carlander from the University of Gothenburg (Gothenburg, Sweden), Luc Arrondel (PSE – Paris School of Economics – Paris, France), Darren Duxbury (Newcastle University Business School, Newcastle, UK), Simon McNair (Leeds University Business School, Leeds, UK), Rob Ranyard (Leeds University Business School, Leeds, UK), and Marlene Haupt (Hochschule Ravensburg-Weingarten, Weingarten, Germany).

Thanks to Annamaria Lusardi (George Washington University and GFLEC – Global Financial Literacy Excellence Center) for her fundamental contributions to the financial literacy studies, for the precious conversations we had in the last years, and for supporting me in many ways in doing my research.

A special thank you goes to Brenda Cude (University of Georgia Athens, Athens, USA) and to Alessandro Carretta (University of Rome "Tor Vergata", Rome, Italy) for being unique mentors: thanks for your guidance and for being a continuous source of learning and inspiration.

Introduction

As with any research study (especially in the case of a book), a study on financial literacy has to deal with the fundamental question concerning the need of the study. Financial literacy regards how much people know about finance, their skills about making a financial decision, as well as their attitude in dealing with financial issues. Under the assumption that the more people are financially literate the more they will be ready to manage their finances and plan for their future, a study on financial literacy can be motivated by the will to investigate how much people are ready to play as aware financial consumers. However, the answer to this question passes by other questions related to the financial knowledge that an individual needs to know in order to make an effective financial decision, and how we can assess the financial literacy of an individual. These are research questions of this study, but before trying to answer these questions there is a preliminary question to be addressed that regards the timing of the study and the reason why a study on financial literacy in Europe is needed now. How much people know about finance, how their knowledge affects their financial behaviors, and what are the possible consequences that different behaviors can have for single persons as well as for a financial system are interesting research questions with relevant implications, but there are several reasons why these questions are today more relevant than in the past, and that explain why financial literacy is now more critical than before.

The need to know about finance in order to manage money in everyday life (e.g. the use of cash and other payments facilities in order to buy goods) and to adjust consumption in an intertemporal perspective by borrowing or investing is not new. In history people have had to manage their finances since the concept of money was developed and the use of money replaced a barter economy. The need to know about finance and the amount of knowledge required to participate in a financial system have dramatically increased in the past years, even if we compare the present with just one or two decades ago. What is new is the number of times we have to make a financial decision, the relevance of these decisions (taking into account the possible consequences of these choices), and the complexity of such decisions. All of these changes make the knowledge and the skills needed to make an aware financial decision definitely much more advanced than before.

A few examples can help to highlight how much the need for financial literacy has increased with passing time. After reform, the welfare state in several developed countries no longer offers a standard public pension system based on a mandatory enrolment and a defined-benefit contribution scheme. The new pension systems, based on a "multi-pillars" scheme, require workers to be active and plan for their retirement by estimating the future pay off of the defined-contribution public pension systems and fill the gap in their retirement goals by contributing to pension funds and to individual retirement plans. The potential lack of knowledge about the functioning of the new pension systems is itself a source of worry that stresses the need to be financially literate. At the same time it is not hard to figure out how much the complexity of pension planning increased after the pension systems reforms in most of the developed countries started in the late '90s.

Investment is another area where the need for knowledge required to make a financial decision has been boosted. The interest rates paid on deposits by banks have dramatically dropped in the last 15 years with the consequence of leaving banks to deal with financial risks and just take a (small) profit from their liquidity before it disappears. In the meantime strategies of the central banks in the post financial crisis era – based on very low interest rates – and after the sovereign debt crisis that caused a downgrade for several (former) triple-A rated countries changed the investor perspective of Government bonds as a safe- and easy-profit investment option. In this new scenario investors approach more sophisticated investment solutions and are called to choose between a wide range of financial products. The need to understand, compare, and select the different available investment options is other evidence that the financial knowledge and skills required to make a financial decision today are much more sophisticated than just a few years ago.

The credit market and the use of debt by households are today more different than in the recent past. The socio-cultural changes in some countries, where the use of debt for purposes not related to homeownership or a few other exceptions (e.g. auto-loans), which represented in the past a stigma and inhibited the development of the consumer credit market, have seen the use of debt and the number of available options bloom. The general growth of household debt, the approach of a new credit market, and the use of different credit products (e.g. revolving credit line, pawn loans, etc.) have increased the financial literacy required to deal with credit providers, as well as the risk of misusing credit and the risk of overindebtedness.

In this new scenario individuals who were previously able to manage their finances and satisfy their financial needs with their essential knowledge about basic financial principles are not able anymore to deal with the market because their financial knowledge and skills are no longer enough to play in a more complex financial system. In the meantime the new financial framework could require actions that were not necessary in the old system (e.g. the need to plan for retirement). Unawareness about the new system can see people rely on the old set of rules without understanding the need to change their financial behaviors (e.g. start saving for retirement and not relying anymore only on the public pension).

These changes in the financial systems happened in a relatively short period of time and require – from a research perspective – to check how much financial knowledge consumers have and test their abilities to make effective financial decisions.

If financial literacy is crucial from a micro-perspective, it is even more interesting from a macro point of view. A financial consumer who is not able to fully understand a financial product can decide to "do nothing", remaining out of the financial system and facing all the negative consequences of the financial exclusion. Otherwise an individual has to "trust" the counterpart of a trade, relying on proxies such as the brand of the financial company (e.g. banks, asset managers, etc.) or the personal feeling the individual has toward the physical counterpart (e.g. bank employees, financial advisors, etc.) with the risk of misinterpreting the characteristics of the financial product or becoming the potential victim of a financial fraud. In such a scenario the need for heavy regulation and strong supervision of the financial system becomes greater. Moreover lack of confidence with some financial products can inhibit individual behaviors even outside the financial system. The chance to be part of an e-commerce transaction (as either a buyer or a seller) for the unbanked or for individuals who do not rely on plastic cards (e.g. credit cards, debit cards, pre-paid cards) is almost null, with the consequence – as a buyer – of not allowing them to shop around and restricting the purchase of a good or a service to a limited set of providers, and the consequence – as a seller – of not having access to a potential new marketplace.

If there are several arguments supporting the need to study financial literacy, this book wants to contribute to the existing knowledge on financial literacy in different manners. The literature review presents and summarizes in a single comprehensive output the state of the art of financial literacy studies, trying **to propose the evolution of research in this field on a systematic basis**. The analysis of the available methodologies to assess financial literacy allows this book **to stress the pro and cons of each measure of financial literacy**, providing methodological insights for future empirical studies (e.g. questionnaire design, survey planning, etc.). A third contribution to financial literacy studies concerns the need to **assess financial literacy using a reasonable number of items** and the need to **keep in mind that the results in the assessment of financial literacy can change a lot when different financial topics are taken into account**. A fourth and fundamental contribution of this study concerns the **empirical measurement of financial literacy in Europe**. The chance to analyze financial literacy by several measures at the same time, taking into account financial knowledge on a wide range of financial topics, offers a unique perspective on the financial literacy of European households. The high quality data collected by the Consumer Finance Research Center (CFRC) offer a unique chance to provide the big picture of financial literacy in the main European countries (the UK, Germany, Italy, France, Spain, and Sweden).

The study is organized in two parts.

The first part is about the methodological issues involved in the assessment of financial literacy. Starting from a detailed analysis of the concepts behind financial literacy, a review of the literature allows a clear definition of financial literacy, stressing what should be included in the core elements of this topic and what should not. In the same part the study analyzes the measurement of financial literacy and the connection between financial literacy and different financial behaviors.

The second part of the study is about financial literacy in Europe. The analysis starts from the results of previous studies, with a special focus on the results of studies promoted by international organizations (OECD, INFE). The further chapters analyze the cases of single European countries according to a standard approach that starts from the presentation of different descriptive statistics of national sample data and provide the results of empirical statistical methodologies used to analyze the determinants of financial literacy. The explanatory power of the main socio-demographic characteristics of individuals (e.g. age, gender, education, income, etc.) has been tested with different regression models. The main results of the study are summarized in the conclusions.

Part I

Financial literacy

A theoretical framework and evidence from previous studies

1 Financial literacy

Definition and measurement

1.1 Financial literacy: a definition

In a study on financial literacy a clear definition of its meaning and understanding of its constructs are pivotal issues, regardless of the aim of the study and the analysis proposed. A definition of financial literacy requires pinpointing the key elements and the peculiarities that make it different from other similar (but different) concepts. The lack of a clear definition paves the way to misunderstanding about what should be taken into account and measured in order to analyze the role of financial literacy in explaining other phenomena, with the risk of testing the relevance of financial literacy by a misleading yardstick.

From the dictionaries

A starting point to develop a definition of financial literacy can be the semantic analysis of the words "financial" and "literacy". The meaning of each word will contribute to shaping the meaning of financial literacy itself. The definition of "literacy" in the Oxford English Dictionary is "*the ability to read and write*" and "*competence or knowledge in specific area*". The same dictionary reports for "financial" "*relating to finance*", where "finance" means "*the management of (large amounts of) money, especially by governments or large companies*". Matching these word definitions, financial literacy can be defined as "competence or knowledge in the management of money". Even though this definition includes the essence of financial literacy, this is not enough to distinguish financial literacy from other concepts and cannot be used as a reference point in a research study.

As the Oxford English Dictionary reports that (1) "economy" is "*the state of a country or region in terms of the production and consumption of goods and services and the supply of money*", (2) "economic" is something "*relating to economics or the economy*", and (3) "economics" is "*the branch of knowledge concerned with the production, consumption, and transfer of wealth*", the distance between the concepts of "financial" and "economic" suggests that the former refers to the use of money, and the latter to production, consumption, and transfer of goods, services, and wealth.

From this basic conceptual explanation it follows that "financial literacy" and "economic literacy" represent different constructs and should not be used interchangeably.

From previous studies

Bearing in mind that the key concepts in financial literacy should be (1) knowledge and (2) competence about (3) the use of money, an analysis of the definition adopted in previous studies will help to build a comprehensive definition of financial literacy by an examination of other elements.

In one of the first studies on financial literacy Noctor et al. (1992) refer to financial literacy as "*the ability to make informed judgements and to make effective decisions regarding the use and management of money*". This definition starts from the ability (competence) but makes a step forward pointing out how financial literacy should be related to making financial decisions. If the word "knowledge" is not mentioned in this definition, it can be argued that it is included by default. If knowledge and competence are different concepts a hierarchic connection between them can be stated due to the fact that knowledge represents a sort of pre-requisite to develop competence, where "competence" means the ability to apply knowledge on practical issues to solve a problem or make a decision. Hence, if it is possible to have knowledge and not be able to apply it (competence), the opposite is not possible, due to the fact that you cannot apply knowledge that you do not have. It follows that, including competence, the definition of Noctor et al. (1992) assumes the relevance of knowledge too and includes the three basic elements of financial literacy: knowledge, competence, and the use of money.

Similar definitions, based on the concept of "ability", were used by Mandell (2008), for whom "*financial literacy refers to the ability of consumers to make financial decision in their own best short and long term interest*", and Servon and Kaestner (2008), for whom "*Financial literacy refers to a person's ability to understand and make use of financial concepts*". Within this first set of definitions, the one of Noctor et al. (1992) is closer than others to the aforementioned word-by-word analysis of financial literacy and suggests the need to refer to financial literacy as a decision making process. This definition was used in several other studies such as Schagen and Lines (1996), Beal and Delpachitra (2003), ANZ (2008), Atkinson and Kempson (2008), and Worthington (2013). In their study Schagen and Lines (1996) tried to figure out which abilities related to the "use of money" have to be considered, arriving at the conclusion that (1) the understanding of key concepts central to money management and (2) a working knowledge of financial institutions, systems, and services are the main abilities to develop in order to be financially literate. In Bowen (2003) there is an attempt to specify the skills within the "use of money". The author talks about financial knowledge "*as the understanding of key financial terms and concepts needed to function daily in American society*", saying that "*it includes knowledge about items related to banking-checking and savings, auto-life-health and homeowners insurance, using credit, taxes, and investing*".

For Vitt et al. (2000) financial literacy is "*the ability to read, analyze, manage and communicate about the personal financial conditions that affect material wellbeing*". Referring to "reading", "analyzing", and "managing", the authors develop the concept of "competence" in specific areas, all related to the use of information. The key role of information as the input of a financial decision making process is quite evident in Mason and Wilson (2000). For these authors financial literacy is "*an individual's ability to obtain, understand and evaluate the relevant information necessary to make decisions with an awareness of the likely financial consequences*". The words "ability" and "understand" recall "competence" and "knowledge" even if the need for access to financial information introduces a new issue and highlights how much knowledge and competences risk being meaningless in a scenario where information is not available. The same issue is stressed by Johnson and Sherraden (2006), who note how the application of knowledge and competence requires access to financial information and financial institutions.

The need to analyze financial literacy in a decision making framework – implicit in the definition of Vitt et al. (2000) – is even more clear in Danes and Haberman (2007), where "*financial literacy is the ability to interpret, communicate, compute, develop independent judgment, and take actions resulting from those processes in order to thrive in our complex financial world*".

If financial literacy should be related to both knowledge and competence, some studies paid more attention to "knowledge", as Kim (2001) did reporting that "*financial literacy is a basic knowledge that people need in order to survive in a modern society*". Similarly the FINRA (2003) adopted a definition of financial literacy as "*the understanding* [knowledge] *ordinary investors have of market principles, instruments, organizations and regulations*". The NCEE (2005) also addresses a pivotal role of knowledge in its definition of financial literacy as "*familiarity with basic economic principles, knowledge about the U.S. economy, and understanding of some key economic terms*". Lusardi and Tufano (2015) defined financial literacy as "*familiarity with the most basic economic concepts needed to make sensible saving and investment decisions*", and Almenberg and Widmark (2011a) refer to financial literacy as "*familiarity with basic financial concepts and products*". Again, Lusardi (2009b) talks about financial literacy as "*the knowledge of basic financial concepts*". Definitions of financial literacy merely shaped around financial knowledge and, on a general basis, studies that use financial knowledge as a proxy of financial literacy are typically the result of the need to fill the gap between available data – usually on financial knowledge – and the information needed, which involves financial skills and competences too. If the need to cope with the lack of data by using financial knowledge for measuring financial literacy is reasonable, a rearrangement of the definition of financial literacy itself that ignores financial abilities and refers simply to financial knowledge is not. Reshaping financial literacy to make it fit with data can have positive effects on the consistency of results in empirical analysis, but risks extending conclusions from knowledge to competence assuming that a broader knowledge involves broader competence, even when people could be confident in answering a test about knowledge but not as confident in making a financial decision. So, a definition of financial literacy should refer to both knowledge and competence (on financial issues), keeping in mind that financial literacy should be assessed within a financial decision process, even if difficulties in measuring all these aspects can necessitate the use of proxies.

The need to stress the different roles of knowledge and ability in financial literacy is evident in different studies. Moore (2003) highlights how individuals can be considered financially literate if they are competent and can demonstrate they used knowledge they have learned. Huston (2010), in a study that reviewed more than 70 studies, arrived at the conclusion that "*financial literacy consists of both knowledge and application* [ability] *of human capital specific to personal finance*". Knowledge and competences are included in a definition as different concepts by the Jumpstart Coalition (2007), and the US Financial Literacy and Education Commission (FLEC) (2007) defined financial literacy as "*the ability to use knowledge and skills* [competence] *to manage financial resources* [money] *effectively for a lifetime of financial well-being*".[1] This last definition clearly includes the three key elements of financial literacy (knowledge, competence, and the use of money), matching the core meaning of these topics. If financial literacy is related to the achievement of financial goals (the "use of money"), the awareness that different goals require different financial knowledge and abilities was included in a definition of financial literacy by Remund (2010) that takes into account both the short-term and the long-term perspectives of the decision making process. We gather from his study that "*financial literacy is a measure of the degree to which one understands key financial concepts* [knowledge] *and possesses the ability and confidence to manage personal finances* [money] *through appropriate, short-term decision-making and sound, long-range financial planning, while mindful of life events and changing economic conditions*".

Financial literacy and financial capability

The need to build a definition of financial literacy including knowledge, abilities, and money does not imply that these topics have to be the only ones.

If financial literacy starts with knowledge, passes by abilities, and arrives at (effective) financial decisions, the chance that other issues could affect this process has to be taken into account and should be included in a more comprehensive definition of financial literacy. Beal and Delpachitra (2003) noted how financial knowledge and competences (skills) can be neutralized by a lack of attitude in the management of financial affairs. A financial background based on a theoretical approach to finance, without the self-confidence to make a financial decision (the so called "attitude"), could make people unable to apply their knowledge and skills in real terms, failing to complete a decision making process. The role of attitude in making decisions is stressed by Atkinson and Messy (2012), for whom "*financial literacy is a combination of knowledge, attitude and behaviour*", and is clear in ASIC (2013), which reports how financial literacy cannot be just related to knowledge and skills, but should take into account even people's attitudes.

If the relevance of attitude in making financial decision is clear, its inclusion within the fundamental concepts of financial literacy is not as clear. Part of the literature supports a definition of financial literacy as a combination of knowledge and skills, referring to attitude and behaviors as part of a broader concept, which includes basic knowledge and abilities, and is called "financial capability". From this point of view financial literacy and financial capability are different concepts, with the latter including the former as a part of it, and should not be used as synonymous. Other studies tend to use the two terms interchangeably under the assumption that the differences between their constructs are limited.

One of the first studies on financial capability was made by the Financial Service Authority (FSA) in the UK (FSA 2005). The study proposes a definition of financial capability based on (1) knowledge and understanding, (2) skills, and (3) confidence and attitudes on financial issues. Attitude differs from knowledge and skills for the ability to make informed decisions regarding personal circumstances, filling the gap between theory and practice. Confidence and attitudes are related to the ability to gather information, the willingness to invest time and other resources to apply knowledge and exercise skills (being aware about the chance to receive advice from others), and the confidence to act on the results. So, the main difference between financial literacy and financial capability involves the ability to make a financial decision in real terms using information from the market. The broader meaning of financial capability is reported by Fessler et al. (2007). In their study financial literacy emphasizes knowledge, understanding, and awareness, while financial capability stresses the relevance of consumer behavior, decision making, and practical abilities. The Central Bank of Ireland (O'Donnell and Keeney 2009) used a financial capability definition as "*knowledge, skills, attitudes and behaviors necessary to manage personal finances and to choose and make appropriate use of financial products*". The study of O'Donnell and Keene (2009) is consistent with the previous definitions, reporting that financial literacy is a narrower concept than financial capability, focused more on knowledge and skills and less on behavior. The difference in behaviors should see capable consumers plan ahead, find and use information, know when to seek advice, and be able to understand and act on this advice. Similarly for Lusardi (2010) and Lusardi and Mitchell (2011) financial capability is "*how well people make ends meet, plan ahead, choose and manage financial products, and possess the skills and knowledge to make financial decisions*". The need to use personal knowledge and skills in the real world is highlighted by Huang et al. (2013) when they note how the concept of financial capability captures the relationship between people's internal ability and their external environments, while Xiao et al. (2013) report that "*financial capability refers to people's ability to manage and take control of their finances*". A definition of financial capability has been developed by the World Bank (2013) too, for which financial capability is "*the internal capacity to act in one's best financial interest given socioeconomic environmental conditions; it therefore encompasses the knowledge, attitudes, skills and behaviors of consumers with regard to managing their resources and understanding, selecting and making use of financial services that fit their needs*". In the same study it is stressed how financial literacy, as "*knowledge and awareness of financial concepts and products*", refers only to one aspect of financial capability.

In an effort to set some reference points before going forward in this study, it can be argued that financial capability is a wider concept than financial literacy from what differs for caring of 'financial attitude', representing the psychological status that makes people feel more or less comfortable when applying their knowledge and abilities in making decisions in finance. Attitude represents a bridge between people and the financial system, making individuals able to apply their financial literacy in real terms. At the same time a lack of knowledge or skills represents a low rate of financial literacy, which leads to a gap in financial capability too. Hence, if financial literacy cannot be enough to predict financial behaviors due to the chance that a lack of attitude could affect financial capability, at the same time a lack of financial literacy is itself a leading indicator of financial behaviors because attitude cannot work with people who are not knowledgeable and/or are not skilled in finance. It follows that studies of financial literacy anticipate the research on financial capability, paving the way for the analysis of attitude, meaning for "attitude" the ability to apply financial literacy in a real financial decision making scenario.

A definition of financial literacy

Bearing in mind the results from previous studies on financial literacy and rearranging them with the arguments proposed in this work, **financial literacy can be defined as knowledge of financial issues and the ability to apply it in a decision making process concerning finance, including awareness of the available sources of information, the functioning of financial products and services, financial intermediaries, and financial markets**. On the other hand, **financial capability is the ability to apply financial literacy in a specific scenario where people have to face financial issues in real terms**. The development of the attitude needed to translate financial literacy into financial capability will be affected by other elements such as motivation, self-confidence, and willingness to cope with financial issues.

Financial literacy and numeracy

In the analysis of previous studies, as in the definition proposed in this work, the role of numeracy and mathematical skills in developing financial literacy has been intentionally omitted. In accordance with Almenberg and Widmark (2011a), **by numeracy we mean the ability to handle numerical information and perform basic calculations**. Similar definitions of numeracy are provided by the Oxford English Dictionary (2017), for which "*numeracy is the ability to understand and work with numbers*", and by the Association of American College and Universities (2018), which defines numeracy as "*a habit of mind, competency, and comfort in working with numerical data*". This study shares the point of view of Hung et al. (2009), recognizing that numeracy applies much more broadly than to just financial issues and represents a much more basic skill set than financial literacy, so it should be treated as a distinct concept and not be included as a part of financial literacy. The influence of numeracy on financial literacy and financial capability has been highlighted in several studies. Remund (2010) considers numeracy – as the ability to calculate numbers – to be part of the basic literacy necessary to become financially literate, and Gustman et al. (2010), in a study on financial literacy in Americans more than 50 years old, tested the hypothesis that financial literacy can be improved by higher levels of numeracy, under the assumption that greater numeracy enhances knowledge that improves financial literacy. Huston (2010) argues that people struggling with arithmetic skills will have problems in the analysis of financial issues, and Almenberg and Widmark (2011a), showing how numeracy is a particularly important determinant of economic outcomes, found that numeracy is strongly correlated with financial literacy, but they consider it to be a different concept. While financial literacy may be easier to attain if grounded in mathematical intuitions, numeracy cannot be referred to as a necessary condition. Evidence from empirical studies shows a high correlation between financial literacy and numeracy. Gilliland et al. (2011), in an analysis of a sample of college freshmen in the US, found that students with higher scores on mathematics have more chances to show high levels of financial literacy. Similar results come from the study of Almenberg and Widmark (2011a) on the Swedish adult population. The authors found that the relationship between numeracy and financial literacy is positive and highly statistically significant. Carpena et al. (2011) analyzed financial literacy and numeracy in India, questioning if numeracy should be included in financial literacy or if it should be separated. Even if their data show a high correlation between the two topics, the authors arrive at the conclusion that numeracy itself cannot be considered as financial knowledge even if they go hand-in-hand. The relevance of numeracy and its relationship with financial literacy are highlighted by the World Bank (2013), which stresses how a number of studies consider it important to collect data on cognitive skills such as numeracy.

If previous studies refer to numeracy as a concept related to but different from financial literacy, other authors treat them differently but assume a closer relationship. Gerardi et al. (2010), in a study on the subprime mortgage crisis, talk about numeracy as "a particular aspect of financial literacy", including numeracy as a building construct of financial literacy. The position of the OECD (2010) on numeracy is more open. If the OECD recognizes a certain level of numeracy as a necessary condition of financial literacy, it on the other hand acknowledges that there are large areas where the content of mathematical literacy and the content of financial literacy do not intersect. The "grey-zone" where numeracy and financial literacy cannot be clearly separated seems to be limited to basic arithmetic as the four operations (addition, subtraction, multiplication, and division) with whole numbers, decimals, and common percentages. The essential role of this knowledge in managing financial issues suggests including it as an intrinsic part of financial knowledge (so also financial literacy), while the use of financial formulae requiring capability with algebra has to be considered separately from financial literacy and included in pure numeracy skills.

1.2 Financial literacy as a relative concept

A clear definition of financial literacy allows us to identify what is relevant in the study of this topic. An application of this definition requires the specification of its contents. If financial literacy is essentially knowledge about financial issues and the ability to apply this knowledge in a decision making process, there is the need to discuss which financial issues to look at in a financial literacy study. Without a specification of the areas of knowledge that should be taken into account, the assumption would be that every issue with a direct or indirect connection with the "use of money" should be included in the assessment of the financial literacy of an individual or a population. The consequence of such a holistic approach is that an individual could be considered to be financially literate only when he/she shows a full degree of knowledge on every single financial topic, without any distinction about how useful this knowledge is (or will be or could ever be) for a single person. The fact that a master's degree in finance – if ever feasible – is not even requested for top academic positions or for the highest positions in financial institutions should lead to the conclusion that financial literacy cannot be addressed as a full degree of knowledge about everything in finance, but should be considered as a relative concept and take into consideration different dimensions. Of course, as in other areas, a clear definition that summarizes what is financial literacy and what is part of it (and what is not) is essential, but this definition needs to be addressed before being applied, by specifying which topic (or group of topics) an individual needs to know and manage in order to make a financial decision.

Comparing financial literacy with medical sciences, we could argue that a measure of literacy that does not refer to specific topics, and that involves the whole knowledge of the field, will consider an individual as financially literate if he/she shows knowledge and abilities on different financial areas such as payment tools (cash, debit card, credit card, bank transfers, etc.), checking accounts, loans and debts, saving and investment, insurance and planning, taxation, currencies and exchange rates, etc. On the other hand, a person should be considered "literate" in medical sciences if he/she is equally skilled in anatomy, pharmacology, dietetics, first aid, orthopaedics, cardiology, neurology, and so on. In both cases the assumption is that literacy has to be assessed while taking into account all the topics that fall into a certain domain (medical or financial). Due to the fact that specialization of knowledge is a natural process that happens when the amount of knowledge in a field grows, and develops different branches of knowledge that differ from others in their utility and their application, it follows that an analysis of financial literacy cannot ignore the fact that a concept of finance as "the use of money" fits well for a comprehensive definition of financial literacy but risks being too wide and simplistic in the analysis of the financial needs of single persons, as in medical sciences a definition of medicine as the science or practice of the diagnosis, treatment, and prevention of disease[2] summarizes the features and the connections between different medical fields, but it is not able to explain the key issues of any single specialization.

Toward an operational definition of financial literacy

The analysis of previous studies shows how the need to operationalize the definition of financial literacy was claimed and different proposals about how to do it were developed. Schagen and Lines (1996), in a study with the aim of discovering the learning needs of adults relating to personal money management, addressed financial literacy using key concepts about money management and the "working knowledge" of financial institutions, systems, and services. As it was an exploratory study – understanding which topics have to be assessed was itself the aim of the paper – the authors analyzed financial literacy from a wide perspective without any reference to specific financial needs. Bowen (2003), in a study on high school students, decided to test financial literacy paying attention only to money management, under the assumption that this is the most relevant topic for teenagers, because their first experiences with finance usually concern spending and money management. The questions used to test financial literacy regarded the use of cheques, ATMs, bank accounts, credit cards, and car insurance. The connection between the items used to assess financial literacy and the everyday needs of the target of recipients (students) shows how the author paid attention to measuring only what is supposed to be relevant, putting the concept of financial literacy into practice. In an exploratory study in the UK, the FSA (2005) analyzed financial literacy consisting of a wide array of topics including budgeting, credit, debts, insurance, saving, and investment. In the same study the understanding of the wider ethical, social, political, and environmental dimensions of finances was tested too. As in Schagen and Lines (1996), the will to shed light on how much people know about finance suggested taking into account different financial topics instead of specific areas of knowledge. Bodie (2006), in a paper that explicitly tried to figure out which topics should be more relevant than others in studies of financial literacy, proposes four general principles to bear in mind: (1) *"there is no free lunch in competitive markets"* (the so called "law of one price"), (2) *"the present value of lifetime consumption can not exceed the present value of lifetime earning and wealth"*, (3) *"It is better to put money in different investments"*, and (4) *"Always remember to take into account of taxes and transaction costs"*. If these economic principles are absolutely relevant in economics as in finance, they represent a sort of golden rule to be applied in almost every financial area. Cude et al. (2006), in a study on the need for knowledge of college students and financial literacy, considered to be financially literate those who are knowledgeable and informed on managing money and assets, banking, investments, credit, insurance, and taxes. An analysis of such different areas provides an overview about financial literacy (as the aim of the study was) even if it probably cannot well fit as a measure of financial literacy when it is applied in a single decision making scenario. There is a preference for analysis that includes very different topics in a study of Lusardi and Mitchell (2006). The study analyzed a sample of Americans approaching the age of retirement using two questions on numeracy,[3] one question on the compound interest,[4] and a last question about the name of the current president of the United States, used as a measure of awareness about future tax and macro-economic prospects. In the same year Worthington (2006), using data from a survey on adult financial literacy in Australia, tested financial literacy by (1) "mathematic literacy" (numeracy), (2) questions on money (what it is, how it's exchanged, and where it comes from and goes), (3) basic financial services (ATMs, credit cards, bank accounts), and (4) risk–return relationship. Even in this case, the wide range of topics is coherent with the purpose of having an overview about financial literacy in the country. In other studies, planned to investigate the level of financial literacy on a nationwide level, Atkinson et al. (2006, 2007) measured financial literacy in the UK by the knowledge and skills on money management, planning ahead, choosing products, and staying informed. The same topics have been used by O'Donnell and Keeney (2009) in Ireland. The choice to diversify the topics in the assessment of financial literacy has been quite common, especially in studies devoted to establishing a baseline for further research. Fessler et al. (2007) analyzed a sample of Austrian households with questions about abilities on money management, planning ahead, making choices, choosing products, getting help, and staying informed. Mandell and Klein (2007) analyzed the high school population in the US evaluating four areas referred to as (1) income, (2) money management, (3) spending and credit, and (4) saving and investing.

More recently some authors tried to set standards about which categories of financial topics have to be used in financial literacy studies. Hill and Perdue (2008), in their methodological paper on financial literacy, suggested organizing financial topics by (1) investment, (2) personal income, (3) taxation, (4) credit and debt management, (5) risk management, and (6) retirement planning. The OECD (2010), in the Programme for International Student Assessment (PISA) project, organized the analysis of financial literacy among youth by (1) money and transactions, (2) planning and managing finances, (3) risk and reward, and (4) financial landscape. The expert group of the study identified even some non-cognitive factors that could affect financial literacy such as access to information and access to financial products.

Reviewing studies on financial literacy Remund (2010) found that (1) budgeting, (2) saving, (3) borrowing, and (4) investing are the terms of the most common operational definition of financial literacy, and this definition was used by Mak and Braspenning (2012) and Dahmen and Rodriguez (2014). Huston (2010) organized financial literacy topics by (1) personal finance basics (time value of money, purchasing power, etc.), (2) borrowing, (3) saving and investing, and (4) protection (insurance, risk management, tax planning, and estate planning). This scheme is close to the one proposed by Lusardi and Mitchell (2014) where the main content areas are (1) financial planning, (2) wealth accumulation, (3) debt, and (4) pensions, while Atkinson (2011) proposes a taxonomy that concerns much more about abilities than other topics and is based on five aspects: (1) making ends meet, (2) keeping track, (3) planning ahead, (4) choosing products, and (5) staying informed.

The main areas of financial literacy

Bearing in mind results from previous studies and trying to summarize the main content areas in finance to be considered in studying financial literacy, the following classification can be proposed:

1 Money management
2 Saving and investment
3 Borrowing and debt
4 Insurance
5 Retirement and planning

Knowledge and abilities in each of these areas do not have to be limited to basic principles, functioning of products and services, and their applications, but should also involve (1) knowledge and abilities in searching for the information needed to make a decision, (2) awareness about where and how to find help and support in making a financial decision in case the individual is not confident about a specific issue (e.g. family members, friends, financial advisors, etc.), and (3) awareness about consumer rights and the legal framework, including knowledge about financial intermediaries and systems. Due to the fact that most of this knowledge and these abilities is common to various financial areas, they can represent a sixth and different area of knowledge that plays a fundamental role in solving problems in each and every other area.

In **"money management"** fall all the knowledge and abilities concerning the use of money in a transactional process, including the use of cash, credit cards, debit cards, and payment services, as well as the management of money related to checking accounts and budgeting. The area related to **"saving and investment"** regards the creation and management of wealth. Basic principles such as time value, inflation, compound interest, the risk–return relationship, and the diversification of risk should be key concepts of this area, which will be related to knowledge and skills on such financial products as saving accounts, bonds, stocks, and mutual funds, as well as the functioning of financial markets and investing decision process. The area **"borrowing and debt"** (or "loans and debt") concerns basic principles and advanced knowledge of borrowing. The compound interest effect and inflation are useful basic knowledge in this area as they are in saving and investment. Knowledge and skills on APRs, fees, and commissions are needed in order to choose between loans, mortgages, credit cards, payday loans, check cashing, pawn shops, and other borrowing options. The "**insurance**" area involves knowledge about risk and the abilities to manage it with reference to health (sickness, injuries, diseases, etc.), properties (damage, theft, destruction, etc.), and behaviors (car crash, professional indemnity insurance, etc.), while in the area "**retirement and planning**" fall all the aspects related to long-term goals, such as retirement needs and planning for specific goals (e.g. education, housing, starting a new business, etc.). Financial literacy in these areas requires knowledge about financial products devoted to these goals (e.g. IRAs, 401(k)s, etc.) and the presence and functioning of tax-shields as well as awareness of the generosity of the welfare system.

Broad measures vs. specific measures

The taxonomy of financial literacy contents in different areas allows us to assess financial literacy more precisely by looking at the case of single individuals (or a group of them) and referring to the related area (or group of areas) of knowledge. Measures of financial literacy that involve contents from all five areas will probably fit well with general purposes, as providing a snapshot about the financial literacy of a population, but will not work as well for the analysis of sub-groups of the population that differ in their needs for financial knowledge and behavior. With regard to people who need to borrow, their need of financial literacy in order to make a decision about borrowing ("can I borrow?", "where can I find a loan?", "which is the best way to borrow?", etc.) suggests that a measure of their financial literacy (as "the knowledge and abilities to take a financial decision") should be assessed in the area "borrowing and debt" but not "saving and investment". The hypothesis is that to understand whether a borrower is able to make a borrowing decision, and for them to be aware about the possible consequences of taking a loan, the assessment should take into account if the borrower knows about borrowing but not if he/she knows about saving and investment.[5] At the same time, people who need to invest their savings have to be considered financially literate if they are able to choose the right investment product and are aware about the risk of their choice, after checking the available information. It follows that their financial literacy has to be assessed with regard to "saving and investment" but not "borrowing and debt". The risk in using a measure of financial literacy based on contents from different areas, when just part of it shows a logical connection with the financial decision to be made, is using a measure that is just partially correlated with the object of the analysis, introducing noise in the data with the consequence of underestimating the role of financial literacy in the financial decision making process.

Basic principles vs. deep knowledge

The need to address financial literacy as a relative concept and to measure it by different topics is clear when the differences between financial topics are used to highlight their relevance in different financial decision making processes.

The need to address financial literacy as a relative concept is not just related to the need to differentiate the topics. A second dimension to take into account concerns **the degree of knowledge and the level of abilities on a single topic**. If a different financial literacy is needed for borrowing compared to investing, it does not mean that financial literacy within these areas cannot differ. A retail investor who is trying to figure out how to reinvest 10,000€ that will be received back from a Government bond that has arrived at maturity and a mutual fund manager who is managing a 10,000,000€ portfolio are technically facing the same investment financial decision (investing), but the hypothesis that they have (and need) the same financial literacy seems inappropriate. The different relevancies of these decisions, due to the different amounts of money and the professional role of a mutual fund manager, will be probably reflected in a different level of financial literacy. This is just an example of how different levels of knowledge and abilities can differentiate people making a financial decision in a single financial area of knowledge, but it helps to stress how an analysis of financial literacy requires taking into account the different degrees of knowledge and abilities of the decision maker. If both the retail investor and the mutual fund manager can be aware about the difference between bond and stock investments, the latter will probably show a much higher knowledge than the former about pricing and forecasting techniques in the stock markets, or will be much more skilled about the connection between stock, bond, and derivative markets. It follows that a measure of financial literacy can be sensitive to these differences, and this highlights differences between people who show different knowledge and skills. The different levels of knowledge and abilities between people do not refer just to retail investors and mutual fund managers, but refer even to people who are facing much more similar decisions. Regardless of how different the knowledge and abilities are within people, **financial literacy has to be assessed keeping in mind that different levels of knowledge and abilities exist**, avoiding minimizing such differences by questioning only basic knowledge or, on the other hand, by testing only advanced skills. In both cases the lack of different grades of difficulty will affect the results. In the first case, measuring financial literacy by very easy items, a retail investor and a fund manager will be assessed as "equally literate" even if they are not. In the second scenario, questioning only very difficult items, the differences between low- and high-literate individuals will be amplified. The circumstance that some issues can be easy for someone and difficult for others recalls **the need to differentiate the level of difficulty in measuring financial literacy by referring to the target of recipients**. So, an analysis of financial literacy of small investors that includes questions they perceive with different levels of difficulty cannot be applied to analyze the financial literacy of mutual fund managers if we assume that their level of knowledge makes all the questions very easy. Hence, the concept of financial literacy has to be addressed not only paying attention to the connection between a topic and a financial decision, but even keeping in mind that knowledge and abilities on the items related to a single topic can be different.

The decision framework

In the selection of the contents to be considered as relevant in a single financial literacy area even the **characteristics of the financial system** have to be taken into account. Two people making the same financial decision can need different financial literacy because some differences in the functioning of their financial systems exist. Countries where the supply of financial products and services related to single financial needs is limited to just a few options will see an individual be considered as financially literate if he/she will be able to choose between them. Having a lack of knowledge about products and services that are not available in his/her financial framework cannot be considered negatively because it is simply useless in this specific scenario and does not affect the result of the decision making process. The same individual, with the same knowledge and ability in finance, will not be as financially literate in a more complex financial framework where the market offers different solutions for the same financial need. If financial literacy concerns the ability to use knowledge in making a financial decision, the knowledge about the available options to solve a problem and the ability to compare them, choosing the one that best fits with personal needs and preferences, are not absolute values, depending on the complexity of the financial system. It follows that **the same level of knowledge and skills can make a person be fully literate in a particular country and be not as literate in another** (if the latter is more complex than the former). At the same time some knowledge and abilities can be useful in a particular financial framework and be useless in others. For instance, the ability to discern between different solutions is not useful when only one of these options is available: people who cannot choose do not have to make any decision. In another case, knowledge and abilities on a topic are unnecessary if in a certain country people do not have financial needs related to this topic. These two scenarios fit with the case of countries that have different welfare states, with one country offering full coverage of retirement needs and another country offering just basic assistance. In the first case, there is no need to choose between different retirement plans due to the fact that there is no need to save for retirement (thanks to the prodigality of the welfare system).[6] So, people have no incentive to develop knowledge and abilities on a financial topic that they simply do not need to know, due to the fact that they will never have the chance to apply them in a decision making process. If in this case financial literacy should not include knowledge on retirement needs within the relevant topics to be assessed, this is not true when people have to take care of their own retirement needs. In this scenario the need to plan for retirement and to choose the best way to achieve it will expect people to be knowledgeable and skilled on this topic, so it should be included in the assessment of financial literacy. The case where knowledge is not needed in one country and is extremely relevant in others clearly highlights **the need to address financial literacy by keeping in mind differences in the financial systems**. However, this is true even when the differences between two financial systems are not so evident. This is the case of countries where the presence of either a strong banking sector or a developed stock market allows private firms to raise capital by taking loans and issuing financial securities. If raising capital from banks or from other investors requires knowledge and abilities on either the banking or security market, the role of these financial sectors in a country can vary, making financial literacy about one of them much more relevant than the other. In countries where the stock market is overwhelmed by the banking system the relevance of financial literacy on financial securities will be less than that on banking issues. On the other hand, a country where stock markets are dominant will see knowledge and skills on financial securities be more relevant than on banking products.

Due to the fact that differences of financial frameworks are usually related to differences in the national regulatory frameworks, the need to address financial literacy by taking into account such differences is usually related with the need to analyze financial literacy in more than one country simultaneously.

Financial literacy as a "relative concept"

At this point we can summarize the arguments about financial literacy as a "relative concept" by saying that financial literacy, as "the need of knowledge in order to make a financial decision", must refer to (1) the selection of the financial area(s) to be included, (2) a consideration of the level of difficulty of the knowledge and abilities to be taken into account, and (3) the variable relevance that knowledge and abilities can have in different financial systems and/ or different countries. Having awareness of these three dimensions of financial literacy allows one to identify what is relevant to assess financial literacy. I have already mentioned the role of financial literacy in making a financial decision; now it is time to stress how much financial literacy matters in the development of financial needs.

Financial literacy and awareness of financial needs

Of course, financial literacy plays a pivotal role in helping consumers make choices and satisfy their financial needs, but we also have to consider the role of financial literacy in the development of these needs, and the chance that financial literacy can help people to become aware of their "**latent financial needs**", meaning for "latent" a financial need that belongs to an individual but is not perceived as relevant or is not perceived at all. Latent financial needs usually refer to long-term planning (e.g. retirement planning), risk management, and other issues that people fail to recognize as relevant until the negative consequences of their actions (or lack of actions) appear. So, if it is true that financial literacy supports people in making a good financial decision, it is also true that financial literacy helps people to realize they even need to make a decision (e.g. planning for retirement, buying an insurance coverage, etc.). It follows that, within the financial areas that matter in the assessment of personal financial literacy, one should include not only the areas where people usually make a financial decision, but all the areas that they need to know, including topics related to latent financial needs. Lack of financial literacy can negatively affect the personal finances of an individual both by their making a mistake in making a decision and by their not making a decision at all when it was needed.

Financial literacy and the dynamics of financial needs

A last argument to threaten financial literacy as a relative concept concerns **the dynamic relationship between time and the need of knowledge**. As the life cycle hypothesis developed by Ando and Modigliani (1963) shows, people change their financial behavior and their financial needs over time in an attempt to balance their saving and consumption. This behavior usually pushes people to acquire debts in the first part of their lives, build their savings during their working age, and "dissave" during retirement. According to the hypothesis that financial literacy has to be assessed by referring to the individuals' need of knowledge, it follows that for young people the area of knowledge related to borrowing will be relevant, while saving and investment skills will become part of the need of knowledge later, until becoming not as relevant after retirement, when financial needs and the need of knowledge decrease. The different needs of knowledge in different stages of the life cycle, together with the development of financial systems that become more and more complex over time, help to shape a degree of preparedness between different cohorts, where the knowledge and abilities developed with previous experiences and different financial needs see adults be on average more financially literate than youth. At the same time the level of knowledge and abilities of the elderly is decreased by the evolution of financial systems. Upgrading financial competences in order to be up to date with the functioning of the market can be meaningless for people on retirement who are no longer involved in saving and investment. The result is a level of preparedness on financial issues that sees adults be the most skilled, followed by the elderly and youth. So, it could be argued that the development of financial literacy is an investment in human capital, motivated by the need to make financial decisions and affected by a rate of decay related to (1) the obsolescence of past knowledge, due to the natural evolution of financial systems, which tend to increase in complexity, and (2) the changing needs of knowledge, which decrease over time, reducing the motivation to invest in learning about new issues.

1.3 How to measure financial literacy

According to the Oxford English Dictionary (2017), "measurement" is "*the act of measuring*"[7] and "to measure" means to "*ascertain the size, amount, or degree of (something) by using an instrument or device marked in standard units*".[8] It follows that the measurement of financial literacy concerns the process by which the degree of knowledge and abilities of an individual (or a group of individuals) on a set of financial issues is assessed by items according to some criteria and by the application of a methodology.

In a study on the measurement of financial literacy Schmeiser and Seligman (2013) highlighted how the measurement of financial literacy is still in its infancy and there are not yet standardized instruments for this. To understand how to measure financial literacy we need to analyze different issues and provide answers to some questions.

The quality of a measure of financial literacy depends on the aim of the measure and its application. Hence, the first issue to take into account is the reason why the measurement is being developed. If financial literacy is a relative concept, in order to develop a measure of financial literacy we need to know **why the measure is needed and how it will be applied**. When the aim of a study is to provide an overview of financial literacy, stressing how much people know about finance or analyzing if financial literacy is related to some non-financial outcomes (e.g. education, stress, risky behaviors, etc.), the inclusion in the study of a wide range of financial topics is meaningful. The will to take into account different aspects of the financial preparedness of an individual is coherent with the analysis of very different topics belonging to such areas as money management, borrowing, saving and investment, and insurance. This is reasonable especially when the target of a study is quite large, including people who differ from each other in their financial needs, previous experiences in finance, and social backgrounds. The same measure of financial literacy is no more reliable if applied in a study with the aim to analyze a single behavior on a specific target of recipients. For instance, the topics to be addressed in a study on the role of financial literacy in the use of credit cards within youths will differ dramatically from the topics in a study whose goal is to summarize the big picture about financial knowledge within a large population. If credit cards can be used as a payment instrument and/or a borrowing facility, financial literacy should refer to money management and borrowing, but not to insurance and planning, due to the fact that these latter topics do not have a logical connection with the objective of the study. So, the same measure of financial literacy, referring to knowledge of different financial areas, fits well in one case (overview of financial literacy) but does not fit anymore in another case (use of credit cards). Of course, the opposite is also true, because a measure developed to analyze a specific financial behavior, such as the use of credit cards, should not be used to measure financial literacy in general terms, due to the fact that a measure built only on money management and borrowing is taking into account only a part of what can be relevant on finance. This approach seems to be coherent with the recommendations provided by the Financial Service Authority in the UK (FSA 2005) about the measuring of financial literacy. In the conclusions of the study it is reported how an overall scale based on knowledge and skills in different financial areas could be inappropriate, supporting the view that measures should be limited to certain selected topics.

With regard to the topics to be taken into account in building a measure of financial literacy one must also think about the **degree of difficulty** tested by the measure, which depends on the aim of the study too. Some studies will request the testing of more advanced knowledge and abilities; in other cases just testing the knowledge of basic financial principles can be enough. On this issue Lusardi (2009a), in a study where financial literacy is analyzed as a tool for informed consumer choice, highlights how basic concepts are not enough to make a financial decision. Saving and investment decisions cannot be competently made simply by applying fundamental financial concepts (that are anyway essential), but awareness of the relationship between risk and return, knowledge about how bonds, stocks, and mutual funds work, and basic asset pricing skills are needed. Again, the need to differentiate between types of knowledge and abilities is stressed by Huston (2011), who suggests measuring separately knowledge, ability, and behaviors and connecting the three results in a scoring grid.

A third question concerns **numeracy** and mathematical skills. It has been already argued that numeracy is relevant but is not part of financial literacy. So, a measure of how much people are able to manage numbers and numerical information can be useful, but should be assessed separately from financial literacy. The role of numeracy and the relevance of measuring it in financial literacy studies have been stressed by different authors. Agnew et al. (2013), studying the role of financial literacy in retirement planning in Australia, found that financial literacy scores are related positively to numeracy skills. Jappelli and Padula (2013), in a study that analyzed financial literacy as an investment in human capital, recognized that a certain level of mathematical competence is a necessary condition for financial literacy, and provided evidence of a positive correlation (0.32) between financial literacy and math skills. The need to test numeracy in assessing financial issues is evident in the study of Nye and Hillyard (2013) too. These authors, in a study on the determinants of financial well-being, used a measure of competency in "financial quantitative literacy" (numeracy) by conducting a specific test made up of 13 items.

If the aforementioned criteria suggest measuring "what is relevant to measure", before thinking about the way to do it, it is useful to set some broad criteria for a scoring system on financial literacy. Results from previous studies[9] agree that a measure of financial literacy should be **relevant, simple**, and **comprehensible**, with the **ability to differentiate** between different people. A measure of financial literacy is relevant if it is based on issues that show a connection with the recipients' needs of financial knowledge. It will be simple and comprehensible if it will be possible to explain the outcomes to a non-technical audience, while the ability to differentiate between different people concerns the need to address different scores to people with different knowledge and abilities, in order to permit comparison across people.

At this point, it is time to discuss how to collect data on single financial literacy items. The use of a questionnaire with one or more questions on a single topic is a standard approach. If it works well to assess knowledge on basic financial principles, or on a financial product or service, a question will not be as effective when specific abilities or skills have to be tested. The risk of assessing abilities by asking questions is to refer to some theoretical scenario that could be too simplistic and could fail in replicating a real decision making framework. In this case an analysis based on a more experimental framework would be more appropriate and could enable people to show their abilities in applying simultaneously different knowledge on different issues to analyze a set of information. Anyway we have to bear in mind that if a virtual scenario can fill the gap between theory and practice, the attempt to replicate reality by using a simulation (even when it is a sophisticated one) will always suffer a lack of engagement of the respondent. With regard to analysis of investment skills, in a trading simulation people are aware that they are not risking real money, with the consequence that the real stress people feel when they think about the possible consequences of their (real) choices is not replicated. Compared with real life, the stress level in a simulation is much lower, and this affects the reliability of the test. The risk is that people will perform well in a simulation, showing abilities that they are not able to show in the real world. How to properly assess abilities, skills, and other behavioral issues while not looking at real behaviors is still an open question. These questions have to be analyzed while being aware that a perfect measure, if ever feasible, should have a chance to be applied in research. Measures that demonstrate an ability to perfectly assess financial abilities and skills, but that require too many resources (time, money, efforts, etc.), risk remaining a theoretical option that is not really available for doing research. If the measurement of abilities and skills is an ongoing topic, the use of questions and interviews is an alternative option that is probably not as effective as others, but represents an affordable methodological tool in financial literacy research. The preference for **questionnaires based on multiple choice questions** had been reported in several studies such as Hung et al. (2009) and FSA (2005). An open and severe criticism about the chance to measure financial abilities by using questions, and with doubts about the chance to assess financial knowledge and financial literacy at all, came from Willis (2008). The author is extremely sceptical about any measure of financial literacy, asserting that life is always much more complicated than a multiple choice question, so any measure of financial literacy is useless in providing information about people's ability to manage their financial resources. If the study represents a useful warning to everyone who cares about financial literacy (stressing how any measure will always be a proxy of the real world) the negative conclusion about the relevance of financial literacy research is probably too pessimistic.

The self-assessment of financial literacy

Asking questions on knowledge and abilities is not the only way to study financial literacy. Several studies used measures of financial literacy coming from one or more **self-assessments**. People are asked to self-assess their level of financial literacy usually by a Likert scale with integer values from zero to an upper limit (e.g. zero-to-five, zero-to-ten, etc.). The risk of directly asking people how much they think they are financially literate is quite evident and is related to the fact that they could underestimate their knowledge or, on the opposite side, be overconfident about their financial skills. The chance that they could misunderstand what it means to be financially literate is another critical issue. However, before rejecting self-assessed measures as a possible analysis of financial literacy, there are some opportunities to be considered. Several studies clearly report that self-assessed measures of financial literacy are not correlated with objective measures (FINRA 2009, Guiso and Jappelli 2009, Jaredi and Mendez 2014, Lusardi and Mitchell 2014). In a study on American adults the data of FINRA (2009) reveal a sharp disconnect between self-reported financial knowledge and responses to financial literacy questions. The study highlights how too often people overestimate their financial literacy and how very few respondents give themselves low scores. The same overconfidence issue came out from the study of Guiso and Jappelli (2009) on the connection between financial literacy and portfolio diversification in Italy, and Lusardi and Mitchell (2014), in a review of different studies, highlighted a general substantial mismatch between people's self-assessed knowledge versus their actual knowledge. If all of these arguments seem to suggest a rejection of self-reported measures of financial literacy, Jaredi and Mendez (2014) noted how subjective measures of financial literacy can be useful even if their correlations with objective measures are little or negative. The authors highlight how a self-assessed measure of financial literacy is even more interesting when it disagrees with other objective measures, because the comparison of what people really know and what they think they know can provide useful information about their awareness and their exposure to risks related with overconfidence. However, their interest in self-assessed financial literacy is limited to this area, and in the conclusions of the study they report that when objective measures exist and are free of errors, then subjective measures will clearly be the less attractive option.

The use of multiple choice questions

The use of questions represents the main instrument to measure financial literacy, even though their application outside the measurement of knowledge can be debated. The central role of questions asks us to pay great attention to some methodological issues about their application in financial literacy studies. The evidence from previous studies suggests that it is best to format questions in financial literacy as multiple choice questions and not to use open answer questions. If an open answer, giving to the respondent the chance to freely answer and provide details about personal opinions and characteristics, represents a source of high quality information, the need to work on the text in order to select and summarize the relevant information suggests that it is best to use this methodological instrument only in qualitative studies or in research projects based on small groups. The answers to multiple choice questions represent the basic information unit to develop a measure of financial literacy. The awareness that some errors of the questions – as single items and as a whole questionnaire – have the potential to negatively affect the result of a study forced the researchers to develop some basic rules in developing a questionnaire on financial literacy.

The motivation behind the development of a measure of financial literacy concerns the will to know how knowledgeable and skilled people are. Due to the fact that people involved in these studies are aware of being studied, the respondents should be allowed to answer a question choosing a "**do not know**" option when they are not able to answer. Without a "do not know" option people have as alternative behaviors a "blank answer" (they simply fail to choose any of the available options) or try to guess by selecting an answer randomly. A blank answer cannot be interpreted as evidence that an individual does not know the right answer, because the respondent could intentionally refuse to answer or simply forget to do it. In this case doubt about why none of the available options were selected represents an issue in the interpretation and the analysis of the data. The alternative hypothesis, that the answer is the result of a random selection process, is even more problematic, because in this case the risk is to confuse knowledge with luck, overestimating the financial literacy of the respondents. Introducing a "do not know" option and explaining to the respondent that the questionnaire does not represent an exam – where the respondent tries the best to obtain the highest score – but is a tool to discern the real level of knowledge and abilities should limit the risk of cheating or guessing behaviors. Similarly, the inclusion within the list of options of a "prefer not to say" or "refuse to say" option will help to resolve the doubt related to a blank answer. Assuming that a respondent who intentionally refused to answer chose the option "prefer not to say", a blank answer can be interpreted as omission due to lack of attention. About the benefit of the "do not know" option in a financial literacy test, Huston (2010) highlights how, choosing this option, the respondents are providing useful information about their level of financial literacy. In admitting they are not able to answer they are showing a level of financial literacy that is particularly low, even lower than that of people who failed the test but tried to answer thinking they knew the answer or were somehow confident that the option they chose was the correct one (even if they were not completely sure about it). The number of "do not know" options can also be a measure of self-confidence about financial issues, providing information about attitude and behavior from a financial capability perspective. The positive correlation between the "do not know" response rate and financial literacy was found by Lusardi and Mitchell (2006), Lusardi and Tufano (2015), and van Rooij et al. (2011a).

In order to analyze specific knowledge using specific variables, multiple choice questions where only one of the available options is right and all the others are undoubtedly wrong[10] are preferred to questions where the selection of more than one option is allowed. The awareness of the respondent that there is one-and-only-one correct answer reduces the complexity of the question from the methodological point of view. This is a desirable issue because a clear understanding of the structure of the test limits the risk that a wrong answer is due to problems with the assessment tool and should make the respondent who is knowledgeable be able to choose the right answer. A multiple choice question where **only one option is the right one** allows the respondent to concentrate on one issue at a time and gives him/her the chance to double-check the answer by checking that the other options he/she rejected are wrong. It follows that in this kind of test a wrong answer has to be accorded to a lack of knowledge. A question where more than one option can be right asks the respondent to assess each option separately without the chance of any confirmation test, making the process more complex. The ability to test knowledge on different aspects of an issue can be addressed by asking different questions. Of course, the preference for developing questions that are easy to understand does not imply that the questions will be easy to answer. The ability to reduce methodological technicalities is related with the aim to shape the difficulty of the question by working on the financial literacy contents, choosing between basic principles or advanced skills within a topic.

The **number of options** in each question is another element to take into consideration. If the "do not know" and "prefer not to say" options should be available in every question by default, the number of options proposed to the respondent as possible right answers can vary from a minimum of two up to a lot of options. A question with only two options is probably easier than a question with three or more and is the only possibility for questions based on an agree-or-disagree structure where the respondent is asked to say if a sentence is true or false. In addition, we have to consider the **chance of guessing behaviors**. If a respondent tries to guess, in this case the risk for the researcher to exchange luck for knowledge increases compared with questions with more options, due to the fact that the respondent has a 50% chance[11] to correctly answer even not knowing the right answer. The chance to be simply lucky falls to around 33% with three options and to 25% in the case of four.[12] If a "do not know" option can limit the risk of guessing, it is probably not enough to completely avoid the problem. People who are thinking of guessing will probably be more prone to do it when they have fewer options available, due to the fact that they know they have more chances to choose the right answer.

Regardless of the number of options chosen for a question, a technical recommendation is **to use the same number of options for all the questions of the survey**. Using a common standard about how many options have to be in a question a researcher can make the assumption that differences between the response rate for a question are not addressed by technicalities or guessing behavior and will be able to consider the data as homogenous.

After the methodological issues about the questions, we can start paying attention to their contents. According to the suggestion to analyze one issue at a time, the **use of jargon**[13] should be limited to questions with the aim to test knowledge about financial terms and expressions. If jargon in questions that are assessing different issues can be used in order to raise the level of difficulty of the question, this approach risks being misleading due to the fact that testing two or more issues at the same time can cause the interpretation of the answers to be unclear. If a correct answer is evidence that the respondent knows all the concepts of the questions (jargon included), the interpretation of a wrong answer does not allow us to know if all the contents are unknown to the respondent or if it is a lack of knowledge with regard to only one issue that made the individual not able to answer correctly (or to not answer at all choosing the "do not know" option).

Several studies provided evidence about another relevant issue referred to as "framing" or "wording".

In a study on the role of financial literacy in stock market participation, van Rooij et al. (2011b), using data from the Netherlands, measured knowledge about the risk of investment in single stocks and mutual funds by using two questions, administered to different samples of individuals. The first question was:

> *"Buying a stock mutual fund usually provides a safer return than a company stock. True or false?"*

And the second was:

> *"Buying a company stock usually provides a safer return than a stock mutual fund. True or false?"*

If the basic principles of investment suggest that a mutual fund is safer than a single stock, results highlighted that the response rate in the first case (63.4%) is double the rate in the second (32.3%), and similar results occur with questions on bond pricing and interest rates[14] and other issues. The same results are reported by Knoll and Houts (2012) in a paper on financial literacy and the financial crisis based on data from American adults. A possible explanation for these results is that people are guessing, and that they answer the true-or-false questions by **preferring the "true" options** as if they are more prone to agree with a sentence than to disagree, regardless of the content of the sentence. This hypothesis is confirmed by Schmeiser and Seligman (2013), who, in an analysis of several waves of the Health and Retirement Study (HRS), representing a large sample of American adults, stressed how the population of their study appear prone to agree in cases where the respondent is asked to agree or disagree, and question variants that require participants to **answer "false" appear consistently more difficult**.[15] The authors arrive at the conclusion that *"the context and frame of a question matter; variation on a question that required the same mathematical skill yielded varying rates of correct responses"*.

The risk that people will guess by using these or other rules of thumbs was stressed by Lusardi and Mitchell (2014), who report as another possible framing effect the attitude to **always pick the first option as the correct answer**. A wording effect was found by Lusardi, Mitchell and Curto (2014) too, in a study on a sample of the American youth population.[16]

Evidence from a previous study suggests taking into account these "framing" or "wording" effects by rotating the options in the questions or by proposing questions in different terms, switching between positive and negative sentences.

The **number of questions to include in the questionnaire** to analyze a financial topic is another dilemma in financial literacy studies. If there is a general consensus about the need of data on financial literacy, authors show different opinions about the chance to study financial literacy by using just a few questions. Chen and Volpe (2005) note how most of their survey had very limited questions on financial literacy. They stress how personal finance covers a broad spectrum of issues, noting how "*a five or ten question survey can hardly touch the surface of these issues*". Moore (2003) reports how several studies demonstrated that financial literacy "*cannot be determined from single, isolated measure of knowledge, experiences or behaviors*", suggesting that measures of financial literacy "*must include a more complex analysis of these factors in aggregate*". More recently Knoll and Houts (2012) support the thesis that financial literacy cannot be measured by using only a few items. They even recognize the need to limit the number of questions in a financial literacy survey in order to reduce the potential for respondent fatigue that could affect the success of the survey. The need to build measures of financial literacy using a reasonable number of items is evident also in the study of Allgood and Walstad (2013) when the authors say that objective measures of financial literacy "*have their limitations when the assessment is done with a just a few test items to serve as a proxy for the full range of financial literacy*". On the other hand, Lusardi (2009a) seems to support the hypothesis that to measure financial literacy by using only a few items is possible – and probably even the only available option – saying that "*given the limited number of questions that can effectively be added to surveys, researchers have to assess financial literacy from only handful of questions*".

Waiting for more generous data on financial literacy, an analysis based on just a few items must be considered, even if the use of financial literacy as a supporting tool to make a financial decision should be limited to studies where a relationship between financial decisions or financial behaviors and the items used to measure financial literacy is reasonable and supported by some theoretical explanations. In other words, the lack of data on some financial topics cannot be managed using very limited measures of financial literacy built on items that do not have any relationship with the aim of the study. A review of the literature shows how different studies used a measure of financial literacy based on the answer to a single question (Hira and Loibl 2005, Atkinson and Kempson 2008, Lusardi and Tufano 2015, Lusardi and Mitchell 2011, Brown and Graf 2013), and Nicolini and Cude (2014) demonstrated how limiting the measure of financial literacy to a single question can be an effective choice when this is the only item related with the financial behavior analyzed. The authors highlighted that adding more items into a financial literacy measure not only can be not useless but can even negatively affect the quality of results by introducing noise in the data. This seems to suggest that more information is not always positive if new items in a financial literacy measure are not related with the aim of the study.

Regardless of the topics, in the case where more than one question is available, an analysis of the **difficulty of each question** is needed. This issue has been taken into account by different authors. For instance, Almenberg and Widmark (2011b) developed a questionnaire with questions showing different levels of difficulty, where the most difficult questions have been proposed to the respondent only if his/her answers to the question on basic principles were correct. A different approach is the one of van Rooij et al. (2011b), who used two sets of questions on the same topics but with different levels of difficulty. These authors developed questions with the aim to make some of them more difficult than others. It can be done in an ex-ante perspective by developing some questions that are more difficult than others or by testing how people react to a question in a focus group or in a one-to-one interview. In other cases (Behrman et al. 2012) the rate of difficulty has been assessed ex-post by the ratio between the number of correct answers and the total number of answers. In this way a question is considered more difficult when less people provided the correct answers.

The presence of more than one question gives the chance to choose between different approaches in the use of data. Responses from a single question can be used separately in a one-by-one analysis. Doing so the researcher treats the **answers to each question as a measure of financial literacy**, and the presence of different questions will provide a set of different measures. On the other hand, data from different questions can be aggregated in a single measure. A criterion to choose between these two approaches is once more related with the aim of the study and the nature of the analyzed topics. If the financial literacy questions concern different topics and the aim of the study is to connect financial literacy with a specific behavior, the use of a single item (question) is reasonable if this is the only one that shows a logical connection with the behavior. It could be the case of a study that the role of financial literacy on the choice between fixed- and floating-rate mortgages is analyzed by a measure of financial literacy based on a single question concerning the functioning of a mortgage, ignoring other questions on such topics as investment or cash management skills that are not related with loans. On the other hand, if the aim of the study was to figure out the existence of a gender gap on financial knowledge in a population, a measure of financial literacy that summarizes various questions on different topics would be appropriate, due to the fact that the aim of the study suggests not restricting the analysis to a specific area of knowledge.

Summary measures of financial literacy

The use of financial literacy measures that take into account more than one question at the same time requires establishing a set of rules by which to summarize the data from different questions.

The most simple and very common criterion is **to sum the number of correct answers** to a set of questions. For each question an index of financial literacy of one unit will be added if the respondent has chosen the correct answer and of zero otherwise. In this approach (1) a wrong answer, (2) a blank answer, and (3) a "do not know" option (when available) are equally treated and will be scored as zero. Indexes of financial literacy like this will range from zero to the number of questions taken into account (e.g. 0–5 or 0–10 if the index summarizes data from five questions or ten questions) and can show only integer values (e.g. a zero-to-five score can be equal to only 0, 1, 2, 3, 4, or 5). Results can be standardized on a zero-to-one scale by dividing the number of correct answers by the total number of questions. These measures of financial literacy, which have been widely used by previous studies,[17] collapse the information from different questions in an ordinal scale making the assumption that people with higher scores are the ones with higher financial literacy.

An index of financial literacy made by the sum of correct answers to a set of questions equally weights data from each question assuming that each question shows the same relevance and difficulty. This hypothesis can be removed by introducing **a set of weights** that could differ for each question by taking into account the different logical connections between the topic analyzed by a question to further the aim of the study or by taking into account the difficulty of the question. The use of a set of weights does not represent a different measure of financial literacy, but it can be seen as a fine tuning of the aforementioned measures that will be more sensitive and more able to differentiate between people who correctly answered the same number of questions but not the same questions. The result is still representing an ordinal scale, but the weights allow us to adjust the financial literacy score by taking into account how much the knowledge or ability measured by a specific question is more relevant in explaining a phenomenon (e.g. the choice between a fixed vs. floating rate mortgage) or is more powerful in explaining the degree of knowledge of an individual (e.g. the correct answer to a difficult question is more valuable than a correct answer to a simple question).

The sum of correct answers to a set of questions is not the only available option to aggregate data on financial knowledge and abilities. Within statistical techniques and procedures based on a **dimensionality reduction approach**, the ones that well fit with the aim to summarize information from a set of questions in order to develop a measure of financial literacy are factor analysis, principal component analysis (PCA), and cluster analysis.

Factor analysis is a statistical method that analyzes the variability between different variables looking for unobserved variables, called "factors", that explain the behavior of the initial set of variables. Due to the fact that the number of factors can range from one up to the number of variables analyzed, the use of these technique in measuring financial literacy can reduce the number of variables by highlighting the presence of two or more questions that should not have to be considered separately because they can be seen as two sides of the same coin (e.g. two questions referring to the same issue of a particular topic). If the factor analysis produces a single factor it means that all the items are related to a common source of knowledge or to a single topic. If two or more factors come out they can be used to identify which questions show a similarity and should be used to develop a single measure of financial literacy. A further aggregation process will start from the original variables and a set of new variables (the factors) that will guarantee the development of indices made by issues that do not overlap. For instance, a set of six financial literacy questions where the first three are related to investment skills and the other three to insurance will be probably summarized in two factors, one for each set of questions, that can be used respectively as a measure of investment financial literacy and a measure of insurance financial literacy, or can be further aggregated in a single measure.

Principal component analysis (PCA) allows us, like factor analysis, to test the presence of possibly correlated variables and, in that case, summarize the behavior of these variables by creating a set of new variables that are linearly uncorrelated.

These new variables, the so called "principal components", can be used as measures of financial literacy or inputs for further analysis, as can be done with factors coming from a factor analysis.

Even if the two techniques (factor analysis and PCA) can be used for the same purpose (to reduce the number of variables) they are not identical – even if they are related – due to differences in the assumptions and the statistical models used to reduce the dimension of the set of data.[18]

In a **cluster analysis**, the observations from a set of variables are grouped in such a way that objects in the same group (a "cluster") are more similar to each other than to those in other groups.[19]

By applying a cluster analysis to data from the answers to a set of financial literacy questions it is possible to identify groups of people who answered the questions similarly. A cluster analysis can be the starting point to look for people with high or low financial literacy. The analysis of different clusters will show who falls in clusters that share a high response rate to financial literacy questions and which kind of people are clustered within low response rate clusters.

Keeping in mind that a measure of financial literacy is a tool to achieve a specific goal, if the aim of a study concerns the development of a measure of financial literacy in order to measure how financially literate an individual is and compare two or more people, this measure should be able to pinpoint how knowledgeable and skilled people are, providing a full scale from the bottom to the top, working as a yardstick. A study could be planned in order to figure out a specific target of a population such as who are the less knowledgeable individuals, because lack of knowledge or a low level of knowledge is supposed to be relevant in order to explain certain phenomena (e.g. overindebtedness, bankruptcy, etc.). In this case the ability of a measure of financial literacy to discriminate between high and very high-literate people is not as relevant (or it could be not relevant at all) compared with the ability to discern between low-literate people and the rest of the population. Here **financial literacy can be measured by developing a dummy variable** equal to one if a respondent fails to answer correctly at least a certain number of questions, and zero otherwise. Under the assumption that people who admit to not knowing the answer by choosing the relative "do not know" option are the ones who show the lowest level of knowledge, a measure of (low) financial literacy based on the number of "do not know" options chosen by a respondent can be another measure of financial literacy.

The need to measure financial literacy while keeping in mind the use of the measure and the reason why it has been developed has been already stressed more than once, and it represents a golden rule in the assessment of financial literacy. If we start from the aforementioned proposals and think about other alternative measures, the available options to measure financial literacy are many – from the use of single questions to indexes that summarize the number of correct answers, passing by measures that fix a threshold on the number of right (or wrong) answers and separate between high and low financially literate people by checking who passes over this threshold. The choice between the available options can be influenced by the desire to compare results from a study with previous results or with results coming from other concurrent studies. Any researcher is aware that there is a **trade off between measures that well fit with the aim of a study and measures that have been already applied** before and that could make the results of the study more interesting, thanks to the chance to easily relate them with the previous literature. If the desire to make a study more relevant and more connected with previous literature is reasonable, on the other hand, there is the risk of choosing a measure of financial literacy merely by using the same measure as previous studies, in order to guarantee a comparability of the results. This risk could affect the quality of the overall results of the study by using a measure that does not fit with the aim of the study.

About international comparisons

A last methodological issue of the assessment of financial literacy and comparability of results concerns the chance to replicate the same study in different countries using the same questionnaire or analyzing the same topics. The fact that the topic of a certain question can be relevant for the citizen of a certain country and not as relevant for others, or even the fact that a question can be quite easy to answer for people living in a certain country and extremely difficult for others, needs to be taken into account before assuming that the same question has the same meaning, the same relevance, and the same explanatory power in different countries. The need to test the comparability of two populations before using the same yardstick to measure their financial literacy is more evident when questions concern topics that go beyond general economic and financial principles, which can be assumed to be relevant in any case. Differences in the functioning of the financial systems, the legal framework, and the culture of people in two or more countries can strongly affect the need of knowledge and the relevance of some topics as can even the familiarity of people with some financial products and services. In this scenario the risk of comparing, by using the same yardstick, two populations that differ in their need of knowledge is to misread the differences in financial knowledge and skills, which could be explained by different social frameworks, causing them to arrive at distorted conclusions.

From the considerations reported about what and how to measure financial literacy, planning the research extremely carefully – keeping in mind clearly the aim of the study and being aware of the need to customize the analysis to the target of recipients and their needs of knowledge – is probably the main conclusion and represents a recommendation for any study on financial literacy. Such flexibility is necessary in either studies with original targets or studies that take inspiration from previous research. If the need of flexibility in the assessment of financial literacy can be seen as a source of fragmentation and an obstacle to the definition of a common yardstick and a unique measure of financial literacy, on the other hand, it could be argued that it represents evidence that **financial literacy is a multidimensional research topic that cannot be standardized in a "one size fits all" approach**.

1.4 Financial literacy measures from previous studies

Interest in financial literacy has grown over time, and many authors have developed different measures of financial literacy. From a review of the literature around 80 studies have been selected and analyzed in order to shed light on the methodological issues related with the measurement of financial literacy. A comparison of previous studies helps to figure out how different measures have been chosen and modelled in order to fit with different scenarios and purposes.

Table 1.1 summarizes the key elements of each study. Information about the data, the aim of the study, and the target of recipients has been reported to help with interpretation of the studies and to better clarify the reasons behind the choice of a measure of financial literacy against alternative options. It also provides a timeline of the evolution in the financial literacy literature. (To download an electronic version of this table please visit the eResource at www. routledge.com/9781138632611.)

Almost all the available options to measure financial literacy have been used. As reported in Table 1.1, financial literacy has been assessed using self-assessment questions, by using the answers to single questions as self-standing measures of financial literacy, adding the number of correct answers to a set of questions, or looking at these measures in order to develop indices of financial literacy that discriminate between people who correctly answered at least a certain number of questions or who were able to provide the correct answer to all of them. In addition, the number of "do not know" answers was used as another measure of financial literacy, and measuring it indirectly by the observation of other related issues has been tried by the use of instrumental variables (IVs).

Table 1.1 Comparison of previous studies on financial literacy and stresses and how they differ in terms of size (number of observations), countries of interest, and topics considered to measure financial literacy

Author(s)	Year	Database	# Obs (rounded)	Country/Area	Target of recipients	Aim of the study	Topics	Basic principles (e.g. Compound interest, Inflation, etc.)	Money management
Lusardi, Mitchell	2011	HRS	-	-	-	Review of the literature on the assessment of FL	Lusardi-Mitchell questions	x	
Huston	2011	-	-	-	-	Review of the literature on the definition of FL	-		
Xu, Zia	2012	-	-	-	-	Summary of FL around the world	Lusardi-Mitchell questions 1) Suppose you had $100 in a savings account and the interest rate was 2% per year. After 5 years, how much do you think you would have in the account if you left the money to grow? (More than $102 | Exactly $102 | Less than $102 | Do not know | Refuse to answer) 2) Imagine that the interest rate on your savings account was 1% per year and inflation was 2% per year. After 1 year, how much would you be able to buy with the money in this account? (More than today | Exactly the same | Less than today | Do not know | Refuse to answer) 3) Please tell me whether this statement is true or false. — Buying a single company's stock usually provides a safer return than a stock mutual fund. | (True | False | Do not know | Refuse to answer)	x	

Source	Year	n	Country	Sample	Description / Purpose	Concepts / Questions		
World Bank	2013	–	–	–	REVIEW OF THE LITERATURE – The purpose of this review is to identify, compare, and contrast existing measurement approaches in the area of financial literacy and capability	Being able to compare and benchmark across countries can yield huge benefits. If a project aims at comparing results internationally, the topics covered and questions asked will have to be adjusted sometimes at the expense of addressing country-specific issues. . . . Just replicating a survey on other countries . . . requires particular caution though because the simple translation of survey instruments developed in other setting is not sufficient. Adequate testing and fine-tuning of the instrument will always be required in order to ensure that the qeustions have the same meaning across countries.		
Lusardi, Mitchell	2014	–	–	–	Review of the literature on the assessment of FL	Lusardi-Mitchell questions	x	
Beal, Delpachitra	2003	842	Australia	College students	Students at the University of Southern Queensland (USQ) in Toowoomba, Queensland,	This research was undertaken as the prelude to a larger project to determine the financial literacy of the Australian population	Basic concepts: Compound interest, Risk and expected return Diversification of portfolio: Achievement of saving, Correct answers, Early withdrawal penalty Markets and instruments: Price of AUD, Definition of 'cash' rate, Historical returns of Australian asset classes, Loan guarantee, Fixed and variable rates Planning: Effectiveness of planning, Bank reconciliation, Expenditure recording, Checking bank statements 'Free' credit	x x

(Continued)

Table 1.1 (Continued)

Author(s)	Year	Database	# Obs (rounded)	Country/Area	Target of recipients	Aim of the study	Topics	Basic principles (e.g. Compound interest, Inflation, etc.)	Money management
							Analysis and decisions: Persistent credit card debt, Source of urgent funding, Monetary problem solving Present value of income stream		
							Insurance: Insurance excess, Risks covered with householders' policies, Vehicle insurance premiums, Risks covered with vehicle CTP policies, Term life insurance benefits		
Worthington	2006	2003 ANZ Survey of Financial Literacy in Australia	3,548	Australia	Australian Adults	Assessment of Financial Literacy in Australia	Money management	Financial products and services	Savings and Investment	Numeracy	Borrowing and debts	Retirement and Planning		x
Agnew, Bateman, Thorp	2013	Specific survey	1,024	Australia	Adults (Australia)	FL and Retirement planning in Australia	Lusardi-Mitchell questions	x	
Behrman, Mitchell, Soo, Bravo	2010	Social Protection Survey (Encuesta de Proteccion Social, EPS)	13,054	Chile	Adults (Chile)	FL and pension accumulation	Lusardi-Mitchell questions + Retirement	x	
Song	2012	Specific survey	1,000	China	Adults (China)	FL and pension contribution	Compound interest	x	
Atkinson, Messy	2012	OECD - INFE	around 1000 obs each country	Czech Republic	Germany	Hungary	Ireland	Norway	Peru	Malaysia	UK	British Virgin Islands		Assessment of FL	Numeracy (division)	Time value	Compound interest	Risk and Return	Inflation	Diversification	x	
Jappelli, Padula	2011	SHARE		Europe	Adults (50+)	FL and Saving decisions	Numeracy		

Author	Year	Survey	N	Country	Population	Title	Questions	
Bigot, Crouette, Muller	2011	CREDOC "Enquete sur la culture financière des Francais"	1,502	France	Adutls (France)	Assessement of FL (France)	Compound interest | Bond | Risk diversification	x
Muller, Weber	2010	"Frankfurter Allgemeine Sonntagszeitung" (German Newspaper) Internet survey on investment fund choice	3,228	Germany	German mutual fund investors	"Who Buys Actively Managed Funds?" (in Germany)	Saving and Investment	
Bucher-Koenen, Lusardi	2011	SAVE survey	2,222	Germany	German Adults	FL and retirement in Germany	Lusardi-Mitchell questions	x
OECD	2013	PISA		International	Young	Assessment of the FL	Money and transactions | Planning and managing finances | Risk and reward | Financial landscape. "It is necessary to select the elements that will best ensure construction of an assessment comprising tasks with an appropriate range of difficulty and a broad coverage of the domain"	x
O'Donnell, Keeney	2009	Irish Financial Capability Study (Central bank of Ireland9	1,529	Ireland	Irish Adults	Asses financial literacy in Ireland	Managing money | Planning ahead | Choosing products | Staying informed	
Monticone	2010	SHIW (Survey on Household Income and Wealth) Banca d'Italia	7,977	Italy	Adults (Italy)	FL and wealth	Lusardi-Mitchell questions	x
Calcagno, Monticone	2011	Unicredit Customers' Survey (UCS) – Private survey	1,686	Italy	Adults (Italy)	FL and Financial Advice	Lusardi-Mitchell questions + Risk	x
Fornero, Monticone	2011	SHIW (Survey on Household Income and Wealth) Banca d'Italia	7,977	Italy	Adults (Italy)	Assess FL in Italy	Lusardi-Mitchell questions	x

(Continued)

Table 1.1 (Continued)

Author(s)	Year	Database	# Obs (rounded)	Country/Area	Target of recipients	Aim of the study	Topics	Basic principles (e.g. Money management, Compound interest, Inflation, etc.)
Sekita	2011	Survey of Living Preferences and Satisfaction (SLPS) by the Osaka University 21st Century Center of Excellence (COE)	5,386	Japan	Adults (Japan)	FL and Retirement planning in Japan	Lusardi-Mitchell questions	x
Atkinson, Kempson	2008	Financial Capability Baseline Survey, 2005	5,328	Kenya	Kenya Adults	Decide how to measure Financial Capability in Kenya		
Crossan, Feslier, Hurnabard	2011	ANZ/Retirement Commission Survey of Financial Literacy 2009	850	New Zealand	Adults (New Zealand)	We compare levels of financial literacy in New Zealand with levels in five other countries	Lusardi-Mitchell questions	x
Beckman	2013	Euro Survey of the Austrian Central Bank		Romania	Adults (Romania)	Assessment of FL (Romania)	Lusardi-Mitchell questions	x
Klapper, Lusardi, Panos	2011	Specific survey of over 1,000 face-to-face interview with Russian individuals	1,600	Russia	Adults (Russia)	Role of FL on financial behavior (looking at the financial crisis)	Lusardi-Mitchell questions	x
Klapper, Panos	2011	Specific survey of over 1,000 face-to-face interview with Russian individuals	1,600	Russia	Adults (Russia)	FL and Retirement planning in Russia	Lusardi-Mitchell questions	x
Almenberg, Save-Soderberg	2011	Survey of the Swedish Financial Supervisory Authority (Finansinspektionen) on FL	1,302	Sweden	Swedish adults aged 18-79	Assess Financial literacy in Sweden	Lusardi-Mitchell questions	x

(Continued)

							Lusardi-Mitchell questions	
Brown, Graf	2013	Survey of University of St. Gallen	1,500	Switzerland	Adults (Switzerland)	FL and retirement planning (Switzerland)		x
Deuflhard, Georgarakos, Inderst	2014	DNB Household Survey	2,000	The Netherlands	Adults (The Netherlands)	FL and Saving account returns	FINANCIAL LITERACY - BASIC	x

(1) Suppose you had 100€ in a savings account and the interest rate was 2% per year. After five years, how much do you think you would have in the account if you left the money to grow? (i) More than 102€; (ii) exactly 102€; (iii) less than 102€; (iv) do not know; (v) refusal.

(2) Suppose you had 100€ in a savings account and the interest rate is 20% per year and you never withdraw money or interest payments. After five years, how much would you have on this account in total? (i) More than 200€; (ii) exactly 200€; (iii) less than 200€; (iv) do not know; (v) refusal.

(3) Imagine that the interest rate on your savings account was 1% per year and inflation was 2% per year. After one year, how much would you be able to buy with the money in this account? (i) More than today; (ii) exactly the same; (iii) less than today; (iv) do not know; (v) refusal

(4) Assume a friend inherits 10,000€ today and his sibling inherits 10,000€ three years from now. Who is richer because of the inheritance? (i) My friend; (ii) his sibling; (iii) they are equally rich; (iv) do not know; (v) refusal.

Table 1.1 (Continued)

Author(s)	Year	Database	# Obs (rounded)	Country/Area	Target of recipients	Aim of the study	Topics	Basic principles (e.g. Compound interest, Inflation, etc.)	Money management
							(5) Suppose that in the year 2010, your income has doubled and prices of all goods have doubled too. In 2010, how much will you be able to buy with your income? (i) More than today; (ii) the same; (iii) less than today; (iv) do not know; (v) refusal. FINANCIAL LITERACY – ADVANCED (1) Which statement describes the main function of the stock market? (i) The stock market helps to predict stock earnings; (ii) the stock market results in an increase in the price of stocks; (iii) the stock market brings people who want to buy stocks together with those who want to sell stocks; (iv) none of the above; (v) do not know; (vi) refusal (2) What happens if somebody buys the stock of firm B in the stock market? (i) He owns a part of firm B; (ii) he has lent money to firm B; (iii) he is liable for firm B debt; (iv) none of the above; (v) do not know; (vi) refusal		

(3) Which statement about mutual funds is correct? (i) Once one invests in a mutual fund, one cannot withdraw the money in the first year; (ii) mutual funds can invest in several assets, for example, invest in both stocks and bonds; (iii) mutual funds pay a guaranteed rate of return which depends on their past performance; (iv) none of the above; (v) do not know; (vi) refusal.

(4) What happens if somebody buys a bond of firm B? (i) He owns a part of firm B; (ii) he has lent money to firm B; (iii) he is liable for firm B_s debts; (iv) none of the above; (v) do not know; (vi) refusal.

(5) Considering a long time period (e.g. 10 or 20 years), which asset normally gives the highest return? (i) Savings accounts; (ii) bonds; (iii) stocks; (iv) do not know; (v) refusal.

(6) When an investor spreads his money among different assets, does the risk of losing money (i) increase; (ii) decrease; (iii) stay the same; (iv) do not know; (v) refusal.

(7) If you buy a 10-year bond, it means you cannot sell it after five years without incurring a major penalty. (i) True; (ii) false; (iii) do not know; (iv) refusal.

(Continued)

Table 1.1 (Continued)

Author(s)	Year	Database	# Obs (rounded)	Country/Area	Target of recipients	Aim of the study	Topics	Basic principles. (e.g. Money Compound interest, management Inflation, etc.)
							(8) Stocks are normally riskier than bonds. (i) True; (ii) false; (iii) do not know; (iv) refusal.	
							(9) Buying a company fund usually provides a safer return than a stock mutual fund. (i) True; (ii) false; (iii) do not know; (iv) refusal.	
							(10) If the interest rate falls, what should happen to bond prices? (i) Rise; ii) fall; (iii) stay the same; (iv) none of the above; (v) do not know; (vi) refusal.	
							(11) Normally, which asset displays the highest fluctuations over time? (i) Savings accounts; (ii) bonds; (iii) stocks; (iv) do not know; (v) refusal.	
Alessie, van Rooij, Lusardi	2011	CentERpanel	2,000	The Netherlands	Adults (The Netherlands)	FL and Retirement planning	Lusardi-Mitchell questions	x
Van Rooij, Lusardi, Alessie	2011	De Nederlandsche Bank (DNB) Household Survey	2,000	The Netherlands	Adults (The Netherlands)	FL and stock market participation	The financial literacy questions are composed of two parts. The first set of questions aims to assess basic financial literacy. These questions cover topics ranging from the workings of interest rates and interest compounding to the effect of inflation, discounting, and nominal versus real values. The second set of questions aims to measure more advanced financial knowledge and covers topics such as the difference between stocks and bonds, the function of the stock market, the workings of risk diversification, and the relationship between bond prices and interest rates	x

Author	Year	Data/Survey	Sample	Country	Population	Topic	Content	
Van Rooij, Lusardi, Alessie	2011	De Nederlandsche Bank(DNB) Household Survey	2,000	The Netherlands	Adults (The Netherlands)	FL, Retirement planning and Wealth	Ability to perform simple calculations | Understanding of how compound interest works | Understanding of the effect of inflation | Time value of money | Money illusion	x
Van Rooij, Lusardi, Alessie	2011	DNB Household Survey by The Netherlands Central Bank	1,508	The Netherlands	Adults (The Netherlands)	FL and Retirement planning in The Netherlands	Lusardi-Mitchell questions + Saving and Investment	x
Bucher-Koenen, Lusardi, Alessie, van Rooij	2012	DATA - US --> FINRA NFCS - NETHERLANDS --> DNB Household Survey (DHS) - GERMANY --> SAVE Study	N.A.	The Netherlands, USA, Germany	Adults	FL and gender gap	Lusardi-Mitchell questions	x
FSA	2005	Financial Capability Baseline Survey, 2005	5,328	UK	British Adults	Assessement of the Financial Capability of British adults	Managing money | Planning ahead | Making choices about financial products | Mortgages | Protection | Savings | Investments | Credit Cards | Loans | Getting help	x
Atkinson, McKay, Kempson, Collar	2006	Financial Capability Baseline Survey, 2005	5,328	UK	British Adults	Assessement of the Financial Capability of British adults	Managing money | Planning ahead | Choosing products | Staying informed	x
Disney, Gathergood	2012	Specific Survey	3,041	UK	Adults (UK)	FL and Credit card use	Simple interest | Compound interest | Credit card use	x

(Continued)

Table 1.1 (Continued)

Author(s)	Year	Database	# Obs (rounded)	Country/Area	Target of recipients	Aim of the study	Topics	Basic principles. (e.g. Compound interest, Inflation, etc.)	Money management
Volpe, Chen, Pavlicko	1996	"students at a mid-sized metropolitan university where the authors teach"	454	US	College students	1) What is college students' knowledge of personal investment? 2) In what areas is investment illiteracy most evident among college students? 3) What is the relationship between illiteracy and gender, academic discipline, and experience?	Risk | Diversification | Financial advisor qualifications | Tax planning | Business math | Impact of interest rate change | Stock | Bond | Mutual fund valuation | Global investing	x	
Chen, Volpe	1998	Specific survey	924	US	College students 14 college campuses. They include both public and private schools, main and branch campuses of large universities, and small community colleges in California, Florida, Kentucky, Massachusetts, Ohio, and Pennsylvania	How an individual's knowledge impacts their opinions regarding personal finance issues and financial decision making.	financial literacy on general knowledge savings and borrowing insurance, and investment	x	
Tennyson, Nguyen	2001	Jumpstart Coalition for Personal Financial Literacy	1,643	US	Students	The study examines the relationship between existing state mandates for personal finance education and student knowledge of personal finance	Income | Money Management | Saving and Investing | Spending and Debt		x

Author	Year	Survey	N	Country	Sample	Purpose	Topics		
Volpe, Kotel, Chen	2002	Specific survey	530	US	Online investors	Assess the FL of online investors	Effect of a distribution from a mutual fund on its net asset value (NAV) | Blue chip stock terminology | Compounding of interest | Beta as a volatility measure | Capital gain tax rate | Portfolio diversification | Stock splits | Financial ratio analysis | Appropriate asset allocation strategies | The relationship between interest rates and bond prices.	x	
Chen, Volpe	2002	Specific survey (to 14 colleges in the US)	924	US	College students	Test differences in financial knowledge between man and women	General knowledge | Saving and borrowing | Insurance | Investments	x	
NASD	2003	Specific survey	1,086	US	Investors	Measurement of investor literacy	Investment		
Bowen	2003	Sample of 64 high school students (Pensylvania)	64	US	College students	The purposes of this study were to determine the financial knowledge of high school juniors/seniors and their parents and the relationship between the teens' and parents' financial knowledge	Money Management | Loans | Insurance		x
Highert, Hogarth, Beverly	2003	FED – Surveys of Consumers (see box, "What's Your Financial IQ?").	1,000	US	Adults	Study the connection between knowledge and behavior	Cash-flow management | General credit management | Saving | Investment | Mortgages		
Agnew	2004	Specific survey	395	US	Mixed	Asset allocation and information overload	INVESTMENT 1 Which of the following types of investments are typically found in a money market fund? Stocks, Bonds or Short Term Securities 2 When is the best time to transfer money into a long-term bond fund? When interest rates are expected to . . . increase, remain stable, decrease, interest rate doesn't matter, don't know		

(Continued)

Table 1.1 (Continued)

Author(s)	Year	Database	# Obs (rounded)	Country/Area	Target of recipients	Aim of the study	Topics	Basic principles. (e.g. Compound interest, Inflation, etc.)	Money management
							3 If you were to invest $1,000 in a STOCK FUND, would it be possible to have less than $1,000 when you decide to withdraw or move it to another fund?		
							4 If you were to invest $1,000 in a BOND FUND, would it be possible to have less than $1,000 when you decide to withdraw or move it to another fund?		
							5 If you were to invest $1,000 in a MONEY MARKET FUND, would it be possible to have less than $1,000 when you decide to withdraw or move it to another fund?		
							6 A stock fund's beta rating can best be described as … . A measure or relative volatility of the fund vs. the S&P 500 index, b. A measure of relative growth vs. the S&P 500 index, c. A measure of the relative capital outflow of the fund vs. the S&P 500 index		
							7 A money market mutual fund is guaranteed by the U.S. government against principal loss		
							8 High yield bond funds are invested in bonds with strong credit ratings		
							9 If you invest in a bond mutual fund with an average maturity of five years, this means that you cannot withdraw your money from the fund within a five-year period without incurring a penalty		
							10 A stock market fund index is actively managed by a fund portfolio manager		

Author	Year	Source	N	Country	Objective	Sample	Items/Questions		
Hira, Loibl	2005	Specific survey	1,519	US	Assess the effect of Financial Education on workplace satisfaction	Employees	(1) I have a very clear idea of my financial needs during retirement (44%). (2) I have a better understanding now of how to invest my money than I did six months ago (43%). (3) I feel more informed now about how to provide for my financial future than I did six months ago (47%). (4) I have a better understanding now of how to manage my credit use than I did six months ago (37%).	x	x
Perry, Morris	2005	1999 Freddie Mac Consumer Credit Survey	10,997	US	Assess the role of FL on financial behavior	Individuals between 20 and 40 years of age with incomes below $75,000 per year	Interest rates | Credit ratings | Managing finance | Investing money	x	
Baron-Donovan, Wiener, Gross, Block-Lieb	2005	Specific survey	42	US	To evaluate one approach employed to prepare instructors of personal financial literacy courses for consumer debtors	Teachers	Credit | Minimum payments | Wise buying/spending habits | Credit reports | Credit scoring | Pay-day loans | Rent-to-own programs | Rights and responsibilities during a bankruptcy case and following the bankruptcy discharge		
Manton, English, Avard, Walker	2006	Specific survey	407	US	To determine how wel Texas high school graduates understand basic consumer financial concepts	College students (Texas, USA)	Functioning of financial products (bank accounts, credit cards, etc.) | Insurance | Investment (Mutual funds, stocks, etc.)	x	
Danes, Haberman	2007	The National Endowment for Financial Education (NEFE) High School Financial Planning Program (HSFPP)	5,329	US	How male and female teenagers answered questions about their financial knowledge	High school students	QUESTIONS "I understand the cost of buying on credit" | "I know key questions to ask when shopping for auto insurance" | "I know about investments (stocks, mutual funds, bonds, etc.)" | "I know the difference between needs and wants"		

(Continued)

Table 1.1 (Continued)

Author(s)	Year	Database	# Obs (rounded)	Country/Area	Target of recipients	Aim of the study	Topics	Basic principles (e.g. Compound interest, Inflation, etc.)	Money management
Mandel, Klein	2007	Jump$tart survey	5,775	US	High school students	Assessment of Financial Literacy in US high school students	Income | Money Management | Spending and Credit | Saving and Investing		x
Robb, James	2008	Specific survey	3,525	US	College students	Personal Financial Knowledge among College Students			
Borden, Lee, Serido, Collins	2008	Specific survey	93	US	College students	Assessment of a financial education program	Credit cards		x
Hill, Perdue	2008	junior and senior-level undergraduate business students at the University of Houston–Clear Lake	170	US	junior and senior-level undergraduate business students	Methodological issues on the measurement of FL	Investments | Personal income taxation | Credit and debt management | Risk management | Retirement planning		x
Sevon, Kaestner	2008	Specific survey (administered by the Center for Survey Research and Analysis at the University of Connecticut)	253	US	Online Banking	FL and online banking	"Basic financial concepts"	x	
Stango, Sinman	2009	Data from real checking accounts and credit cards	N.A.	US	Adults (USA)	Use of checking accounts and credit cards	Interest	x	
Lusardi, Tufano	2009	Survey by Taylor Nelson Sofres (TNS) Global	1,000	US	Adults	Debt literacy and overindebtedness	Compound interest	x	
Robb, Sharpe	2009	Specific survey	3,884	US	College students	To examine the role that knowledge of personal finance concepts and principles may play in college students' decision to revolve a credit card balance	1) Which of the following credit card users is likely to pay the GREATEST dollar amount in finance charges per year, if they all charge the same amount per year on their cards? - Someone who always pays off their credit card bill in full shortly after it is received - Someone who only pays the minimum amount each month (%)*		

- Someone who pays at least the minimum amount each month, and more when they have more money
- Someone who generally pays their card of in full, but occasionally will pay the minimum when they are short on cash
- Don't know

2) Which of the following types of investment would best protect the purchasing power of a family's savings in the event of a sudden increase in inflation?
    - A 25 year corporate bond
    - A house financed with a fixed-rate mortgage
    - A 10-year bond issued by a corporation
    - A certificate of deposit at a bank
    - Don't know

3) Which of the following statements best describes your right to check your credit history for accuracy?
    - A car loan
    - A home equity loan
    - A credit card loan
    - A student loan
    - Don't know

4) Which of the following loans is likely to carry the highest interest rate?
    - A car loan
    - A home equity loan
    - A credit card loan
    - A student loan
    - Don't know

(Continued)

Table 1.1 (Continued)

Author(s)	Year	Database	# Obs (rounded)	Country/Area	Target of recipients	Aim of the study	Topics	Basic principles. (e.g. Compound interest, Inflation, etc.)	Money management
							5) Which of the following is TRUE about the annual percentage rate (APR)? - APR is expressed as a percentage on a semi-annual basis - APR does not take into account all loan fees - APR is not an accurate measure of the interest paid over the life of the loan - APR should be used to compare loans 6) A high-risk and high-return investment strategy would be most suitable for: - An elderly retired couple living or a fixed income - A middle-aged couple needing funds for their children's education in two years - A young married couple without children - All of the above because they all need high returns - Don't know		
Lusardi	2010	FINRA Foundation NFCS (National Financial Capability Study)	25,000	US	American Adults	Understand how financially capable are Americans	Lusardi-Mitchell questions	x	

Clark, Sandler, Morrill, Allen	2010	The Retirement Expectations Survey (REXs)	1,701	US	Near to retirement American adults	Effect of knowledge on planned retirement age	Questions	
							1) "Buying a single company stock usually provides a safer return than a stock mutual fund". True/false --> LUSARDI-MITCHELL	x
							2) Imagine that the interest rate on your savings account was 1% per year and inflation was 2% per year. After 1 year, would you be able to buy more than, exactly the same as, or less than today with the money in this account? --> LUSARDI-MITCHELL	
							3) What is the earliest age that you can start Social Security benefits?	
							4) What is the age that you can receive a full or unreduced Social Security benefit ("normal retirement age")?	
							5) If you start Social Security benefits at the earliest possible age, you will receive a benefit that is ___ percent of the benefit you would have received at the normal retirement age.	
							6) Is the reduction in Social Security benefits for early retirement permanent or does the reduction end when you reach the normal retirement age?	
							7) After you start receiving Social Security benefits, these benefits are: a) the same for the rest of my life b) increased annually by the rate of inflation	

(Continued)

Table 1.1 (Continued)

Author(s)	Year	Database	# Obs (rounded)	Country/Area	Target of recipients	Aim of the study	Topics	Basic principles. (e.g. Money Compound interest, management Inflation, etc.)
							c) increased annually but by less than the rate of inflation	
							d) increased annually but by more than the rate of inflation	
							e) Don't know	
							8) What is the earliest age that you will be eligible for Medicare?	
							9) Can you take a lump sum distribution of some or all of your pension plan (do not include income for your 401(k) account)?	
							10) Does your company offer you the opportunity to stay in the company health plan after you retire?	
							11) Does your company offer any type of phased retirement, flexible work options, or the opportunity to work part-time after you retire?	
							12) The monthly pension benefit that you will receive from your current employer will:	
							a) stay the same for the rest of your life	
							b) be increased annually by the rate of inflation	
							c) be increased annually by the same rate as wages for active workers	
							d) don't know	
							13) Are you covered by a pension plan offered by your company?	
							14) What is the earliest age that you can retire and start receiving benefits from the plan?	

Authors	Year	Survey / Dataset	Sample	Country	Population	Focus	Measurement	
Fonseca, Mullen, Zamarro, Zissimopoulos	2010	RAND American Life Panel (ALP)	2,500	US	Adults (Americans)	FL and gender gap	Basic financial concepts	Investing	Life insurance	Annuities	x
Yoong	2011	ALP (American Life Panel)	2,500	US	Adults	FL and stock market participation	Lusardi-Mitchell questions	x
Lusardi, Mitchell	2011	FINRA Foundation NFCS (National Financial Capability Study)	1,488	US	Adults (USA)	FL and Retirement planning in the US	Lusardi-Mitchell questions	x
Utkus, Young	2011	Specific survey	900	US	Adults	FL and 401(k) loans	Compound interest	Credit card debt	Stock market risk	Investment returns	x
Brumcont, Lin, Lusardi	2011	FINRA NFCS	25,000	US	Adults (Americans)	FL in the US (geographical differences)	Lusardi-Mitchell questions	x
Bumcrot, Lin, Lusardi	2011	FINRA Foundation NFCS (National Financial Capability Study)	25,000	US	American Adults	Assess the geographical differences on FL in the US	Lusardi-Mitchell questions	x
de Bassa Scheresberg	2013	FINRA NFCS	4,500	US	Young Adults (Americans 25–34)	FL and financial behavior	Lusardi-Mitchell questions	x
Huang, Nam, Sherraden	2013	SEED for Oklahoma Kids experiment	2,651	US	Child	Assessment of FE programs	Lusardi-Mitchell questions	x
Lusardi, de Bassa Scheresberg	2013	FINRA Foundation NFCS (National Financial Capability Study)	25,000	US	American Adults	FL and the High-cost to borrowing	Numeracy	Knowledge of the effects of inflation	Understanding of risk diversification	x
Mottola	2013	FINRA Foundation NFCS (National Financial Capability Study)	25,000	US	American Adults	FL, Woman and credit cards	Lusardi-Mitchell questions	x
Xiao, Chen, Chen	2013	FINRA Foundation NFCS (National Financial Capability Study)	25,000	US	American Adults	FL and financial satisfaction	"financial capability was measured by three variables: perceived financial capability, financial literacy, and financial behavior".	x
Nye, Hillyard	2013	Specific survey	267	US	American Adults	FL and financial behavior	Numeracy	x

(Continued)

Table 1.1 (Continued)

Author(s)	Year	Database	# Obs (rounded)	Country/Area	Target of recipients	Aim of the study	Topics	Basic principles. (e.g. Money management Compound interest, Inflation, etc.)
Schmeiser, Seligman	2013	HRS	N.A.	US	Adults	FL and financial behavior	Lusardi-Mitchell questions	x
Moore	2003	Telephone survey sponsored by the Washington State (USA)	1,423	US (Washington State)	Washington State residents	to evaluate consumers' financial literacy and mortgage experiences in Washington state	Assessment of FL (Washington state, USA)	x
Gustman, Steinmeier, Tabatabai	2012	HRS 2004		USA	Adults (Americans)	FL and pension wealth	Lusardi-Mitchell questions	x
Knoll, Houts	2012	RAND ALP 2006 HRS FINRA NFCS	2,539	USA	Adults (Americans)	Assessment of FL (Romania)	Lusardi-Mitchell questions + OTHER QUESTIONS	x
Jappelli, Padula	2013	Sharelife		Europe			4 question Numeracy + 1 question compound interest	x

(Continued)

Table 1.1 (Continued)

Author(s)	Saving and Investment	Borrowing and Debts	Insurance	Retirement and Planning	# of questions	Type of Index	Self-assessment	Sum of correct answers	All correct (dummy)	At least "n" correct answers	one-by-one	Instrumental Variable (IV)	Number of "Do not know"
Lusardi, Mitchell					3	1) Each question as different variable 2) The "do not know" as variable					x		x
Huston					–	–							
Xu, Zia					3	SUMMARY OF PREVIOUS STUDIES – NO ORIGINAL MEASURES							
World Bank						1) Each question "one-by-one"; 2) Sum of correct answers; 3) Weighted average by using larger weights to the questions that fewer people answered correctly; 4) Factor analysis		x			x		
Lusardi, Mitchell					3	Sum of correct answers		x					
Beal, Delpachitra	x		x		25	Sum of correct answers … then dummy High–Low FL with treshold the median of correct answers		x		x			
Worthington	x	x		x	28	Sum of correct answers … and 3 percentile for high–middle–low FL		x					
Agnew, Bateman, Thorp	x				3	1) "all three correct" … using Lusardi-Mitchell; 2) sum of correct answers; 3) each of the three question as separate variable; 4) sum of "do not know"		x	x		x		x

(Continued)

Table 1.1 (Continued)

Author(s)	Saving and Investment	Borrowing and Debts	Insurance	Retirement and Planning	# of questions	Type of Index	Self-assessment	Sum of correct answers	All correct (dummy)	At least "n" correct answers	one-by-one	Instrumental Variable (IV)	Number of "Do not know"
Behrman, Mitchell, Soo, Bravo				x	12	FL SCORE --> PRIDIT approach --> This approach involves a two-step weighting scheme, where the first step links each individual's responses on particular questions to others' performance on the same questions. The goal is to determine which questions are more difficult (ones that few people answer correctly) and give more credit to particularly difficult questions (which few people can answer). --> A simple aggregation would simply assign zero credit for an incorrect answer and a full point for each correct answer; by contrast, PRIDIT applies a negative penalty for an incorrect answer and a greater penalty for a question that most of the population answered correctly.--> The second PRIDIT step applies a principal components analysis to take into account correlations across questions -->						**Macro-economic conditions and family backgrounds**	

Thus if answering question 3 correctly means most people tend à Conversely, if question 5 were a question that distinguished well between people, that question would be judged more informative about relative financial literacy than questions 3 and 4 and hence receive greater weight. In this way, the resulting PRIDIT scores indicate how financially literate an individual is in relation to the average population and to specific questions asked —> While the PRIDIT score we have computed is positively correlated with a simple ¡percentage correcti tally, the PRIDIT approach incorporates additional information about the relative difficulty of each question and the value–added of each question. Furthermore, the PRIDIT score allows us to determine which questions are driving results. Accordingly in what follows we use the PRIDIT scores thus generated.

(Continued)

Table 1.1 (Continued)

Author(s)	Saving and Investment	Borrowing and Debts	Insurance	Retirement and Planning	# of questions	Type of Index	Self-assessment	Sum of correct answers	All correct (dummy)	At least "n" correct answers	one-by-one	Instrumental Variable (IV)	Number of "Do not know"
Song					5	the index will measure the distance of the answer to the correct answer … measuring financial "illiteracy"		x					
Atkinson, Messy					22	Sum of correct answers (sum of three scores on Knowledge, Behavior, Attitudes)		x					
Jappelli, Padula					4	Instrumental Variable (IV) for FL –> Math performance in school						Math performance in school	
Bigot, Crouette, Muller					10	Dummy if at least 5 correct answers			x				
Muller, Weber	x				8	Sum of correct answers + Self.assessment (Likert 1-5)	x	x					
Bucher-Koenen, Lusardi					3	(1) dummy if all 3 answers are correct (2) number of correct answers		x	x				
OECD					N.A.	N.A.							
O'Donnell, Keeney				x	N.A.	Factor Analysis + PCA (Principal Components Analysis) + Cluster Analysis							
Monticone					3								

						Age of fist use of financial products (mutual funds, stocks, etc.9
						Individual and average regional [national language] skills (Japanese)
Calcagno, Monticone	8	1) Sum of correct answers; 2) Instrumental Variable (IV) for FL —> Age of first use of financial products (mutual funds, stocks, etc.)		x		x
Fornero, Monticone	3	1) sum of correct answers; 2) dummies for answering correctly one question (each test included separately); 3) dummies for answering correctly two questions (each couple separately);4) the number of DK; 5) dummy for answering at least one DK		x	x	
Sekita	3	1) Dummy for "All three responses correct"; 2) sum of correct answers; 3) Self-assessment (1–5 scale)	x	x	x	
Atkinson, Kempson	–	CITATION....There are many ways of using survey data to create a financial capability score or scale of capability. The most common ones include: 1 Identifying a particular question, or questions of relevance and reporting the responses – this is the simplest approach but does not give an overall picture.		x		

(Continued)

Table 1.1 (Continued)

Author(s)	Saving and Investment	Borrowing and Debts	Insurance	Retirement and Planning	# of questions	Type of Index	Self-assessment	Sum of correct answers	All correct (dummy)	At leat "n" correct answers	one-by-one	Instrumental Variable (IV)	Number of "Do not know"
						2 Summing the responses from a number of questions in order to provide a single measure – this is relatively easy to do, but is most appropriate where there are clear right and wrong answers, for example, when measuring levels of knowledge. 3 Undertaking statistical analysis of a number of questions to identify underlying patterns in the responses – which is most appropriate when creating a score from a range of attitudes and behaviors. ...WEIGHTS –> When summing replies it would be possible to treat some questions as more, or less, important than others by 'weighting' them before adding the scores together.							

...FACTOR ANALYSIS
—> Statistical approaches
to creating scores
typically involve
a method of data
reduction known as
factor analysis, which
identifies questions with
correlated responses that
can be described by a
single latent variable —>
However, it should be
noted that it can only
be used with questions
that have a natural order
to their responses (e.g.
Likert scale)

...CLUSTER ANALYSIS
—> Cluster analysis has
also been used by various
analysts, including
those in the UK and
the Netherlands, to
identify segments of the
population with similar
patterns of financial
capability. This technique
assigns people to groups
by identifying those
who give broadly similar
responses to a range
of questions. —> The
benefit of this approach
is that there is no need
to make assumptions
about the types of people
who exhibit particular
types of behaviors

(Continued)

Table 1.1 (Continued)

Author(s)	Saving and Investment	Borrowing and Debts	Insurance	Retirement and Planning	# of questions	Type of Index	Self-assessment	Sum of correct answers	All correct (dummy)	At least "n" correct answers	one-by-one	Instrumental Variable (IV)	Number of "Do not know"
Crossan, Feslier, Hurnabard					3	Indices "question by question" Index equal to 1 if all the three questions are correct			x		x		
Beckman					3	1) Dummy for "all three questions correct"; 2) Sum of correct answers; 3) Each question as a different variable		x	x		x		
Klapper, Lusardi, Panos					4	1) A continuous index of financial literacy using principal component analysis (PCA) to reduce the information from the four survey questions 2) Number of correct responses in the financial literacy questions 3) The responses to a question of self-assessment of an individual's financial literacy ("On a scale from 1 to 7, where 1 means very low and 7 means very high, how would you assess your overall financial knowledge?").	x	x				1) Number of newspapers 2) Number of universities across the region	
Klapper, Panos					3	1) Dummy for "All three responses correct"; 2) sum of correct answers; 3) Dummy for each question "one by one"			x		x		

Author					
Almenber, Save–Soderberg	3	FL INDEX 1 –> financial literacy is a dummy variable that equals one if a respondent correctly answered all three financial literacy questions FL INDEX 2 –> financial literacy variable is the number of correct answers to the three financial literacy questions FL INDEX 3 –> we elaborate with the number of do not know responses as a measure of financial literacy. –> We find a clear negative and statistically significant association between being less financially literate, measured as the number of don't know responses, and planning.	x	x	x
Brown, Graf	3	1) Dummy for "all three questions correct"; 2) Each question as a different variable		x	x
Deuflhard, Georgarakos, Inderst	5 basic questions + 11 sophisticated questions	Factor Analysis	x		
Alessie, van Rooij, Lusasrdi	3	Instrumental Variable (IV) for FL –> Financial experiences of siblings and parents	**Financial experience of sibling and parents**		

(Continued)

Table 1.1 (Continued)

Author(s)	Saving and Investment	Borrowing and Debts	Insurance	Retirement and Planning	# of questions	Type of Index	Self-assessment	Sum of correct answers	All correct (dummy)	At least "n" correct answers	one-by-one	Instrumental Variable (IV)	Number of "Do not know"
Van Rooij, Lusardi, Alessie	x				16 (5 basic + 11 advanced)	We summarize all of the information about financial literacy resulting from our two sets of questions into a financial literacy index. We first combine the information we have available by performing a factor analysis on the 16 questions in the financial literacy module the factor analysis indicates there are two main factors with different loading on two types of questions: The simple literacy questions (first five questions) and the more advanced literacy questions (remain-ing 11 questions).		x					
Van Rooij, Lusardi, Alessie					16 (5 basic + 11 advanced)	1) "basic index"; 2) Factor Analysis; 3) Self-assessment	x	x					
Van Rooij, Lusardi, Alessie	x				5 basic questions + 11 sophisticated questions	1) "basic index"; 2) Factor Analysis	x	x					
Bucher-Koenen, Lusardi, Alessie, van Rooij					3 Lusardi-Mitchell + other (total 18)	1) Self-assessment; 2) All correct answers; 3) At least 1 "do not know"	x		x				
FSA	x	x			8	Assigning a score to each question and adding these up to give an overall score for each respondent.		x					

Study			no single indicator of financial capability		Factor Analysis			
Atkinson, McKay, Kempson, Collar			x					
Disney, Gathergood				3	1) Sum of correct answers ("We sum the number of correct answers to the three financial literacy questions to generate a financial literacy score which ranges from 0 to 3"); 2) each question as a separate variable; 3) all three questions rights (dummy)	x	x	x
Volpe, Chen, Pavlicko	x			10	Sum of correct questions (10 points each question (scale 0–100))	x		
Chen, Volpe	x	x		36	Sum of correct answers … then dummy High–Low FL with treshold the median of correct answers	x		
Tennyson, Nguyen	x			31	Sum of correct answers	x		
Volpe, Kotel, Chen	x			10	1) One-by-one; 2) Sum of correct answers; 3) Dummy if above the mean; 4) Dummy if above the median	x	x	x
Chen, Volpe	x			36	Sum of correct answers	x	x	
NASD	x			10	Dummy if more than 7 on 10		x	x
Bowen	x	x		19	No summary index			
Hilgert, Hogarth, Beverly	x	x		28	Sum of correct answers	x		
Agnew	x			10	Sum of correct answers	x		
Hira, Loibl			x	4	Each question one-by-one			
Perry, Morris	x			4	Self-assessment (sum of value of each question . . . Likert scale)	x		

(Continued)

Table 1.1 (Continued)

Author(s)	Saving and Investment	Borrowing and Debts	Insurance	Retirement and Planning	# of questions	Type of Index	Self-assessment	Sum of correct answers	All correct (dummy)	At least "n" correct answers	one-by-one	Instrumental Variable (IV)	Number of "Do not know"
Baron-Donovan, Wiener, Gross, Block-Lieb	✗				16	Sum of correct answers		✗					
Manton, English, Avard, Walker	✗	✗			20	Sum of correct answers		✗					
Danes, Haberman	✗	✗	✗		4	Self-assessment (Likert scale)	✗						
Mandel, Klein	✗	✗			31	"Financial literacy score" (sum of correct answers)		✗					
Robb, James					6	Sum of correct answers		✗					
Borden, Lee, Serido, Collins		✗			7	Sum of correct answers		✗					
Hill, Perdue	✗			✗	50	Adjusted Score = C − [I/(n−1)] where C is the number of correct answers, I is the number of incorrect answers, and n is the number of available answers on each question. On a test with five possible answers on each question, the average random score of test takers with no knowledge of the subject should be 20 percent. However, the adjusted score for these people would be 20 − [80/(5−1)] = 20 − 20 = 0 indicating that zero is the correct score for a person who knows nothing on the topic and is only guessing.		✗					

Author				N.A.			Measure of financial literacy		Knowledge on bond pricing
Sevón, Kaestner				N.A.			N.A.		
Stango, Sinnan				1			No indices		
Lusardi; Tufano	x			3			Self-assessment + one-by-one	x	
Robb, Sharpe	x			6		x	Sum of correct answers		
Lusardi	x			5			Self-assessment + "OTHER"	x	
Clark, Sandler, Morrill, Allen			x	14		x	Sum of correct answers		
Fonseca, Mullen, Zamarro, Zissimopoulos	x	x		23			23= 13 items scale from Lusardi and Mitchell (2006) + 10 new items; Lusardi-Mitchell 2006 (Numeracy | Compound interest | Inflation | Stock market | Stocks | Bonds | Mutual funds and diversification); Stocks; Bonds; Insurance and annuities (4 questions)		
Yoong				3		x	"Do not know" as a sort of "NEGATIVE FL INDEX"		x
Lusardi, Mitchell				3	x	x	1) Dummy for "All three responses correct"; 2) Sum of correct answers		
Utkus, Young				4	x	x	Dummy if all answers (to four questions) right, and zero otherwise		
Brumcont, Lin, Lusardi				5	x	x	Sum of correct answers		
Bumcrot, Lin, Lusardi				5	x	x	Sum of correct answers		
de Bassa Scheresberg			x	3	x	x	1) Dummy for "all three questions right"; 2) Each question separately; 3) Rate of do not know; 4) self-assessment; 5) Math ability	x	x

(Continued)

Table 1.1 (Continued)

Author(s)	Saving and Investment	Borrowing and Debts	Insurance	Retirement and Planning	# of questions	Type of Index	Self-assessment	Sum of correct answers	All correct (dummy)	At least "n" correct answers	one-by-one	Instrumental Variable (IV)	Number of "Do not know"
Huang, Nam, Sherraden					3	1) Sum of correct answers; 2) All three answers correct		x	x				
Lusardi, de Bassa Scheresberg					5	1) A dummy for correctly answering each financial literacy question (numeracy, knowledge of the effects of inflation, and understanding of risk diversification); 2) A dummy if "all of the five questions" are correct; 3) Self-assessed knowledge of math (scale 1–7)	x		x		x		
Mottola					5	Sum of correct answers		x					
Xiao, Chen, Chen					5	Self-assessmente (Likert 1–7)	x	x					
Nye, Hillyard					13	Sum of correct answers		x					
Schmeiser, Seligman					N.A.	Item Response Theory (IRT) "Item Response Theory (IRT) is a promising avenue for developing more useful financial literacy instruments. —> we suggest that future financial literacy survey efforts be designed with IRT-based identification in mind"							

Moore	x	21 (15 general knowledge questions; 6 knowledge on financial markets questions)	Sum of correct answers (on 12 questions)	x
Gustman, Steinmeier, Tabatabai		3	sum of correct answers	x
Knoll, Houts		20	"By using IRT, the current analysis uses individuals' answers to inform which questions to include in the scale in the first place, rather than simply confirming relationships between these answers and other financially relevant outcomes post hoc"	x
Jappelli, Padula		5	Sum of correct answers	x

The measures

From a comparison of the **measures** it is quite evident how the practice of using the sum of correct answers to different questions in order to measure financial literacy is the most popular approach. Almost 60% of the studies (46 of 78) used this measure to assess financial literacy. The practice of stressing the ability of people to correctly answer all the questions is quite common too (17 of 78), as is the use of answers to single questions as distinct measures of financial literacy (15 of 78) and self-assessed measures (12 of 78). The use of instrumental variables (IVs) in order to capture the effect of financial literacy on a specific outcome, by using a variable that is correlated with financial literacy but is not affected by endogeneity issues,[20] is becoming more and more popular. If it is not the most used option of all (7 of 78), it represents one of the most preferred in recent years.

The financial topics

If we look at the **topics** taken into account, almost three-fourths of the studies (55 of 78) included basic principles as a reference point or as part of a bigger set of topics in the assessment of financial literacy. **Compound interest**, **risk diversification**, and **inflation** are the most frequent topics. The broad areas of application of such general items make them perfectly match with financial literacy measures developed to be applied in studies that try to provide a big picture about financial literacy in a wide population. In most of the cases (41 of 55) these topics represent the only ones used to assess financial literacy, while in others (14 of 55) they are used with items that can be referred to specific topics (e.g. money management, saving and investment, etc.).

When a **specific area of knowledge** has been taken into account, saving and investments is the one that received the most attention. More than 20 studies included questions on saving and investments (23 of 78). If most of the time this has not been the only area of interest, in some cases (10 of 23) it has been the focus of the analysis or it represented the only topic that has been matched with items on general issues.

Other areas of interest were money management (13 of 78) and borrowing and debt (12 of 78), which most of the time (8 of 13) have been part of the same study and/or included in the same measure. The other areas – insurance, and retirement and planning – were not analyzed as often as the previous ones. Both of them have been analyzed in seven studies and most of the time together with other areas of interest. Only three studies paid attention exclusively to financial literacy on retirement and planning, while there were no studies within the ones taken into account that focused on insurance.

Several studies tried to pay attention to the role of different areas of knowledge in the measurement of financial literacy and the correlation between them by statistical methodologies in order to test the hypothesis that the ability to answer different questions and knowledge on different topics can attributed to the same source of knowledge. The desire to summarize financial literacy identifying some key factors and skills suggested most of the time to use factor analysis (8 of 78), even if principal component analysis (PCA) and cluster analysis have been applied too. The output of these techniques usually does not represent itself as a measure of financial literacy, but is used in other steps. The added value of these methodologies is the chance to clearly identify the source of knowledge and avoid overestimating the relevance of a single issue by the use of several items that can be related to the same issue.

An analysis of the studies that used **more than one measure of financial literacy at the same time** shows how this practice is not new (Chen and Volpe 2002, Volpe et al. 2002, Beal and Delpachitra 2003) and has become more and more frequent in recent years, when the number of measures adopted in order to test the effect on the result of the study increased. For instance, in the early 2000s the studies that included more than one measure of financial literacy used two measures (Beal and Delpachitra 2003) or three (Volpe et al. 2002). More recently some studies arrived to test even four measures at the same time (Fornero and Monticone 2011, de Bassa Scheresberg 2013, Agnew et al. 2013), and the use of three measures is no more exceptional (Sekita 2011, Disney and Gathergood 2012, Beckman 2013, Lusardi and de Bassa Scheresberg 2013).

An analysis of **the number of items** used to assess financial literacy allows further considerations. Still referring to the 78 studies of the sample, the average number of items concerning financial literacy is 10.47. The distribution of the data shows a great variance and even a large gap between the study with the lowest number of items (one item: Stango and Zinman 2009) and the one with the highest number (50 items: Hill and Perdue 2008). Most of the studies based their analysis on just a few questions as attested by the median[21] of the sample being equal to 5.

As has been already stressed, the number of items is not itself an index of the quality of a measure of financial literacy, because it is the use of the measure that will provide evidence about the sense of a study. At the same time developing and indexing financial literacy simply using three or five items on basic topics dramatically shrinks the possible applications of this measure to studies whose aim is to provide an overview about the general level of financial literacy in a population. Any analysis with more specific purposes risks being affected by a measure of financial literacy that is not able to provide more than a basic scale on very general issues. The risk in using such an analysis is that the weakness of the measure of financial literacy, due to the lack of information caused by not using a large enough number of items, will underestimate the effect of financial literacy because such an index will not be able to highlight the connection between financial literacy and the object of the study.

The number of items to be used in a study is ceiled by the number of available items. The lack of available data on financial literacy from specific surveys and the practice of adding questions on financial literacy to previous surveys (usually to be within the budget limit) restrict the chance to study financial literacy to just a few options, making, in most of cases, the preference for a very simple measure be a forced choice.

The lack of resources to develop bigger surveys and the will to make the results from a study comparable with results of a previous one are probably reasons behind the success of a set of three questions introduced for the first time in the 2004 wave of the Health and Retirement Study (HRS) and then replicated in several other surveys and experiments. These questions have been developed by Annamaria Lusardi and Olivia Mitchell and are usually referred to as "the Lusardi–Mitchell questions". The original version of the questions is the following (see Box 1.1), but they are usually adjusted in the values and the currencies, in order to let them be more familiar for the target of recipients of the survey.

The review of the literature behind this section shows how at least 31 of the 78 studies taken into account are totally based on or include, as part of the questions on financial literacy, **the Lusardi–Mitchell questions**. The number

---

Box 1.1   The Lusardi–Mitchell questions

Compound interest

Suppose you had $100 in a savings account and the interest rate was 2% per year. After 5 years, how much do you think you would have in the account if you left the money to grow?

- more than $102
- exactly $102
- less than $102

Inflation

Imagine that the interest rate on your savings account was 1% per year and inflation was 2% per year. After 1 year, would you be able to buy with the money in this account?

- more than today
- exactly the same as today
- less than today

Risk diversification

Do you think that the following statement is true or false? "Buying a single company stock usually provides a safer return than a stock mutual fund".

- True
- False

Source: Documentation of the Health and Retirement Study (HRS) – 2004 (http://hrsonline. isr.umich.edu/index.php?p=docs)

of studies based on this set of questions is a result of only the ones that explicitly refer to these questions or that reproduce the same contents, but the influence of the Lusardi-Mitchell questions on the measure of financial literacy is even bigger when one thinks of the studies that used just a few of them or that used them in order to develop more sophisticated questions. These questions have more than one element of strength. The lack of jargon[22] and the use of round numbers allow one to focus the attention of the respondent on a single issue. At the same time the options do not require any mathematical skills, making the intuition about the general effect of the core principle (compound interest, purchase power and inflation, risk diversification) sufficient to identify the correct answers. The very basic nature of these issues and their relevance, due to their effects on a plethora of financial cases (e.g. investment, borrowing, money management, etc.), represent other positive aspects of this set of questions. The fact that the questions do not refer to a specific financial system or a single country makes them ready to be replicated in studies related to different countries. Any measure of financial literacy based on the Lusardi-Mitchell questions will benefit from their simplicity and their relevance. At the same time we should keep in mind that an analysis of very basic principles will lead to a measure of financial literacy that is just as basic and that should be used to test the financial literacy in very general terms. If people who fail to correctly answer these simple questions can be considered financially illiterate, the opposite is not true. Three questions are probably not enough to judge an individual as "financially literate" simply because the knowledge of such basic principles can be used only as a pre-requisite for further analysis that is needed to test more advanced knowledge and skills.

The instrumental variable approaches

The lack of items to be directly used in a financial literacy measure can be one of the reasons behind the attempt to measure the effect of financial literacy on different financial outcomes by using **instrumental variables**. This methodology requires us to use a variable that does not represent itself as a measure of financial literacy but is highly correlated with financial literacy and, at the same time, is not affected by the variable used to measure the subject of the study. When available, these variables can be a good substitute for direct measures of financial literacy and can pass over the doubts about the role of financial literacy in explaining the behavior of other variables when the reverse hypothesis concerning the case that financial literacy could be the result of (or – at least – could be affected by) these variables cannot be ignored. Within the 78 studies in seven cases an instrumental variable (IV) approach has been used as a substitute or together with other measures of financial literacy.

Behrman et al. (2012) in a study on the role of financial literacy on pension accumulation in Chile introduced as part of their study some instrumental variables such as (1) **attendance of primary school** in an urban area, (2) **macro-economic conditions** around the time of school leaving/labour market entry, and (3) **family background variables** (e.g. paternal and maternal schooling attainment, poor economic background when child, respondent worked when under 15 years of age). For each of these variables the authors explain the hypothesis behind their use as instrumental variables for financial literacy. For attendance of primary school in an urban area the assumption is that school in such areas is on average better than school in rural areas. From this the authors assume that attendance of primary schools in urban areas can be a good predictor of knowledge and skills, including on financial issues. A poor macro-economic condition is supposed to be related with financial literacy in a negative sense. People who lived in a poor country when they were young could be negatively affected in their schooling attainment, and their financial literacy in school could be affected too. The family background is supposed to be relevant because a poor family economic background could reduce the chance to learn from parents and siblings.

Klapper et al. (2013), using data from Russia, used the **number of newspapers** sold and the **presence of universities** in a specific area as instrumental variables in a study on the role of financial literacy in explaining different financial behaviors (e.g. use of bank accounts, level of unspent income, use of credit, etc.). The assumption is that people with higher financial literacy are more interested than others in being informed by buying newspapers and that the presence of a university enhances the learning-from-peers effect.[23]

Calcagno and Monticone (2011) studied the relationship between financial literacy and the demand for financial advice using data from the Italian market. In their study they used as an instrument for financial literacy **the age at which the individual first traded a given financial product** (Government bonds, stocks, or mutual funds). The assumption is that the use of financial products is strongly related to financial literacy, while it is not related to the extent of delegation.

In a study on the relationship between financial literacy and retirement planning in the Netherlands, Alessie et al. (2011) used the **financial experience of siblings and parents** as an instrument for financial literacy. In this case the assumption is once more related with a learning-from-peers effect, because the authors assume that people living with financially literate people will learn by the interaction with them. Sekita (2011) decided to use individual and average regional language skills (Japanese) as an instrument for financial literacy, assuming that people with a lack of knowledge of (native) language skills will show lower levels of financial literacy too.

Yoong (2011), in a study on the role of financial literacy in stock market participation in the US, decided to use as an instrument for financial literacy **knowledge of other financial topics**. The author tested different hypotheses and decided to use the knowledge about bond pricing as the main instrument. The assumption is that knowledge on bond pricing is related with financial literacy but should not determine the stock market participation decision. The instrumental role of knowledge on bond pricing is supported by the assumption that stock market participation could improve knowledge on stock pricing, but not on bond pricing.

Jappelli and Padula (2011), in their analysis of saving decisions and financial literacy in a sample of European individuals, used as an instrument for financial literacy a measure of **numeracy**, under the assumption that higher levels of numeracy are related with higher levels of financial literacy. The variable they used for numeracy does not come from questions about mathematical issues but represents math performance in school.

The geographical distribution of financial literacy studies

An analysis of previous measures of financial literacy allowed the assessment of different levels of attention paid by different countries. The fact that 50% of the studies (39 of 78) analyzed data from the US is crystal clear evidence about the leading role of American studies on this issue and on financial literacy studies overall. The most studied country, after the US, seems to be the Netherlands, due to the fact that five studies analyzed the role of financial literacy on such different outcomes as saving account returns (Deuflhard et al. 2014), retirement planning (Alessie et al. 2011), stock market participation (Van Rooij et al. 2011a), and wealth (Van Rooij et al. 2011a). The presence of a free-to-access national survey with several types of information about financial literacy issues[24] played a key role in the development of these studies. Australia, the UK, and Italy have been studied three times each, while in other cases only one study has been found for each country (Chile, China, France, Ireland, Japan, Kenya, New Zealand, Romania, Sweden, Switzerland), except for Germany and Russia, where two studies have been found. The **lack of studies that try to compare different countries** is another issue. There are only five studies based on assessment of an international database that use data from different countries in the same study.

The available data

A last remark on the analysis of financial literacy is about **the size of the database** used in previous studies. As reported in Table 1.1, within the studies that provide detailed information about the data used measuring financial literacy, a comparison between different studies shows that the sample sizes are quite different. Baron-Donovan et al. (2005) tried to evaluate in their study an approach employed to prepare instructors of personal financial literacy courses for consumer debtors by analyzing 42 observations, which represents the smallest database of the sample. On the other side, the biggest sample is the FINRA Foundation National Financial Capability Study (NFCS) that includes around 25,000 observations on American adults and has been used in several studies (Lusardi 2010, Lusardi and Mitchell 2011, Bumcrot et al. 2013, de Bassa Scheresberg 2013, Mottola 2013, Xiao et al. 2013). Taking into account all the studies with available data about the sample sizes, on average the studies used databases with 4,368 observations. The fact that the median is just 1,694 highlights how some studies relied on much smaller samples than others.

The studies analyzed in this section are far from being a comprehensive review of the literature about financial literacy. Many other studies on financial literacy have been realized. Because the specific aim of this section was to stress how financial literacy has been measured, the lack of quantitative measures of financial literacy in some studies or the fact that there was not enough information about the use of these measures suggested that these research works not be included in the list of references.

Notes

1 The same definition was used two years later by Hung et al. (2009) and Murphy (2013).
2 Oxford English Dictionary (2017).
3 The two questions were:

    1 *"If the chance of getting a disease is 10 percent, how many people out of 1,000 would be expected to get the disease?"*
    2 *"If 5 people all have the winning number in the lottery and the prize is 2 million dollars, how much will each of them get?"*

4 *"Let's say you have 200 dollars in a savings account. The account earns 10 percent interest per year. How much would you have in the account at the end of two years?"*
5 The reference is to knowledge and abilities that are typical of a specific area and not to general principles that can be useful in more than one area.
6 In a similar scenario, a government that declares as mandatory contribution to a public pension system that is able to pay pensions that meet the financial needs of people on retirement will make knowledge and abilities on an alternative solution useless.
7 Oxford English Dictionary (2017).
8 Oxford English Dictionary (2017).
9 FSA (2005), Lusardi and Mitchell (2014), Atkinson and Kempson (2008).
10 A wrong option should be objectively wrong, without the chance to be considered right in some cases or partially right because it cites only some elements of the right answer while missing others.
11 In a question with two options where only one is right the odds of answering correctly are estimated as the ratio between the number of correct answers to the sum of options, equal to 1 on 2. So 0.5 or 50%.
12 In these cases the odds are equal to 1 on 3 (0.333 or 33.3%) and 1 on 4 (0.25 or 25%).
13 According to the Oxford English Dictionary (2017) we refer to jargon as "*special words or expressions used by a profession or group that are difficult for others to understand*".
14 In this case the two "twin" questions were:

    "If the interest rate rises, what should happen to bond prices?" (rise | fall | stay the same | none of the above)

    and

    "If the interest rate falls, what should happen to bond prices?" (rise | fall | stay the same | none of the above)

    In the first case 30.5% of respondents answered correctly (when the interest rate rises bond prices fall), while in the second case only 18.9% chose the right answer (when the interest rate falls bond prices rise).

15 An example of a question affected by a framing effect cited in the paper is "if you start out with $1,000 and earn an average return of 10% per year for 30 years, after compounding, the initial $1,000 will have grown to MORE than $6,000. True or false?" The alternative question differs by using "LESS than $6,000" as the reference point.

16 In the study, one set of respondents was asked whether the following statement is true or false: "*If you invest for the long run, the annual fees of mutual funds are important*"; the second group was asked: "*If you invest for the long run, the annual fees of mutual funds are unimportant*". Results support the hypothesis that people tend to deny a sentence, saying that it is false, very rarely.

17 An analysis of the measures of financial literacy in previous studies is included in the next paragraph.

18 For an analysis of the difference between factor analysis and principal component analysis see Bartholomew et al. (2008).

19 Bailey (1994).

20 The use of measures of financial literacy in order to explain some financial behaviors has been criticized on account of endogeneity issues. For instance, the hypothesis that people with higher knowledge about a product (e.g. credit cards) will be more prone to use it, due to the fact that their knowledge makes the product more familiar and lets it be considered as part of the available options, could be opposed to the hypothesis that the use of a product increases the knowledge about the key elements and the functioning of the product by a learning by doing process. The basic intuition about the use of instrumental variables that are related with financial literacy but that do not receive any influence from the use of a financial product has been taken into consideration when the possible endogeneity problem could be an issue.

21 The median is the value showed by the observation between the 2nd and the 3rd quartile of the distribution.

22 What is a bank account, what inflation means, and what are stocks and mutual funds are the main underlying issues. The use of these words on a regular basis by a general population minimizes the risk that the respondent is aware of a concept but does not choose the right answer or does not answer at all just because he/she does not know the words used to identify this concept.

23 The underlying assumption, confirmed by other studies, is that people with higher education are more financially literate.

24 All the studies used the De Nederlandsche Bank (DNB) Household Survey, promoted by the Dutch central bank.

References

Agnew, J., Bateman, H., Thorp, S. (2013). Financial Literacy and Retirement Planning in Australia. *Numeracy Advancing Education in Quantitative Literacy*, 6(2), *article* 7. DOI: http://dx.doi.org/10.5038/1936-4660.6.2.7

Alessie, R., van Rooij, M., Lusardi, A. (2011). Financial Literacy, Retirement Preparation and Pension Expectations in the Netherlands. *Journal of Pension Economics and Finance*, 10(4), 527–545.

Allgood, S., Walstad, W. (2013). Financial Literacy and Credit Card Behaviors: A Cross-Sectional Analysis by Age. *Numeracy Advancing Education in Quantitative Literacy*, 6(2), *article* 3. DOI: http://dx.doi.org/10.5038/1936-4660.6.2.3

Almenberg, J., Widmark, O. (2011a). Numeracy and Financial Literacy Among Swedish Adults. *Swedish Financial Supervisory Authority (Finansinspektionen), Report*

Almenberg, J., Widmark, O. (2011b). Numeracy, Financial Literacy and Participation in Asset Markets. *SSRN*, DOI: http://dx.doi.org/10.2139/ssrn.1756674

Ando, A., Modigliani, F. (1963). The "Life Cycle" Hypothesis of Saving: Aggregate Implications and Tests. *The American Economic Review*, 53(1), 55–84.

ANZ (2008). ANZ Survey of Adult Financial Literacy in Australia. www.anz.com/Documents/AU/Aboutanz/AN_5654_Adult_Fin_Lit_Report_08_Web_Report_full.pdf

ASIC Australian Securities and Investments Commission (2013). Shaping a National Financial Literacy Strategy for 2014–16. *National Financial Literacy Strategy (Australia), consultation paper 206*. www.asic.gov.au/cp

Association of American College and Universities (2018). Quantitative Literacy VALUE Rubric. *e-book*. http://secure.aacu.org/imis/ItemDetail?iProductCode=E-VRQNTLIT

Atkinson, A. (2011). *Measuring Financial Capability Using a Short Survey Instrument: Instruction Manual*. Bristol: Personal Finance Research Centre.

Atkinson, A., Kempson, E. (2008). *Measuring and Improving Financial Capability: Designing an Approach for Kenya*. Personal Finance Research Centre – University of Bristol

Atkinson, A., McKay, S., Collard, S., Kempson E. (2007). Levels of Financial Capability in the UK. *Public Money & Management*, 27(1), 29–36.

Atkinson, A., McKay, S., Kempson, E., Collard S. (2006). Levels of Financial Capability in the UK: Results of a Baseline Survey. *Financial Service Authority, Consumer Research*, 47.

Atkinson, A., Messy, F. (2012). Measuring Financial Literacy: Results of the OECD/International Network on Financial Education (INFE) Pilot Study. *OECD Publishing, OECD Working Paper on Finance, Insurance and Private Pensions, N. 15*. DOI: http://dx.doi.org/10.1787/5k9csfs90fr4-en

Bailey, K. (1994). Numerical Taxonomy and Cluster Analysis. *Typologies and Taxonomies*, 34. ISBN 9780803952591.

Baron-Donovan, C., Wiener, R., Gross, K., Block-Lieb, S. (2005). Financial Literacy Teacher Training: A Multiple-Measure Evaluation. *Journal of Financial Counselling and Planning*, 16(2), 63–75.

Bartholomew, D.J., Steele, F., Galbraith, J., Moustaki, I. (2008). *Analysis of Multivariate Social Science Data. Statistics in the Social and Behavioral Sciences Series* (2nd ed.). Boca Raton, FL: Taylor & Francis. ISBN 1584889608.

Beal, D., Delpachitra, S.B. (2003). Financial Literacy Among Australian University Students. *Economic Papers*, 22(1), 65–78.

Beckmann, E. (2013). Financial Literacy and Household Savings in Romania. *Numeracy Advancing Education in Quantitative Literacy*, 6(2), *article* 9. DOI: http://dx.doi.org/10.5038/1936-4660.6.2.9

Bodie, Z. (2006). A Note on Economic Principles and Financial Literacy. *Networks Financial Institute at Indiana State University Working Paper, 2006-PB-07*.

Behrman, J., Mitchell, O.S., Soo, C., Bravo, D. (2012). Financial Literacy, Schooling, and Wealth Accumulation. *American Economic Review Papers and Proceedings*, 102(3), 300–304.

Bodie, Z. (2006). A Note on Economic Principles and Financial Literacy. *Networks Financial Institute at Indiana State University Working Paper, 2006-PB-07*.

Bowen, C. (2003). Financial Knowledge of Teens and Their Parents. *Journal of Financial Counselling and Planning*, 13(2), 93–102.

Brown, M., Graf, R. (2013). Financial Literacy and Retirement Planning in Switzerland. *Numeracy Advancing Education in Quantitative Literacy*, 6(2), *article* 6. DOI: http://dx.doi.org/10.5038/1936-4660.6.2.6

Bumcrot, C., Lin, J., Lusardi, A. (2013). The Geography of Financial Literacy. *Numeracy Advancing Education in Quantitative Literacy*, 6(2), *article* 2. DOI: http://dx.doi.org/10.5038/1936-4660.6.2.2

Calcagno, R., Monticone, C. (2011). Financial Literacy and the Demand for Financial Advice. *Journal of Banking and Finance*, 50, 363–380.

Carpena, F., Cole, S., Shapiro, J., Zia, B. (2011). Unpacking the Causal Chain of Financial Literacy. *World Bank, Policy Research Working Paper, No. 5798.*

Chen, H., Volpe, R. (2002). Gender Differences in Personal Financial Literacy Among College Students. *Financial Services Review*, 11, 289–307.

Chen, H., Volpe, R. (2005). Financial Literacy, Education and Services in the Workplace. *Quest (Business Quest): A Journal of Applied Topics in Business and Economics.* www.westga.edu/~bquest/2005/workplace.pdf

Cude, B., Lawrence, F.C., Lyons, A.C., Metzger, K., LeJeune, E., Marks, L., Mactmes, K. (2006). College Students and Financial Literacy: What They Know and What We Need to Learn. *Eastern Family Economics and Resource Management Association, 2006 Conference.*

Dahmen, P., Rodriguez, E. (2014). Financial Literacy and the Success of Small Businesses: An Observation from a Small Business Development Center. *Numeracy Advancing Education in Quantitative Literacy*, 7(1), *article* 3. DOI: http://dx.doi.org/10.5038/1936-4660.7.1.3

Danes, S., Haberman, H. (2007). Teen Financial Knowledge, Self-Efficacy, and Behavior: A Gender View. *Journal of Financial Counselling and Planning*, 18(2), 48–60.

de Bassa Scheresberg, C. (2013). Financial Literacy and Financial Behavior among Young Adults: Evidence and Implications. *Numeracy Advancing Education in Quantitative Literacy*, 6(2), *article* 5. DOI: http://dx.doi.org/10.5038/1936-4660.6.2.5

Deuflhard, F., Georgarakos, D., Inderst, R. (2014). Financial Literacy and Savings Account Returns. *MPRA Munich Personal RePEc Archive.* DOI: http://dx.doi.org/10.2139/ssrn.2358564

Disney, R., Gathergood, J. (2012). Financial Literacy and Consumer Credit Use. *CFCM – Centre for Finance and Credit Markets, Working Paper, 12/01*

Fessler, P., Schürz, M., Wagner, K., Weber, B. (2007). Financial Capability of Austrian Households. *Monetary Policy & the Economy*, Q3–07, 50–67.

FINRA (2003). NASD Investor Literacy Research: Executive Summary. www.finrafoundation.org/web/groups/foundation/@foundation/documents/foundation/p118411.pdf

FINRA (2009). Financial Capability in the United States National Survey Executive Summary. *FINRA Investor Education Foundation. www.usfinancialcapability.org/downloads/NFCS_2009_Natl_Exec_Sum.pdf*

Fornero, E., Monticone, C. (2011). Financial Literacy and Pension Plan Participation in Italy. *Journal of Pension Economics and Finance*, 10(4), 547–564.

FSA (2005). Measuring Financial Capability: An Exploratory Study. *Financial Service Authority, Consumer Research*, 37.

Gerardi, K., Goette, L., Meier, S. (2010). Financial Literacy and Subprime Mortgage Delinquency: Evidence from a Survey Matched to Administrative Data. *Federal Reserve Bank of Atlanta Working Paper, 2010–10.*

Gilliland, D., Melfi, V., Sikorskii, A., Corcoran, E., Melfi, E. (2011). Quantitative Literacy at Michigan State University, 2: Connection to Financial Literacy. *Numeracy Advancing Education in Quantitative Literacy*, 7(1), *article* 6. DOI: http://dx.doi.org/10.5038/1936-4660.4.2.6

Guiso, L., Jappelli, T. (2009). Financial Literacy and Portfolio Diversification. *CSEF – Centre for Studies in Economics and Finance, Working Paper, No. 212.*

Gustman, A., Steinmeier, T., Tabatabai, N. (2010). Financial Knowledge and Financial Literacy at the Household Level. *Michigan Retirement Research Center, Working Paper, 2010–23.*

Hill, R., Perdue, G. (2008). A Methodological Issue in the Measurement of Financial Literacy. *Journal of Economics and Economic Education Research*, 9, 150–162.

Hira, T.K., Loibl, C. (2005). Understanding the Impact of Employer-Provided Financial Education on Workplace Satisfaction. *Journal of Consumer Affairs*, 39(1), 173–194.

Huang, J., Nam, Y., Sherraden, M. (2013). Financial Knowledge and Child Development Account Policy a Test of Financial Capability. *Journal of Consumer Affairs*, 47(1), 1–26.

Hung, A., Parker, A.M., Yoong, J. (2009). Defining and Measuring Financial Literacy. *RAND Working Paper, WR-708.*

Huston, S. (2010). Measuring Financial Literacy. *Journal of Consumer Affairs*, 44(2), 296–316.

Jappelli, T., Padula, M. (2011). Investment in Financial Literacy and Saving Decisions. *CSEF Centre for Studies in Economics and Finance, W-272.*

Jappelli, T., Padula, M. (2013). Investment in Financial Literacy, Social Security and Portfolio Choice. *CSEF Centre for Studies in Economics and Finance, Working Paper, No. 330.*

Jaredi, S., Mendez, F. (2014). On the Advantages and Disadvantages of Subjective Measures. *Journal of Economic Behavior and Organization*, 98, 97–114.

Johnson, E., Sherraden, M.S. (2006). From Financial Literacy to Financial Capability Among Youth. *Center for Social Development Working Paper, 06-11.*

Jumpstart Coalition (2007). National Standards in K-12 Personal Finance Education. *Jumpstart Coalition.* http://education.howthemarketworks.com/wp-content/uploads/2015/11/2015_NationalStandards.pdf

Kim, J. (2001). Financial Knowledge and Subjective and Objective Financial Well-Being. *Consumer Interests Annual*, 47, 1–3.

Klapper, L., Lusardi, A., Panos, G. (2013). Financial Literacy and Its Consequences: Evidence from Russia During the Financial Crisis. *Journal of Banking and Finance*, 37(10), 3904–3923.

Knoll, M.A.Z., Houts, C.R. (2012). The Financial Knowledge Scale: An Application of Item Response Theory to the Assessment of Financial Literacy. *Journal of Consumer Affairs*, 46(3), 381–410.

Lusardi, A. (2009a). Financial Literacy: An Essential Tool for Informed Consumer Choice? *Networks Financial Institute at Indiana State University Working Paper, 2008 -WP-13.* DOI: 10.3386/w14084

Lusardi, A. (2009b). U.S. Household Savings Behavior: The Role of Financial Literacy, Information and Financial Education Programs. *Published in Foote, C., Goette, L, Meier, S. (eds) Policymaking Insights from Behavioral Economics: Federal Reserve Bank of Boston*, 109–149.

Lusardi, A. (2010). Americans' Financial Capability. *Report Prepared for the Financial Crisis Inquiry Commission.*

Lusardi, A., de Bassa Scheresberg, C. (2013). Financial Literacy and High-Cost Borrowing in the United States. *Global Financial Literacy Excellence Center (GFLEC) Research Paper.* www.usfinancialcapability.org/downloads/HighCostBorrowing.pdf?utm_source=.

Lusardi, A., Mitchell, O.S. (2006). Financial Literacy and Retirement Preparedness: Evidence and Implications for Financial Education. *Michigan Retirement Research Center, Working Paper, 2006-144.*

Lusardi, A., Mitchell, O.S. (2011). Financial Literacy and Retirement Planning in the United States. *Journal of Pension Economics and Finance*, 10(4), 509–525.

Lusardi, A., Mitchell, O.S. (2014). The Economic Importance of Financial Literacy: Theory and Evidence. *Journal of Economic Literature*, 52(1), 5–44.

Lusardi, A., Mitchell, O.S., Curto, V. (2014). Financial Literacy and Financial Sophistication in the Older Population: Evidence from the 2008 HRS. *Journal of Pension Economics and Finance*, 13(4), 347–366. DOI: 10.1017/S1474747214000031

Lusardi, A., Tufano, P. (2015). Debt Literacy, Financial Experiences, and Overindebtedness. *Journal of Pension Economics and Finance*, 14(04), 332–368.

Mak, V., Braspenning, J. (2012). Errare humanum Est: Financial Literacy in European Consumer Credit Law. *Journal of Consumer Policy*, 35, 307–332.

Mandell, L., (2008). *Financial Education in High School. Published in Lusardi, A. (eds) Overcoming the Saving Slump*. Chicago, IL: University of Chicago Press, 257–279.

Mandell, L., Klein, L. (2007). Motivation and Financial Literacy. *Financial Services Review*, 16, 105–116.

Mason, C., Wilson, R. (2000). Conceptualising Financial Literacy. *Loughborough University Business School (UK), Research Series Paper 2000-7*. ISBN 1 85901 168 3.

Moore, D. (2003). Survey of Financial Literacy in Washington State: Knowledge, Behavior, Attitudes and Experiences. *Washington State University Social and Economic Sciences Research Center, Technical Report 03–39*.

Mottola, G. (2013). In Our Best Interest: Women, Financial Literacy, and Credit Card Behavior. *Numeracy Advancing Education in Quantitative Literacy*, 6(2), *article* 4. DOI: http://dx.doi.org/10.5038/1936-4660.6.2.4

Murphy, J.L. (2013). Psychosocial Factors and Financial Literacy. *US Social Security Administration – Social Security Bulletin*, 73(1), 73–81.

NCEE National Council for Economic Education (2005). *What American Teens & Adults Know about Economics*. Washington, DC: NCEE. www.councilforeconed.org/cel/WhatAmericansKnowAboutEconomics_042605-3.pdf

Nicolini, G., Cude, B. (2014). Financial Literacy, Low Incomes and Financial Stress in US Households. *Bancaria Forum*, (4), 41–60.

Noctor, M., Stoney, S., Stradling, R. (1992). Financial Literacy: A Discussion of Concepts and Competences of Financial Literacy and Opportunities for Its Introduction into Young People's Learning. *Report prepared for the National Westminster Bank*. London: National Foundation for Education Research.

Nye, P., Hillyard, C. (2013). Personal Financial Behavior: The Influence of Quantitative Literacy and Material Values. *Numeracy Advancing Education in Quantitative Literacy*, 6(1), *article* 3. DOI: http://dx.doi.org/10.5038/1936-4660.6.1.3

O'Donnell, N., Keeney, M. (2009). Financial Capability: New Evidence for Ireland. *Central Bank of Ireland Research Technical Paper 1/RT/09*.

OECD (2010). PISA 2012 Financial Literacy Framework. www.oecd.org/finance/financial-education/PISA2012FrameworkLiteracy.pdf

Oxford University (2017). *Oxford English Dictionary*. Oxford, UK: Oxford University Press.

Remund, D.L. (2010). Financial Literacy Explicated: The Case for a Clearer Definition in an Increasingly Complex Economy. *Journal of Consumer Affairs*, 44(2), 276–295.

Schagen, S., Lines, A. (1996). *Financial Literacy in Adult Life: A Report to the Natwest Group Charitable Trust*. Slough, Berkshire: National Foundation for Educational Research.

Schmeiser, M., Seligman, J. (2013). Using the Right Yardstick: Assessing Financial Literacy Measures by Way of Financial Well-Being. *Journal of Consumer Affairs*, 47(2), 191–374.

Sekita, S. (2011). Financial Literacy and Retirement Planning in Japan. *Journal of Pension Economics and Finance*, 10(4), 637–656.

Servon, L.J., Kaestner, R. (2008). Consumer Financial Literacy and the Impact of Online Banking on the Financial Behavior of Lower-Income Bank Customers. *Journal of Consumer Affairs*, 42(2), 271–305.

Stango, V., Zinman, J. (2009). Exponential Growth Bias and Household Finance. *Journal of Finance*, 64, 2807–2849.

US FLEC United States Financial Literacy and Education Commission (2007). *Taking Ownership of the Future: The National Strategy for Financial Literacy*. www.mymoney.gov/pdfs/add07strategy.pdf

van Rooij, M., Lusardi, A., Alessie, R. (2011a). Financial Literacy and Retirement Planning in the Netherlands. *Journal of Economic Psychology*, 32, 593–608.

van Rooij, M., Lusardi, A., Alessie, R. (2011b). Financial Literacy and Stock Market Participation. *NBER Working Paper, No. 13565.*

Vitt, L.A., Anderson, C., Kent, J., Lyter, D.M., Siegenthaler, J.K., Ward, J. (2000). *Personal Finance and the Rush to Competence: Financial Literacy Education in the U.S.* Middleburg, VA: Fannie Mae Foundation. www.isfs.org/documents-pdfs/rep-finliteracy.pdf

Volpe, R., Kotel, J., Chen, H. (2002). A Survey of Investment Literacy Among Online Investors. *Journal of Financial Counselling and Planning*, 13(1), 1–16.

Willis, L.E. (2008). Against Financial Literacy Education. *Iowa Law Review*, 94, 197–285.

World Bank (2013). Financial Capability Surveys Around the World. http://documents. worldbank.org/curated/en/693871468340173654/pdf/807670WP0P14400Box037982 0B00PUBLIC0.pdf

Worthington, A. (2006). Predicting Financial Literacy in Australia. *Financial Services Review*, 15, 59–79.

Worthington, A. (2013). Financial Literacy and Financial Literacy Programmes in Australia. *Journal of Financial Services Marketing*, 18, 227–240.

Xiao, J., Chen, C., Chen, F. (2013). Consumer Financial Capability and Financial Satisfaction. *Social Indicators Research*, 118(1), 415–432.

Yoong, J. (2011). Financial Illiteracy and Stock Market Participation: Evidence from the RAND American Life Panel. *Published in Financial Literacy Implications for Retirement Security and the Financial Marketplace.* New York, NY: Oxford University Press, 76–10.

2 Financial literacy and financial behavior

2.1 The role of financial literacy in the financial decision making process

The interest on financial literacy from academics, policy makers, supervisory authorities, and other institutions is essentially motivated by the **assumption that financial literacy plays a role in the explanation of people's financial behaviors** and that, working on financial literacy, it is possible to affect financial behaviors. Even studies that simply proposed an assessment of the financial literacy of a population or a subgroup (e.g. college students, the elderly, etc.), without looking for any connection with specific financial behavior, have been motivated by the will to assess how much people are prepared to make a financial decision or to be aware about their financial status. It follows that the study of financial literacy represents an intermediate step – or a tool to be used – in order to achieve different final goals such as financial well-being, prevention of financial troubles, and financial stability of individuals, communities, or (in a broader perspective) national and international targets. The positive effect of financial literacy on financial behaviors should be the driver to achieve purposes on an individual or a general basis.

The typical research hypothesis of financial literacy studies is that better knowledge on a financial issue will help a subject to make a better financial decision, being more aware about the possible consequences that could follow from making this decision. The point of view in the present study is that the connection between financial literacy and financial behavior (looking at the former as a driver of the latter) cannot be summarized in a cause-effect relationship where it is possible to predict what an individual will do only knowing how much he/she knows about finance. It does not mean that the approach to the topic is less optimistic compared with studies that assume a leading role for financial literacy on financial behaviors, but it is based on less enthusiastic and more balanced expectations that are motivated by different arguments.

The basic assumption that the person who is more knowledgeable about finance and who knows how to use his/her knowledge to make a financial decision will be in a better condition in making a choice about finance is out of the question. At the same time the assumption that financially literate people will make a good financial decision by definition is not as obvious. As reported by Mason and Wilson (2000), financial literacy can only ensure individuals are informed to make decisions; it cannot ensure that the "right" decision is actually made. A first argument to support the hypothesis that **financial literacy itself is not a guarantee of a good financial decision** concerns the presence of **behavioral biases** that could deviate the decision toward a not optimal choice. Studies of behavioral finance (e.g. Mak and Braspenning 2012; Korniotis and Kumar 2011) have found evidence about the chance that well informed and skilled people can make a decision that does not fit with a pure rational outlook. Cognitive errors and psychological biases could affect the decision of a fully financially literate individual. Of course, it does not mean that financial literacy is meaningless in a financial decision making process, but these results support the hypothesis that financial literacy matters but is not the only driver of the process.

A second argument is about the **possibility to determine a financial decision as the "right choice" on absolute terms**. If there are some cases where the choice between alternative options shows a clear preference for one of them, in other cases the choice between different options depends on several elements that have to be taken into account and that make an option optimal for a particular individual and not as good for another. The elements that affect the decision making process and push individuals to behave differently concern **the differences between people** about their risk attitudes, their intertemporal consumption preferences, their perception about market conditions, and other issues related with personal characteristics. The FSA (2005) described how an individual's personality can have a key role in different financial behaviors by stressing whether individuals are organized, their ability to resist temptations, and their attitude to comparing products and shopping around before making a decision. For instance, the decision to save more in order to benefit from a higher income when on retirement or to enjoy a higher standard of living today is a decision that cannot be interpreted in a right-or-wrong sense, due to the fact that it depends on personal preferences. Behrman et al. (2012) stressed the role of further personal issues like intelligence and motivation as possible explanation variables of financial behaviors.

The **socio-economic framework** is another element that can affect a financial decision. The presence of a more or less generous welfare state is probably a key element in the decision about how much to save for retirement. People living in a country where the government ensures a very generous public pension will not perceive the need to save for retirement as a top priority, while people living in a country where the level of post-retirement income is the result of private contributions to some pension schemes will be affected in their decision to save by the awareness of the need to do it.

Besides personal preferences, and the features of the legal system and the social framework, a third element that is able to affect the result of a financial decision making process is the presence of other **external constraints**. The chance that people are aware – thanks to their financial literacy – that a specific behavior is objectively the most desirable, but they are not able to behave coherently with their will, due to the presence of some difficulties, cannot be ignored. For instance, the need to save for retirement in countries where the pension systems are based on private contribution schemes can be quite evident to all, but people do not save due to a lack of income and the need to cope with other upcoming needs.

The example of saving for retirement shows how a financial decision cannot be interpreted as good or bad without taking into account how much information is available to people, their ability to understand and interpret this information (financial literacy), their preferences, their attitudes, the socio-economic framework they are living in, and their perception about the possible consequences of their behavior.

The aforementioned considerations suggest approaching the role of financial literacy in the financial decision making processes not referring to a financial decision or a financial behavior as "good or bad", but looking at the role of financial literacy in **making people be more aware about the possible consequences of their choices**. The hypothesis about the connection between financial literacy and financial behaviors is that financial literacy plays a key role in helping people be aware about the possible consequences of their actions. It follows that, despite other elements that can affect the financial behavior of an individual, high financial literacy will positively affect the quality of the result of a decision making process.

Being aware that financial literacy is not the only thing that explains a financial behavior (and being aware that it could even not be the main one) does not mean that it is not a key variable to work on, in order to analyze how people make their decisions in finance and to guide them toward better results. The positive effect of financial literacy on the quality of a financial decision cannot be enough to ensure an optimal result; however, a **lack of financial literacy represents a strong predictor of a low quality decision**. A choice between alternative options (e.g. "*which is the financial product that best fits with my need?*") without the knowledge about the features and the functioning of each option risks being driven by heuristic approaches if not even by a random process. The fact that the choice between different items needs to account for what these items are and what the differences are between them leads to the conclusion that an adequate level of financial literacy represents a necessary condition to making a good financial decision, even if its contribution to the decision making process can be minimized or eliminated by other elements. At the same time a lack of financial literacy can be seen as a strong predictor of a low quality decision.

The key role of financial literacy in making a financial decision is even more relevant when taking into account that a lack of financial literacy can **inhibit the beginning of the process** itself. As suggested by studies on behavioral changes (Prochaska et al. 1992), the decision to change a certain status or change a specific habit, adopting a new behavior by taking an action, is just the final step of the entire process of change that contemplates different "stages of change".[1] The decision to do something follows previous steps relating with the awareness that a change is needed and preparedness for the change by collecting information about the best way to do it. In this transition, from a state of mind where the need to change is not perceived at all (precontemplation) to the awareness of the need (contemplation), the role of financial literacy can be determinate, due to the fact that the ignorance about the consequences related to a lack of action (e.g. lack of saving for retirement due to a lack of knowledge about the functioning of the pension system or a misinterpretation about its rules) could inhibit any decision, leading to results that are even worse than the ones related to a bad decision (e.g. doing nothing – not having a pension at all – is worse than doing something, even if it is not the best thing to do like investing in the stock market by putting all the money in the stocks of a single company instead of contributing to a pension fund). If in the case of financial decisions with short-term effects, the awareness about a need can be developed by having a bad experience (e.g. to understand the benefit of having a bank account after experiencing a theft of cash at home), in the case of a long-term decision (e.g. saving for retirement, saving for children's education, etc.) the "school of hard knocks" does not give the chance to repair the effect of a lack of knowledge because the awareness of the need arrives when it is too late to repair. Evidence about the positive role of financial literacy on the self-awareness of financial needs is reported by Almenberg and Säve-Söderberg (2011), who used a sample of Swedish adults to test the differences in financial literacy between planners and non planners, finding higher levels of financial literacy within the planners group. Clark et al. (2010) used a sample of American adults near retirement to test the effect of knowledge on planned retirement age. The results confirm that people with higher financial literacy are more aware about their real eligible retirement age and are more ready to go on to retirement. Positive effects on financial planning skills are also reported by Bucher-Koenen and Lusardi (2011) studying the effect of financial literacy on individual planning for retirement in Germany. Further evidence has been found for the US in the study of Nye and Hillyard (2013) that confirmed how more quantitatively literate consumers make more forward-looking financial choices.

The chance to use financial literacy to help people make better financial decisions has been discussed in the literature, and some authors have arrived at the conclusion that the hypothesis to use financial literacy in order to improve financial behavior is misleading and does not represent an available option. The most fierce **attack of the financial literacy studies** is the one of Willis (2008). The author proposed different arguments to support her thesis. The first one is related with the fact that the financial marketplace is constantly changing at a very rapid pace. If it is tough for regulators to keep up with the pace of financial innovation, it is almost impossible for consumers, so "*financial literacy is chasing a moving target it will never reach*" (p. 219). At the same time banks and other financial institutions have so much more knowledge, skills, information, and resources than their clients to make the assumption about financial literacy as a solution to fill this gap simply unrealistic. Another argument against financial literacy concerns the presence of different biases that affect consumer financial behaviors and that could neutralize the effect of financial literacy. The lack of motivation and interest of people for financial issues is reported as another critical point. If people are not interested to learn about finance, the attempt to help them by improving their knowledge risks being worthless. At the same time financial literacy can be seen as an investment in human capital that, as with other investments, becomes reasonable only if its cost-benefit analysis suggests that the latter returns are greater than the former costs. The fixed costs related to a learning process become reasonable only if the benefits coming from the application of the acquired knowledge are great enough, with the risk of making the investment in financial literacy not convenient for un-wealthy people. The fact that a low level of financial literacy can even affect perception about the benefits coming from learning about finance, underestimating the value of the investment, contributes to reducing the chance that people will engage in a learning process.

The supposed fallacy of financial literacy expectations, supported by Willis (2008), is summarized in a single sentence, where the author stresses how *"Consumers generally do not serve as their own doctors and lawyers and for reasons of efficient division of labour alone, generally should not serve as their own financial experts"* (Willis 2008, p. 198).

More recently Fernandes et al. (2013) reviewed the literature about financial literacy on financial behavior with an analysis of 155 papers covering 188 prior studies. Their empirical approach seems to support the assumption that financial literacy cannot be used to explain consumer financial behavior. The authors reported that interventions to improve financial literacy explain just a few of the variances in financial behavior, especially when one controls for psychological traits.

The point of view of some authors about financial literacy is even more negative, arriving to the conclusion that financial literacy is not only ineffective in order to improve financial behavior, but is even a dangerous thing. Willis (2008) reported how giving people just a bit of knowledge and information they become overconfident about their ability to use them in order to make a financial decision, and other studies (Gamble et al. 2013) found that overconfidence is greater with fraud victims.

Nevertheless several authors replied to the criticism about financial literacy in different manners. For instance, Lusardi and Mitchell (2014) replied to Willis (2008) noting how the fact that an individual will hardly become a financial expert does not imply that financial literacy is not worthy at all. So, if people will not be their own financial expert it does not mean that they will not benefit from their financial literacy, as people who attend a course on literature will benefit from it even if it will not make them into professional writers. It could be even said that the basic principles of financial literacy need to be known in making the most of daily financial decisions (e.g. *"is it better to pay cash by making a withdrawal at an ATM, or should I pay by credit card?"*), as the basic principles of medicine need to be known to solve some basic problems (e.g. *"if I have a bit of fever from a cold should I take an aspirin, or should I go to the hospital and ask a doctor?"*). Improving their financial literacy, people are not necessarily trying to be their own financial expert, and investing in financial literacy is not in conflict with the use of a financial advisor. As noted by Collins (2012) financial advice more often serves as a complement to, rather than a substitute for, financial literacy. The need to choose a financial advisor and to be aware about one's own financial needs is evidence that financial literacy is useful and necessary even if there is an external support. About this issue, Collins (2012) found that consumers with low financial literacy – those individuals who may be most likely to make financial mistakes without advice – are among the least likely to seek it.

About the low influence of financial literacy in explaining financial behavior, Carpena et al. (2011) highlight that not only the way financial literacy is measured matters (number of items, relationship between topics and behavior, etc.), but even the behavioral change could be an issue. If improvements in financial literacy are required to change financial behavior, then it would be difficult to detect behavioral outcomes, since these would be situated at the end of the causal chain. For instance, financial literacy on pension planning could be effective if people start thinking about saving for retirement, figuring out that this is a real need, even if the behavioral outcome "start saving for retirement" is not reported, if no changes happen, and people are not enrolled in any saving plan. The point in time and how a behavioral change is measured are quite relevant.

A last dilemma about the role of financial literacy on explaining financial behavior concerns the so called "**reverse causality**" hypothesis. Several authors analyzed the relationship between financial literacy and financial behavior in order to figure out if a cause–effect relationship exists and what is the main direction of the effect. Hilgert and Hogarth (2002) used data from a sample of American adults[2] and arrived at the conclusion that it is not clear where the causation lies, whether knowledge comes from having experience with financial products or experience with financial products follows a basic knowledge of the principles of these types of products. In more recent studies, some clear results seem to have been found. In a study on the relationship between financial literacy and retirement planning in the US, Lusardi and Mitchell (2007) used information[3] on individuals' past financial literacy, prior to entering the job market, finding that those who were financially literate when young are more likely to plan for retirement, which shows that it is literacy that affects planning and not the other way around. Similarly van Rooij, Lusardi, and Mitchell (2011), in a study on the role of financial literacy in retirement planning in the Netherlands,[4] used information on economic education acquired in school and showed that the nexus of causality goes from financial literacy to planning, while Pahnke and Honekamp (2010) found that financial literacy leads to greater retirement planning in Germany. There are also studies that arrived at opposite conclusions, such as Gustman et al. (2010), who found how pension wealth is more likely to cause pension knowledge in the US, rather than the other way around.

2.2 The new challenges of financial literacy between personal financial behaviors and social outcomes

The previous paragraph discussed the chance to use financial literacy in order to help people make their financial decisions. The assumptions that people with more financial literacy are more aware about the consequences of their financial behaviors and will be more ready to make a financial decision pave the way for the use of financial literacy as a driver of desirable financial outcomes such as the avoidance of financial frauds, the awareness of long-term financial needs, and the ability to recognize the best option between different solutions available on the financial markets. The need and the will to support people's financial literacy can be motivated both from an individual micro-economic perspective, looking at how much an individual can benefit from being financially literate, and a macro-economic perspective, analyzing the positive effect on the functioning of a financial system from the presence of knowledgeable and skilled financial consumers.

From the individual perspective, financial literacy represents a self-protection tool, against both financial frauds and wrong decisions, and a decision making tool to be used in order to improve the quality of a financial decision. The analysis of financial literacy as a "human capital" investment has been already introduced in the present study, presenting the decision to acquire and develop this kind of capital in a cost–benefit analysis framework, and stressing how people will choose to invest in their knowledge and develop their skills in finance if they have the perception that the efforts and the resources required to develop their financial literacy will be rewarded somehow in the future. The perception of the potential benefits of financial literacy is pivotal to provide people with the right **motivation to learn**. Without the belief that financial literacy is essential to manage one's own finances, any effort to change financial behaviors by improving financial literacy is vain.

Financial literacy is an investment of time, energy, and other resources, and the expected returns of this investment depend on the estimated value added to future financial outcomes coming from financial literacy. The benefits from the use of financial literacy can involve a single strategically relevant financial decision (e.g. the decision to be enrolled in a saving plan for retirement and the choice of a single pension scheme) or a sequence of small financial decisions to be made on a daily basis (e.g. the use of credit cards, cash, or other payment options). Helping people in developing **awareness of the need** to be financially literate represents the first challenge of financial literacy. This challenge has to cope with at least two issues. The first concerns the chance that **low financial literacy could represent itself an obstacle to figuring out the possible benefit of financial literacy**. For instance, Bhattacharya et al. (2014) conducted an experiment with a European brokerage bank, proposing a no-cost financial advice service to the bank's most active clients. Results show that clients who participated in the financial advice service were among the ones with the highest financial literacy.

A second obstacle to convincing people to invest in developing their financial literacy is the "**hyperbolic discounting**" bias. As reported by Laibson (1997) people tend to perceive as more relevant the things that will happen in the very short term compared with events that will produce their outcomes in the mid and long term. The preference for instant gratification versus long-term goals is far from being linear and seems to follow a time-decay rate that is much more similar to a hyperbolic trend, due to the fact that the marginal utility time-decay effect is very high in the very short term (e.g. the perceived utility of a sum of money today is much higher than the perceived utility of the same amount of money tomorrow, which is much higher than the utility on day three) and becomes very low in the mid and long term (e.g. the perceived utility for a sum of money that will be available in a year is just a bit higher than the utility of the same amount in two years), making the perception of happenings in the short term seem much more relevant than events in the near future. The consequence of this distortion in the perceived utility function makes things that will happen in the very short term be perceived as much more relevant than things that will happen in the future. It follows that the cost of an investment that must be paid immediately has to be compensated by very high future benefits in order to let the investment be perceived as reasonable. If one looks at the development of financial literacy as an investment, where the initial costs of learning will be rewarded by returns only in the long term, the presence of the "hyperbolic discounting" bias dramatically reduces the motivation to learn by shrinking the perceived utility of financial literacy.

The need to motivate people to learn and the presence of the hyperbolic discounting bias are both elements that stress the need to reduce as much as possible the time gap between learning and the application of the acquired knowledge about finance. If any plan with the aim to develop financial literacy in a long-term view is praiseworthy, the risk that people will fail in appreciating the value of this knowledge can be the reason behind a lack of motivation.

The need to motivate people to learn represents only the first challenge of financial literacy, which can be seen as a part of a consumer (self-)protection strategy or a consumer interest movement's tool devoted to protecting consumers by education. However, there are other new challenges as regards financial consumers and their financial literacy.

If the need to know about finance in order to make a financial decision is not a new topic, the growing relevance of financial literacy is motivated by more than one reason, such as the development of financial systems and radical changes in welfare state policies in many countries.

The welfare state policies implemented by most of the developed countries, after World War II, and devoted to building a wide public safety net – regarding the job market, the pension system, and public healthcare coverage – represented part of a social framework where people do not need to care about present and future needs because they can take advantage of the benefits ensured by the government.

We can think of the case of generous and mandatory **public pension schemes**, based on defined benefit plans, where public and private workers do not have any uncertainty about their retirement age or the amount of their pensions, and (overall) where they are sure that the purchasing power of these pensions will allow them to maintain the standard of living of pre-retirement age. In such a positive scenario there is no need to take care about pension planning, and, as a consequence, there is no need to develop knowledge and skills about this topic, due to the fact that no financial decisions have to be made by individuals enrolled in the public pension system on a mandatory basis. For instance, Crossan et al. (2011), in an analysis of the New Zealand pension system, stressed how payment by the government of the so called "New Zealand Superannuation" – a universal flat-rate pension to people aged 65 and over, irrespective of their assets, income, or employment status – might suggest that financial literacy need play only a minor role in retirement planning.

Demographic changes, such as the improvement of people's life expectancies, the reduction of births, and the increase of the old-age dependency ratio,[5] forced the governments of most countries to change the prodigality of their public pension systems by reducing their benefits and introducing (or enhancing) a "multi-pillars" system, where the public pillar is complemented by private institutions – such as pension funds – or individual retirement accounts.

Data from an OECD study[6] on pension systems around the world show that more than 30 countries introduced some pension system reform during 2009–2013 (Table 2.1).

Table 2.1 Overview of pension reform measures in 34 OECD countries, 2009–2013

	Coverage	Adequacy	Sustainability	Work incentives	Administrative efficiency	Diversification/ security	Other
Australia	x	x	x	x	x		x
Austria	x	x	x				x
Belgium				x			
Canada	x		x	x		x	x
Chile	x	x			x	x	x
Czech Republic			x	x		x	
Denmark				x	x		
Estonia		x	x	x	x	x	
Finland	x	x	x	x		x	
France	x	x	x	x			x
Germany		x	x	x			
Greece		x	x	x	x		
Hungary		x	x	x		x	x
Iceland							x
Ireland	x		x	x		x	x
Israel	x	x				x	
Italy		x	x	x	x		
Japan	x	x	x		x		x

(Continued)

Table 2.1 (Continued)

	Coverage	Adequacy	Sustainability	Work incentives	Administrative efficiency	Diversification/ security	Other
Korea	x		x		x		
Luxembourg	x		x	x			
Mexico		x			x	x	
Netherlands						x	
New Zealand		x	x				x
Norway		x	x	x			
Poland	x		x	x		x	
Portugal	x	x	x	x		x	
Slovak Republic			x		x	x	
Slovenia	x	x	x	x	x	x	x
Spain		x	x	x			
Sweden		x	x	x	x	x	
Switzerland		x				x	
Turkey				x		x	x
United Kingdom	x	x	x	x	x	x	x
United States	x	x	x				

Source: OECD (2013), Pensions at a Glance 2013: OECD and G20 Indicators, OECD Publishing, p. 21 (http://dx.doi.org/10.1787/pension_glance-2013-en)

In the same study a taxonomy of different types of retirement-income provision (Figure 2.1) was used to compare different pension systems, especially in their non voluntary parts.

The main distinction is between three "tiers" (or "pillars"), where the first two are the mandatory or quasi-mandatory parts of the pension systems. The "**first tier**" is designed to ensure pensioners achieve some absolute, minimum standard of living and based on a redistributive scheme, the "**second tier**" is designed to achieve some target standard of living in retirement compared with that when working, while the "**third tier**" ensures individuals will save more for retirement on a voluntary basis and usually with a tax-shield effect. Within the first pillar a "**basic scheme**" can pay the same amount of money to every retiree (so called "flat rate") or benefits whose value depends on years of works, not on past earnings. In a "resourced-tested" or "**targeted**" plan the poorer pensioners receive higher benefits coming from a reduction to the better-off retirees, and the benefits depend either on income from other sources or on both income and assets. A "**minimum pension**" is quite similar to a "targeted" plan because the value of entitlements takes account only of pension income but not of income from savings. In a **defined benefit (DB) plan** the retirement income depends on the number of years of contributions and on individual earning. A very similar approach called a "**points scheme**" is used in some countries (France, Germany, Estonia, and Slovakia). In this scheme workers earn pension points based on their earnings each year, and at retirement, the sum

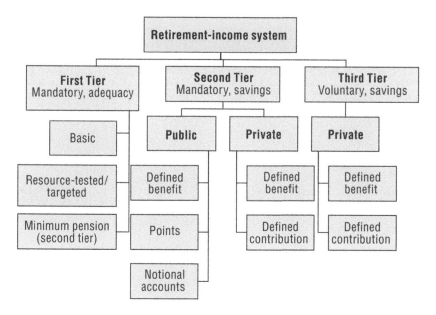

Figure 2.1 Taxonomy of different types of retirement-income provision

Source: OECD (2013), Pensions at a Glance 2013: OECD and G20 Indicators, OECD Publishing, p. 121 (http://dx.doi.org/10.1787/pension_glance-2013-en)

of pension points is multiplied by a pension-point value to convert them into regular pension payments. In a **defined contribution (DC) plan** the contributions flow into an individual account, and it is the accumulation of contributions and investment returns that is usually converted into a pension-income stream at retirement. Something similar to a DC plan is the "notional account plan" or the "**notional defined contribution plans**" (NDC) – used in Italy, Norway, Poland, and Sweden – where the accounts are "notional" because they exist only on the books of the managing institution.

The structure of the retirement-income provision in the OECD countries and other major economies is summarized in Table 2.2.

The chance to rely on the pension system in order to maintain the standard of living or working age in retirement can be assessed looking at the data about the "gross pension replacement rates" (Table 2.3) that show which percentage of the pre-retirement income is guaranteed from the system after retirement. The fact that differences in the pre-retirement income may affect the ratio is taken into account by showing data about the average earning (1.0) and data for people with just half of that earning (0.5) or showing values that are above the average for more than 50% (1.5).

Comparing the data between different income ranges, it can seem like individuals who can rely on the pension system in order to comfortably live in

Table 2.2 Structure of retirement-income provision

OECD members	Public			Public	Private
	Targeted	Basic	Minimum	Type	Type
Australia	X				DC
Austria				DB	
Belgium	X		X	DB	
Canada	X	X		DB	
Chile	X		X		DC
Czech Republic		X	X	DB	
Denmark	X	X			DC
Estonia		X		Points	DC
Finland			X	DB	
France			X	DB+points	
Germany	X			Points	
Greece			X	DB	
Hungary				DB	
Iceland	X	X			DB
Ireland		X			
Israel		X			DC
Italy	X			NDC	
Japan		X		DB	
Korea	X	X		DB	
Luxembourg	X	X	X	DB	
Mexico			X		DC
Netherlands		X			DB
New Zealand		X			
Norway			X	NDC	DC
Poland			X	NDC	DC
Portugal			X	DB	
Slovak Republic			X	Points	DC
Slovenia			X	DB	
Spain			X	DB	
Sweden			X	NDC	DC
Switzerland	X		X	DB	DB
Turkey			X	DB	
United Kingdom	X	X	X	DB	
United States				DB	

OECD *members*	Public			Public	Private
	Targeted	*Basic*	*Minimum*	*Type*	*Type*
Other major economies					
Argentina		X		DB	
Brazil				DB	
China		X		NDC/DC	
India				DB + DC	
Indonesia				DC	
Russian Federation		X		NDC	DC
Saudi Arabia			X	DB	
South Africa	X				

Source: OECD (2013), Pensions at a Glance 2013: OECD and G20 Indicators, OECD Publishing, p. 121 (http://dx.doi.org/10.1787/pension_glance-2013-en)

retirement are just a few. As reported by the OECD (2013), this conclusion can be even stronger taking into account that pre-retirement earnings are not estimated as the earnings of the last working year, but are reported as the average earnings throughout the worker's career. It means that if people move up the earnings distribution as they get older, then their earnings just before retirement would be higher than they were on average over their lifetime and the replacement rates calculated on individual final earning would be lower.

The need to cope with pension issues is reinforced by data on public expenditure on old-age (and survivors) benefits. Data from 1990 to 2009 (Table 2.4) show how several countries increased the percentage of their GDP devoted to feeding the pension system, and, in most of the cases, this triggered the rearrangement of system rules introduced by the recent pension system reforms.

Another source of uncertainty about the prodigality of the pension system with today's workers (the "future retirees") comes from the age structure of the population, as reported by the data of the United Nations (Department of Economic and Social Affairs) reported in Table 2.5 (United Nations 2013).

In this new scenario the need to know about the structure and the functioning of the pension system is no more useless, and financial literacy is more relevant due to the relevance of saving for retirement and the need to choose between different ways to do it (e.g. "*Which is the pension scheme that best fits with my needs? How much should I contribute on a monthly basis?*"). The risk that people, ignoring the functioning of the new pension systems and relying on the generosity of benefits paid to the old generations (who are actually in retirement), will not perceive the need to save for retirement and will not take any

Table 2.3 Gross pension replacement rates from public, mandatory private, and voluntary private pension schemes

Percentage of individual earnings

	Public			Mandatory private			Voluntary DC			Total mandatory			Total with voluntary		
	0.5	1	1.5	0.5	1	1.5	0.5	1	1.5	0.5	1	1.5	0.5	1	1.5
Australia	52.4	13.6	0.6	38.7	38.7	38.7				91.1	52.3	39.4			
Austria	76.6	76.6	74.0							76.6	76.6	74.0			
Belgium	58.2	41.0	30.2				15.1	15.1	11.2	58.2	41.0	30.2	73.3	56.2	41.4
Canada	63.1	39.2	26.1				33.9	33.9	33.9	63.1	39.2	26.1	97.0	73.1	60.1
Chile	20.4	4.8	0.0	36.9	37.2	37.3				57.3	41.9	37.3			
Czech Republic	71.8	43.5	34.1				39.2	39.2	39.2	71.8	43.5	34.1	111.0	82.8	73.4
Denmark	68.0	30.6	18.1	52.6	47.9	46.4				120.7	78.5	64.4			
Estonia	40.4	27.4	23.0	24.8	24.8	24.8				65.2	52.2	47.9			
Finland	64.1	54.8	54.8							64.1	54.8	54.8			
France	64.8	58.8	47.5							64.8	58.8	47.5			
Germany	42.0	42.0	42.0				16.0	16.0	16.0	42.0	42.0	42.0	58.0	58.0	58.0
Greece	75.4	53.9	46.7							75.4	53.9	46.7			
Hungary	73.6	73.6	73.6							73.6	73.6	73.6			
Iceland	25.9	6.5	4.3	65.8	65.8	65.8				91.7	72.3	70.1			
Ireland	73.4	36.7	24.5				43.0	43.0	43.0	73.4	36.7	24.5	116.4	79.7	67.5
Israel	44.5	22.2	14.8	59.3	51.1	34.1				103.7	73.4	48.9			
Italy	71.2	71.2	71.2							71.2	71.2	71.2			
Japan	49.8	35.6	30.8							49.8	35.6	30.8			
Korea	59.2	39.6	29.2							59.2	39.6	29.2			
Luxembourg	77.7	56.4	53.0							77.7	56.4	53.0			
Mexico	30.7	3.8	2.5	24.7	24.7	24.7				55.5	28.5	27.2			

Netherlands	59.1	29.5	19.7	35.3	61.1	69.7	14.1	14.1	14.1	94.4	90.7	89.4	95.3		
New Zealand	81.1	40.6	27.0	5.5	6.8	7.2	8.3	11.3	16.5	81.1	40.6	27.0	71.6	54.7	41.2
Norway	57.9	45.7	34.3	24.3	24.3	24.3				63.4	52.5	41.6		63.8	58.1
Poland	24.5	24.5	24.5	24.3	24.3	24.3				48.8	48.8	48.8			
Portugal	67.5	54.7	54.1							67.5	54.7	54.1			
Slovak Republic	45.9	37.6	35.1	28.3	28.3	28.3				74.2	65.9	63.4			
Slovenia	62.0	39.2	36.7							62.0	39.2	36.7			
Spain	73.9	73.9	73.9							73.9	73.9	73.9			
Sweden	48.6	33.9	25.7	21.7	21.7	42.2				70.2	55.6	67.9			
Switzerland	49.3	32.0	21.4	14.9	23.1	15.4				64.3	55.2	36.8			
Turkey	73.5	64.5	64.5							73.5	64.5	64.5			
United Kingdom	55.2	32.6	22.5				34.5	34.5	34.5	55.2	32.6	22.5	89.7	67.1	57.0
United States	49.5	38.3	33.4				37.8	37.8	37.8	49.5	38.3	33.4	87.4	76.2	71.2
OECD34	**57.4**	**40.6**	**34.5**				**34.5**	**34.5**	**34.5**	**70.1**	**54.0**	**48.0**	**88.9**	**67.9**	**58.6**
Other major economies															
Argentina	115.2	90.4	82.1							115.2	90.4	82.1			
Brazil	55.4	57.5	61.7							55.4	57.5	61.7			
China	97.9	77.9	71.2							97.9	77.9	71.2			
India	75.6	55.8	49.2							75.6	55.8	49.2			
Indonesia			14.1	14.1	14.1	14.1				14.1	14.1	14.1			
Russian Federation	30.6	30.6	30.6	17.3	17.3	17.3				47.9	47.9	47.9			
Saudi Arabia	100.0	100.0	100.0							100.0	100.0	100.0			
South Africa	0.0	0.0	0.0				54.5	54.5	54.5	0.0	0.0	0.0	54.5	54.5	54.5
EU27	59.2	47.0	41.3							69.0	57.6	53.0		54.5	54.5

Source: OECD (2013), Pensions at a Glance 2013: OECD and G20 Indicators, OECD Publishing, p. 137 (http://dx.doi.org/10.1787/pension_glance-2013-en).

Table 2.4 Public expenditure on old-age and survivors benefits

| | Public expenditure on cash benefits for old-age and survivors | | | | | | | | Level in net terms (% of GDP) | Total inc. non-cash (% of GDP) |
| | Level (% of GDP) | | | | | Change | Level (% of total government spending) | | | |
	1990	1995	2000	2005	2009	1990-2009	1990	2009	2009	2009
Australia	3.0	3.6	3.8	3.3	3.5	14.7%	8.5	9.4	3.4	5.1
Austria	11.4	12.3	12.2	12.4	13.5	18.3%	22.1	25.5	11.8	14.0
Belgium	9.1	9.3	8.9	9.0	10.0	10.2%	17.4	18.7	8.9	10.2
Canada	4.2	4.7	4.3	4.1	4.5	7.4%	8.5	10.3	4.3	4.5
Chile		6.7	7.3	5.7	3.6				3.5	3.6
Czech Republic	5.8	6.1	7.2	7.0	8.3	42.9%		18.5	8.3	8.6
Denmark	5.1	6.2	5.3	5.4	6.1	19.3%	9.2	10.5	4.5	8.2
Estonia			6.0	5.3	7.9			17.6	7.8	8.1
Finland	7.3	8.8	7.6	8.4	9.9	36.3%	15.1	17.7	8.3	11.1
France	10.6	12.0	11.8	12.4	13.7	29.2%	21.4	24.2	12.8	14.1
Germany	9.7	10.5	11.1	11.4	11.3	15.7%		23.4	10.9	11.3
Greece	9.9	9.7	10.8	11.8	13.0	31.2%		24.2	13.0	13.2
Hungary			7.6	8.5	9.9			19.4	9.9	10.5
Iceland	2.2	2.4	2.2	2.0	1.7	−21.3%		3.4	1.6	2.2
Ireland	4.9	4.3	3.1	3.4	5.1	5.2%	11.5	10.5	4.8	5.6

Country										
Italy	10.1	11.3	13.5	13.9	15.4	53.3%	19.1	29.8	13.5	15.6
Japan	4.8	6.1	7.3	8.7	10.2	111.4%		19.1	9.5	11.8
Korea	0.7	1.2	1.4	1.5	2.1	193.5%	3.7	6.5	2.1	2.4
Luxembourg	8.2	8.8	7.5	7.2	7.7	−6.1%	21.6	17.8	6.9	7.7
Mexico	0.5	0.7	0.9	1.2	1.7	269.0%		7.3	1.7	1.7
Netherlands	6.7	5.8	5.0	5.0	5.1	−23.9%	12.2	9.9	4.7	6.1
New Zealand	7.4	5.7	5.0	4.3	4.7	−36.7%	14.0	11.1	4.0	4.7
Norway	5.6	5.5	4.8	4.8	5.4	−5.2%		11.5	4.4	7.4
Poland	5.1	9.4	10.5	11.4	11.8	129.1%		26.4	10.8	11.8
Portugal	4.9	7.2	7.9	10.3	12.3	151.9%		24.8	11.6	12.5
Slovak Republic		6.3	6.3	6.2	7.0			16.9	7.0	7.4
Slovenia			10.5	9.9	10.9			22.1	10.9	11.0
Spain	7.9	9.0	8.6	8.1	9.3	17.3%		20.1	9.0	9.9
Sweden	7.7	8.2	7.2	7.6	8.2	6.8%		15.0	6.2	10.8
Switzerland	5.6	6.7	6.6	6.8	6.3	11.9%	18.6	19.5	6.4	6.6
Turkey	2.4	2.7	4.9	5.9	6.8	188.7%		16.8	6.8	6.9
United Kingdom	4.8	5.4	5.3	5.6	6.2	28.1%	11.6	12.1	5.9	6.8
United States	6.1	6.3	5.9	6.0	6.8	12.6%	16.4	16.3	6.4	6.9
OECD	**6.1**	**6.7**	**6.9**	**7.0**	**7.8**	**27.0%**		**16.6**	**7.3**	**8.3**

Source: OECD (2013), Pensions at a Glance 2013: OECD and G20 Indicators, OECD Publishing, p. 171 (http://dx.doi.org/10.1787/pension_glance-2013-en)

Table 2.5 Old-age dependency ratio (ratio of population aged 65+ per 100 population 25–64)

Countries	Old-age dependency ratio (ratio of population aged 65+ per 100 population 25–64)												
	1950	1955	1960	1965	1970	1975	1980	1985	1990	1995	2000	2005	2010
OECD countries													
Australia	16.1	17.1	18.2	18.9	18.2	18.9	20.2	20.8	21.9	23.0	23.3	24.2	25.1
Austria	19.4	21.6	23.8	26.9	29.1	31.2	32.6	27.6	28.8	27.8	27.9	28.9	32.3
Belgium	20.7	21.8	23.1	25.6	27.9	29.1	29.3	26.2	28.4	29.9	31.7	32.2	31.8
Canada	16.4	17.1	17.3	18.0	18.3	18.5	19.5	20.1	21.0	22.1	22.9	23.6	25.3
Chile	10.4	11.3	12.5	13.5	13.8	14.3	14.2	13.8	13.6	14.1	14.9	16.1	17.9
Denmark	17.7	19.5	21.6	23.7	25.4	27.2	29.0	29.6	29.8	28.3	26.9	27.5	31.4
Estonia	22.9	21.5	20.5	21.3	23.0	24.4	24.5	21.9	22.3	26.2	29.0	31.9	32.3
Finland	13.9	14.5	15.5	17.2	19.4	21.2	23.2	23.5	24.7	26.1	27.5	29.4	31.7
France	22.5	23.0	23.4	25.2	28.0	28.8	29.3	25.8	27.9	29.4	30.6	31.6	32.1
Germany	18.2	20.1	22.3	24.1	26.9	30.1	31.1	27.1	27.2	27.0	28.8	34.5	38.1
Greece	15.2	15.9	16.9	17.6	22.6	24.9	26.7	26.4	26.4	29.0	31.5	33.9	33.9
Hungary	15.4	16.1	17.5	20.2	22.7	25.0	26.6	22.6	26.0	27.5	28.5	28.1	29.8
Iceland	16.7	17.2	18.9	20.8	21.8	22.1	22.8	22.2	22.3	23.1	23.2	22.8	23.3
Ireland	24.0	24.2	25.4	26.5	26.9	26.2	26.1	25.6	25.5	24.4	22.4	20.8	20.6
Israel	8.4	9.4	10.6	13.1	15.9	18.9	20.9	20.5	20.9	22.3	22.5	21.9	22.1
Italy	16.9	17.8	18.9	20.1	22.3	24.7	27.2	25.6	28.3	30.7	32.8	35.1	36.5
Japan	12.3	12.6	12.7	13.2	14.1	15.0	16.9	18.9	21.9	26.3	30.9	35.9	42.8
Korea	7.6	9.2	10.2	9.3	9.0	9.3	9.6	9.7	10.2	11.2	13.3	16.2	18.8
Luxembourg	18.1	19.0	19.8	21.7	24.4	26.0	26.3	24.5	23.9	24.9	25.3	26.0	24.8

Mexico	9.9	9.6	10.1	11.1	11.9	12.2	12.2	11.8	12.1	11.9	12.0	12.2	13.1
Netherlands	16.3	17.8	19.4	21.1	22.5	22.9	23.5	23.5	24.1	23.9	24.2	25.3	28.2
New Caledonia	9.0	9.0	8.8	8.7	8.8	10.3	10.7	11.2	11.5	11.4	12.4	14.0	18.7
Norway	18.1	19.6	22.1	25.0	27.5	28.9	30.7	32.1	33.0	31.2	28.8	27.6	28.2
Poland	11.3	11.6	12.2	14.5	18.1	20.6	21.2	18.3	19.8	22.1	23.9	24.6	23.6
Portugal	15.6	16.3	17.2	18.3	21.1	23.0	24.9	25.3	27.5	29.2	30.6	31.2	32.2
Slovakia	14.1	14.0	14.3	17.4	20.0	22.3	22.7	18.6	21.0	21.9	22.0	21.0	21.2
Slovenia	14.9	15.1	15.9	18.3	20.3	22.4	23.0	18.7	20.0	22.4	25.5	27.2	28.8
Spain	15.3	16.0	16.8	18.2	20.5	22.2	24.0	25.0	27.6	29.8	31.3	29.5	29.7
Sweden	18.9	20.5	22.6	25.0	27.1	29.8	32.2	34.0	35.1	34.0	32.7	32.6	35.1
Switzerland	18.0	18.9	20.0	21.4	22.8	24.6	27.1	26.6	26.9	26.4	27.5	28.2	30.1
Turkey	8.1	8.7	8.5	10.1	11.1	12.7	13.2	11.6	11.5	12.3	13.8	14.2	14.5
UK	20.2	21.4	22.7	24.3	27.0	29.0	30.9	30.6	31.1	30.4	29.8	30.1	31.4
US	16.6	18.2	19.7	21.3	21.9	22.9	23.8	24.0	24.4	24.3	23.7	23.4	24.6
Other major economies													
Argentina	9.0	10.3	11.8	13.4	15.1	16.7	18.1	19.3	20.5	21.9	22.4	22.0	22.2
Brazil	8.2	8.6	9.3	10.2	10.7	11.2	11.4	10.9	10.9	11.6	12.2	13.1	13.7
China	10.3	10.0	9.9	9.4	10.8	12.3	12.8	13.4	13.2	13.0	13.3	14.3	15.0
India	7.8	8.1	7.9	8.5	8.9	9.5	9.7	9.8	9.9	10.0	10.4	10.8	11.1
Indonesia	10.8	10.2	9.6	9.0	9.1	9.8	10.2	10.0	9.8	10.1	10.5	10.5	10.4
Russian Federation	11.1	11.7	12.8	13.3	15.9	18.3	20.3	18.5	19.1	23.1	23.2	25.5	22.9
Saudi Arabia	9.2	9.9	10.4	10.4	10.2	9.6	8.5	7.1	7.3	6.5	8.8	6.9	6.1
South Africa	9.1	9.9	10.4	10.7	9.7	9.1	8.7	8.5	8.5	8.4	8.0	9.9	11.6

Source: United Nations (2013). World Population Prospects: The 2012 Revision, DVD Edition. United Nations, Department of Economic and Social Affairs, Population Division (https://esa.un.org/unpd/wpp/publications/Files/WPP2012_Volume-II-Demographic-Profiles.pdf)

action highlights the role of financial literacy as a tool to develop awareness of financial needs before being a tool to make a financial decision.

Worries about people's awareness about the need to take care about retirement have been cited in different studies. Lusardi and Mitchell (2011) looked at the switching from defined benefits (DB) to defined contributions (DC) plans in the US as a reason to improve financial literacy. Xiao et al. (2013) motivated their study on financial literacy in the US by the American socio-economic trend featuring a weakening in the safety net which requires more individual responsibility for long-term economic security. Schmeiser and Seligman (2013) analyzed the growth of 401(k) plans[7] assessing financial literacy of the US population as increasingly important.

In Europe, Brown and Graf (2013) highlight how household finance in Switzerland is characterized by increased individual responsibility for retirement planning, and Bucher-Koenen and Lusardi (2011) see in the transformation of the German public pension system, from a monolithic system to a multi-pillar system, a source of potential problems for low-literate individuals. These worries are confirmed by Honekamp (2012) in a study on retirement saving in Germany, where the author highlights how, until the pension reform in 2001, most Germans relied almost solely on their statutory pension entitlements. In a study on the Dutch pension landscape van Rooij et al. (2011) reported an increase in the official pension age from 65 to 67, looking at the chance that further increases could be realized (to ensure the stability of the pension system due to an increase in longevity) as a source of uncertainty that needs to be managed in a retirement planning strategy. The need to cope with a new financial framework and the risk of not being ready due to a lack of financial knowledge seem to be issues even in Russia. Klapper et al. (2013) analyzed the Russian pension system reform in 2005, which was based on a decreasing role of the state and a shift from a publicly managed distributive system to one supplemented by a privately managed mandatory funded component. In their study the authors stressed how the growth of private contribution after a few years is low and how the lack of experience of previous generations about the need to save for retirement can be a possible explanation for that. Increasing longevity and growing old-age dependency ratios were the main reasons behind the pension reforms in Italy and Japan. Fornero and Monticone (2011) studied the Italian pension system, while Sekita (2011) did it for the Japanese one, arriving at the same conclusion that the policy to fix contribution rates and then to adjust the benefit level, reducing them when the populations continue to age, implies that individuals must take more responsibility for their own financial well-being after retirement. The fact that in a survey promoted by the Pension Fund Association of Japan in 2007 about half of participants in defined contribution pension plans admitted that they did not understand the contents of their pension plans and they did not know how their contribution was allocated is clear evidence of a lack of financial literacy.

The **healthcare system** is another part of the welfare state model that has been remodelled in recent years. In some countries the role of the public system in assisting people with all their healthcare needs – not referring just to emergencies, and including even injuries, sickness, surgeries, and other physical and mental needs – has been revisited by introducing (or reinforcing) private contribution to provision of benefits, or by shrinking access to the system (e.g. using waiting lists).

Data from the World Health Organization report that the governments of all the main developed countries increased during the years studied the resources for the healthcare systems. It can be seen looking at data on the general government expenditure on health as a percentage of total government expenditure (Table 2.6) and looking at how these resources represent a big part of the total expenditure on health (Table 2.7).

If the amount of money spent by public systems has grown during these years, and it did more than the private expenditure on health (Table 2.8), two things must be taken into account.

The first is that the uptrend of life expectancy (Table 2.9) increased both the demand for treatment for a growing number of system users and the circumstance that the elderly are required to spend on average more than the youth. Moreover, a growing amount of money spent by healthcare systems does not imply a better quality of service. As reported by Björnberg (2015), in a report for the Health Consumer Powerhouse about the quality of the services provided in the healthcare systems in Europe, there is a rather vague correlation between financial resources and high quality care, due to the fact that many other assets are essential to delivering good performance, such as a culture of responsibility, a civic climate of trust and accountability, the absence of corruption, etc. In the same study, the countries ranked as those offering the best healthcare value for money spent are several medium and low income ones.

These results are supported by the European Commission (2014),[8] which reported how European citizens are on average dissatisfied with the quality of the healthcare in their country (Table 2.10). The same data show how this average is the mean between countries with a very high satisfaction (Belgium 97%, Austria 96%, Finland 94%) and others widely dissatisfied (Romania 25%, Greece 26%, Bulgaria 29%).

The accessibility of the system seems to be an issue for many countries, as reported by Table 2.11. For instance, the chance to have a computer tomography scan (CT scan) within 7 days from the request is an issue for most of the countries, included the UK, Sweden, Italy, and Spain. Data show that access to major elective surgery (within 90 days of the request) is supposed to be difficult in almost one in three cases (10 of the 29 European countries).

In this scenario, where the coverage guaranteed by the system is not complete, where the risk of not being served on time by the system or the quality of the benefits is perceived as a real issue, the need to cope with these issues has reinforced the need for financial literacy in order to plan for medical needs, to save for that, and to decide how to do it (e.g. health insurance, etc.).

Table 2.6 General government expenditure on health as a percentage of total government expenditure

General government expenditure on health as a percentage of total government expenditure (WHS7_113)

OECD members	1995	2000	2005	2010	2012	OECD members (continued)	1995	2000	2005	2010	2012
Australia	13.1	15.1	16.7	17.2	17.8	New Zealand	13.3	15.6	17.2	20.2	20.3
Austria	12.5	14.6	15.7	16.5	16.9	Norway	14.2	18.0	19.1	18.9	17.8
Belgium	11.2	12.3	14.7	15.0	15.0	Poland	8.4	9.4	9.9	11.0	11.1
Canada	13.3	15.1	17.6	18.3	17.4	Portugal	11.2	14.9	15.1	13.8	12.5
Chile	12.7	14.1	12.6	15.4	15.2	Slovakia	11.0	9.4	13.8	14.5	14.7
Denmark	11.3	13.6	15.6	16.4	16.1	Slovenia	11.1	13.2	13.4	13.0	13.1
Estonia	13.7	11.3	11.5	12.3	11.7	Spain	12.1	13.2	15.3	15.4	15.0
Finland	9.2	10.6	12.4	12.1	12.3	Sweden	10.6	12.6	13.7	14.8	15.1
France	15.2	15.5	16.0	15.9	15.9	Switzerland	14.4	15.4	18.4	21.0	20.6
Greece	9.6	10.1	12.8	12.4	11.4	Turkey	10.7	9.8	11.3	12.8	12.8
Germany	15.0	18.3	17.7	18.6	19.1	UK	13.1	15.1	15.3	15.8	16.1
Hungary	11.0	10.6	11.8	10.5	10.3	US	16.6	17.4	19.3	19.7	19.9
Iceland	16.1	18.4	18.6	14.8	15.7	**Other major economies**					
Ireland	11.6	14.7	17.0	13.8	12.4	Argentina	15.3	14.7	14.0	17.4	22.5
Israel	9.7	9.2	9.4	10.4	10.4	Brazil	8.4	4.1	4.7	10.7	7.6
Italy	9.8	12.7	14.2	14.7	14.2	China	15.2	10.5	9.9	12.1	12.5
Japan	15.6	16.0	17.6	19.4	19.4	India	7.6	7.4	6.9	6.8	9.4
Korea	7.1	9.7	11.3	13.7	13.6	Indonesia	4.8	4.5	4.4	6.8	6.9
Luxembourg	13.0	16.9	16.2	14.4	13.5	Russian Federation	9.0	12.7	11.8	9.7	10.3
Mexico	15.1	16.6	16.5	15.3	15.8	Saudi Arabia	4.7	8.6	8.1	5.7	5.7
Netherlands	10.5	11.4	15.7	18.8	19.7	South Africa	10.1	13.2	12.6	12.5	12.9

Table 2.7 General government expenditure on health as % of total expenditure on health

General government expenditure on health as % of total expenditure on health (WHS7_149)

OECD members	1995	2000	2005	2010	2012	OECD members (continued)	1995	2000	2005	2010	2012
Australia	65.8	66.8	66.9	67.8	66.9	New Zealand	77.2	78.0	79.7	83.2	82.7
Austria	73.5	75.6	75.3	74.7	75.6	Norway	84.2	83.6	83.8	84.9	85.1
Belgium	76.8	74.6	76.1	75.1	75.9	Poland	72.9	70.0	69.4	71.6	70.1
Canada	71.3	70.4	70.2	70.8	70.1	Portugal	62.6	66.6	68.0	65.9	62.6
Chile	38.2	43.3	39.0	48.1	48.6	Slovakia	88.5	89.4	74.4	64.5	70.5
Denmark	82.5	83.9	84.5	85.1	85.5	Slovenia	77.7	74.0	72.7	74.0	73.3
Estonia	89.8	77.4	76.9	79.6	79.9	Spain	72.2	71.6	70.9	74.2	73.6
Finland	71.7	71.3	73.8	74.8	75.4	Sweden	86.7	84.9	81.2	81.5	81.7
France	79.7	79.4	77.7	76.9	77.0	Switzerland	53.6	55.4	59.5	65.2	61.7
Germany	81.4	79.5	76.6	76.7	76.3	Turkey	70.3	62.9	67.8	75.1	73.9
Greece	51.0	60.0	59.3	67.9	67.5	UK	83.9	79.1	81.0	83.6	82.5
Hungary	84.0	70.7	70.0	64.8	63.6	US	45.1	43.1	44.2	47.6	46.4
Iceland	83.9	81.1	81.7	80.7	80.7	**Other major economies**					
Ireland	72.5	75.1	76.0	69.6	64.5	Argentina	59.8	53.9	53.5	64.0	69.2
Israel	69.2	64.0	60.5	61.8	61.7	Brazil	43.0	40.3	40.1	47.0	46.4
Italy	72.8	74.2	77.9	78.5	78.2	China	50.5	38.3	38.8	54.3	56.0
Japan	82.3	80.8	81.6	82.1	82.5	India	26.0	26.0	22.1	28.2	33.1
Korea	38.6	50.4	53.3	56.5	54.4	Indonesia	35.7	36.2	28.8	37.7	39.6
Luxembourg	92.4	85.1	84.9	85.5	84.5	Russian Federation	73.9	59.9	62.0	58.5	61.0
Mexico	42.1	46.6	45.0	49.0	51.8	Saudi Arabia	52.6	72.1	72.7	65.5	65.8
Netherlands	71.0	63.1	64.7	79.6	79.8	South Africa	39.6	41.3	38.4	46.6	47.9

Source: World Health Organization (WHO) – World Statistic Health – Global indicator (different years)

Table 2.8 Private expenditure on health as a percentage of total expenditure on health

Private expenditure on health as a percentage of total expenditure on health (WHS7_147)

OECD members	1995	2000	2005	2010	2012	OECD members (continued)	1995	2000	2005	2010	2012
Australia	34.2	33.2	33.1	32.2	33.1	New Zealand	22.8	22.0	20.3	16.8	17.3
Austria	26.5	24.4	24.7	25.3	24.5	Norway	15.8	16.4	16.2	15.1	14.9
Belgium	23.2	25.4	23.9	24.9	24.1	Poland	27.1	30.0	30.6	28.4	29.9
Canada	28.8	29.7	29.8	29.2	30.0	Portugal	37.4	33.4	32.0	34.1	37.4
Chile	61.8	56.7	61.0	51.9	51.4	Slovakia	11.5	10.6	25.6	35.5	29.5
Denmark	17.5	16.1	15.5	14.9	14.5	Slovenia	22.3	26.0	27.3	26.0	26.7
Estonia	10.2	22.6	23.1	20.4	20.1	Spain	27.8	28.4	29.1	25.8	26.4
Finland	28.3	28.7	26.2	25.2	24.6	Sweden	13.4	15.1	18.8	18.5	18.3
France	20.3	20.6	22.3	23.1	23.1	Switzerland	46.4	44.6	40.5	34.8	38.3
Germany	18.6	20.5	23.4	23.3	23.7	Turkey	29.7	37.1	32.2	24.9	26.1
Greece	45.5	40.0	36.8	32.2	32.5	UK	16.1	20.9	19.1	16.5	17.5
Hungary	16.0	29.3	30.0	35.2	36.4	US	54.9	57.0	55.8	52.4	53.6
Iceland	16.1	19.0	18.3	19.3	19.4	**Other major economies**					
Ireland	27.5	24.9	24.0	30.4	35.6	Argentina	40.2	46.1	46.5	36.0	30.8
Israel	30.8	36.0	39.5	38.2	38.3	Brazil	57.0	59.7	59.9	53.0	53.6
Italy	27.2	25.8	22.1	21.5	21.8	China	49.5	61.7	61.2	45.7	44.0
Japan	17.7	19.2	18.4	17.9	17.5	India	74.0	74.0	77.9	71.9	66.9
Korea	61.4	49.6	46.7	43.5	45.6	Indonesia	64.3	63.9	71.2	62.3	60.4
Luxembourg	7.6	14.9	15.1	14.5	15.5	Russian Federation	26.1	40.1	38.0	41.5	39.0
Mexico	57.9	53.4	55.0	51.0	48.2	Saudi Arabia	47.4	27.9	27.3	34.5	34.2
Netherlands	29.0	36.9	28.1	12.9	13.4	South Africa	60.4	58.7	61.6	53.4	52.1

Source: World Health Organization (WHO) – World Statistic Health – Global indicator (different years)

Table 2.9 Life expectancy at age 60 (both sexes combined) from 1950 to 2010

Life expectancy at age 60 (both sexes combined) 1950-2010

OECD members	1985-1990	1990-1995	1995-2000	2000-2005	2005-2010
Australia	20.55	21.46	22.42	23.57	24.61
Austria	19.77	20.54	21.31	22.39	23.23
Belgium	19.75	20.70	21.36	22.04	22.93
Canada	21.09	21.72	22.13	23.03	23.80
Chile	19.42	20.14	21.02	22.33	22.75
Denmark	19.70	19.75	20.08	20.97	21.92
Estonia	17.91	17.49	18.05	18.86	19.85
Finland	19.52	20.21	21.13	22.13	23.19
France	21.15	22.15	22.69	23.51	24.53
Germany	19.62	20.27	21.11	22.08	22.89
Greece	20.17	21.21	21.72	22.44	22.91
Hungary	17.01	17.25	17.88	18.77	19.40
Iceland	21.38	21.98	22.09	23.33	23.74
Ireland	18.31	19.15	19.68	21.11	22.66
Israel	20.01	20.86	21.76	22.69	23.60
Italy	20.50	21.38	22.22	23.23	24.09
Japan	22.09	22.76	23.64	24.85	25.51
Korea	17.76	18.90	19.81	21.25	23.10
Luxembourg	19.52	20.52	21.09	22.11	22.69
Mexico	19.97	20.54	21.13	21.47	22.08
Netherlands	20.56	20.85	21.21	21.85	22.95

OECD members (continued)	1980-1985	1985-1990	1995-2000	2000-2005	2005-2010
New Zealand	19.53	20.79	21.53	22.58	23.58
Norway	20.33	20.87	21.60	22.46	23.42
Poland	17.79	17.99	18.72	19.82	20.48
Portugal	19.73	20.08	20.77	21.60	22.45
Slovakia	17.36	17.69	18.22	18.88	19.44
Slovenia	18.56	19.08	19.96	20.94	22.23
Spain	21.15	21.83	22.39	23.09	24.21
Sweden	20.90	21.52	22.21	22.86	23.60
Switzerland	21.40	22.00	22.74	23.61	24.51
Turkey	17.94	18.41	18.85	19.33	20.00
UK	19.29	20.02	20.71	21.77	22.93
US	20.48	21.07	21.34	21.85	22.77
Other major economies					
Argentina	18.62	19.19	19.84	20.27	20.86
Brazil	17.93	18.96	19.82	20.51	21.10
China	17.56	17.75	17.93	19.26	19.63
India	15.05	15.21	15.72	16.24	16.75
Indonesia	15.94	16.32	16.70	17.07	17.43
Russian Federation	17.81	17.03	16.63	16.26	17.28
Saudi Arabia	17.22	17.40	17.76	18.12	18.49
South Africa	14.74	15.23	15.40	15.31	15.22

Source: United Nations, Department of Economic and Social Affairs, Population Division (2013). World Population Prospects: The 2012 Revision

Table 2.10 Satisfaction with the healthcare system

"How would you evaluate the overall quality of healthcare in YOUR COUNTRY?"

Country	Total "Good"	Country	Total "Good"
Belgium	97%	Cyprus	73%
Austria	96%	**EU**	**71%**
Malta	94%	Lithuania	65%
Finland	94%	Ireland	62%
The Netherlands	91%	Croatia	59%
Luxembourg	90%	Italy	56%
Germany	90%	Portugal	55%
France	88%	Slovakia	50%
Denmark	87%	Latvia	47%
Sweden	86%	Hungary	47%
UK	85%	Poland	32%
Czech Republic	78%	Bulgaria	29%
Spain	77%	Greece	26%
Slovenia	73%	Romania	25%
Estonia	73%		

Source: European Commission (2014) "Special Eurobarometer 411 – Patient Safety and Quality of Care 2014"

Another challenge of financial literacy is related to the **job market**, its flexibility, and the need to take into account periods of unemployment during working life, as well as the need to be aware that a financial decision could be affected by the risk of losing a job and not being able to find a new one in a short period of time. For instance, a spending vs. saving decision should take into account that present income can overestimate permanent income[9] when the risk of unemployment exists. People who ignore that, due to a lack of knowledge, risk not saving enough for "rainy days", or they could invest in time constrained financial products, with the risk of not being able to use this money in case of need.

The changes in the welfare state are not the only relevant changes for financial consumers. The **complexity of the financial system** has grown worldwide in recent years and represents another challenge for financial literacy. The number of financial products offered by financial institutions and the chance to choose between different options within the same product require people to be able to understand the functioning of these products, compare different solutions, and recognize the pro-and-cons of each of them, in order to choose the most appropriate. For instance, falling interest rates in financial markets and the downgrading of several Government bonds' ratings nudged retail investors to change their investment strategies, causing them to not look anymore at Government bonds as a low-risk and high-yield investment and search for alternative and more profitable investment solutions, making a new need for financial literacy bloom (see Box 2.1).

Table 2.11 Assessment of health system accessibility (waiting time for treatment) by European consumers

	Assessment of health system accessibility (waiting time for treatment) by European consumers					
	Family doctor same day access	Direct access to specialist	Major elective surgery < 90 days	Cancer therapy < 21 days	CT scan < 7 days	A&E waiting times
Austria	+	+	=	+	+	=
Belgium	+	+	+	+	+	+
Bulgaria	+	=	+	=	−	=
Croatia	+	=	−	+	−	+
Cyprus	+	−	−	+	−	+
Czech Republic	+	=	=	−	+	+
Denmark	+	=	+	+	=	+
Estonia	−	=	=	+	=	=
Finland	−	−	+	+	+	+
France	+	=	+	+	=	−
Germany	=	+	+	+	=	=
Greece	−	+	=	−	=	=
Hungary	+	=	=	=	−	+
Ireland	=	−	−	−	−	−
Italy	+	=	=	=	−	−
Latvia	+	+	−	=	−	=
Lithuania	−	−	=	−	−	−
Luxembourg	+	+	+	+	−	=
Malta	+	−	−	+	−	−
Poland	−	=	−	−	−	=
Portugal	+	−	+	+	=	+
Romania	−	−	=	−	−	−
Slovakia	+	+	−	+	=	=
Slovenia	=	=	−	−	−	=
Spain	−	−	−	=	−	=
Sweden	−	−	=	=	−	−
Switzerland	+	+	+	+	+	+
The Netherlands	+	−	+	=	+	+
UK	−	−	=	=	−	−

Source: Björnberg (2014). Health Consumer Powerhouse Euro Health Consumer Index 2014 Report

Note: "+" positive opinion; "=" neutral opinion; "−" negative opinion

Box 2.1 Government bond yields and rating

Data from the European Central Bank (ECB Statistical Data Warehouse) show that interest rates of ten-year Government bonds with rating AAA within the Euro area in recent years (Figure 2.2) constantly dropped from 2.25% (Jun. 2014) to 0.49% (Sep. 2017). Data from Standard & Poor's (2017) ratings highlight that in most of the cases a downgrading on Government bonds occurred, pushing some of them under the investment grade threshold.

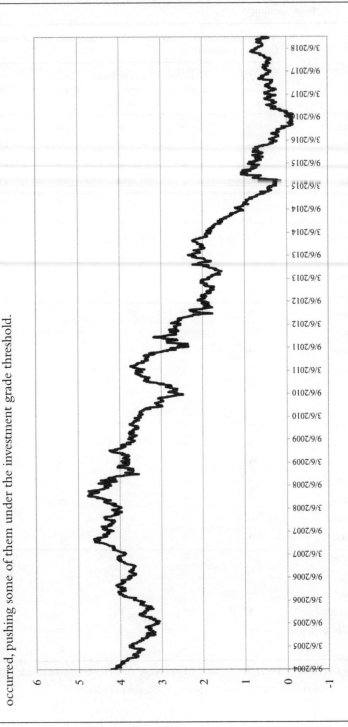

Figure 2.2 Yield curve spot rate, ten-year maturity – Government bond, nominal, all issuers whose rating is AAA – Euro area (changing composition)

Source: ECB Statistical Data Warehouse (http://sdw.ecb.europa.eu/)

Sovereign ratings in local currencies (Feb. 2017)

OECD members	2017 (Feb.)	2015 (Feb.)	2012 (Feb.)	2010 (Feb.)	Variation 2017 vs. 2010
Australia	AAA	AAA	AAA	AAA	=
Austria	AA+	AA+	AA+	AAA	−
Belgium	AA	AA	AA	AA+	−
Canada	AAA	AAA	AAA	AAA	=
Chile	A+	AA+	AA−	A+	=
Denmark	AAA	AA−	AAA	AAA	=
Estonia	AA−	AA−	AA−	A−	+
Finland	AA+	AA+	AA+	AAA	−
France	AA	AA	AA	AAA	−
Germany	AAA	AAA	AAA	AAA	=
Greece	B−	B−	B	BB+	−
Hungary	BBB−	BB	BB	BBB−	=
Iceland	A	BBB−	BBB−	BBB−	+
Ireland	A+	A	A	AA	−
Israel	A+	A+	A+	A	+
Italy	BBB−	BBB−	BBB−	A+	−
Japan	A+	AA−	AA−	AA	−
Korea	AA	AA−	A+	A	+
Luxembourg	AAA	AAA	AAA	AAA	=
Mexico	BBB+	A	BBB+	BBB	+
Netherlands	AAA	AA+	AA+	AAA	−

OECD members (continued)	2017 (Feb.)	2015 (Feb.)	2012 (Feb.)	2010 (Feb.)	Variation 2017 vs. 2010
New Zealand	AA	AA+	AA	AA+	−
Norway	AAA	AAA	AAA	AAA	=
Poland	BBB+	A	A−	A−	−
Portugal	BB+	BB	BB	A−	−
Slovakia	A+	A	A	A+	=
Slovenia	A+	A−	A−	AA	−
Spain	BBB+	BBB	BBB	AA+	−
Sweden	AAA	AAA	AAA	AAA	=
Switzerland	AAA	AAA	AAA	AAA	=
Turkey	BB	BBB	BB+	BB	=
UK	AA	AAA	AAA	AAA	−
US	AA+	AA+	AA+	AAA	−
Other major economies					
Argentina	B	CCC+	SD	B−	+
Brazil	BB	BBB+	BBB−	BBB−	−
China	AA−	AA−	AA−	A+	+
India	BBB−	BBB−	BBB−	BBB−	=
Indonesia	BBB−	BB+	BB+	BB	+
Russian Federation	BB+	BB−	BB+	BBB	−
Saudi Arabia	A−	AA−	AA−	AA−	−
South Africa	BB+	BBB+	BBB−	BBB+	−

Source: Standard & Poor's service ratings

Legend: The values of S&P ratings from top (low-risk) to bottom (default) is: "AAA"; "AA+"; "AA"; "AA−"; "A+"; "A"; "A−"; "BBB+";
"BBB"; "BBB−"; "BB+"; "BB"; "BB−"; "CCC+"; "CCC"; "CCC−"; "D"

The OECD (2013), in a document of the Programme for International Student Assessment (PISA) project, stressed how in all the countries of the program a growing number of consumers have access to a wide range of financial products and services from a variety of providers and delivered through various channels. In the same document a big concern is expressed about the need to protect consumers by giving them enough financial literacy. Similar concerns have been expressed in several other studies (Lusardi and Mitchell, 2011, Bumcrot et al. 2013, Sekita 2011, Honekamp 2012). For instance, Klapper et al. (2011) analyzed the development of consumer credit in Russia, noting how this industry has grown very fast, passing from US$10 billion in 2003 to more than US$170 billion in 2008, accounting for more than 10% of the GDP in 2008 versus less than 1% in 2003. In their conclusions the authors highlight how their findings suggest that rapid growth of consumer credit combined with a low level of financial literacy (and the shock of the global financial crisis) might end up being a dangerous mix.

An inadequate level of financial literacy on an individual basis is not only an issue from a consumer protection perspective, but it represents something negative even from a macro-economic point of view. Keeping in mind that a community is made of individuals, the need to address financial literacy even from a **macro-economic perspective** is quite clear. A low level of financial literacy within the demand side of the market (financial consumers) can have negative consequences for the functioning of the market itself. Consumers who show a lack of knowledge, sometimes even about basic principles, are not able to distinguish between different financial products, reducing the effect of competition between issuers, financial institutions, and other subjects belonging to the supply side of the financial markets. The hypothesis that competition in the market will guarantee its efficiency can be denied by a lack of knowledge of financial consumers. Moreover, as reported by Honekamp (2012), *"Financial literacy is not only vital for the individual but also for market efficiency. Financial literate consumers also encourage competition between the financial institutions in the market. This entails innovation and ensures that financial products meet the requirements of the consumers"* (p. 2).

During his administration, the US President Barack Obama (2010) argued in his Presidential Proclamation of Financial Literacy Month that *"Our recent economic crisis was the result of both irresponsible actions on Wall Street, and everyday choices on Main Street. Large banks speculated recklessly without regard for the consequences, and other firms invented and sold complex financial products to conceal risks and escape scrutiny. At the same time, many Americans took out loans they could not afford or signed contracts without fully understanding the terms. Ensuring this crisis never happens again will require new rules to protect consumers and better information to empower them"*.[10]

At the same time the need to protect consumers from predatory behaviors (e.g. predatory lending, high-cost of borrowing, financial frauds, etc.) requires regulatory and monitoring efforts that could be otherwise limited to a basic and more neutral approach if the consumers would be able to self-protect themselves. It does not mean that financial literacy can be a substitute for financial regulation, but, as noted by Rutledge (2010), it can potentially be an effective form of consumer protection. If financial literacy cannot solve all the problems in consumer finance, it can help to avoid some of the worst financial consumer abuses.

At the same time the effect of low financial literacy risks affecting the **more knowledgeable and skilled people** too. If we consider some financial businesses, such as insurance and banking, they are based on the hypothesis of risk-diversification and work well only if a reasonable number of people join the market and participate in the system. The chance that just a small fraction of the population (the most knowledgeable) will ask for insurance and banking products and services can make the business be not sustainable, denying these people the chance to satisfy their financial needs (e.g. saving, investing, hedging), or will see financial intermediaries raise the pricing of their services in order to make their business profitable.

A last issue related to lack of financial knowledge concerns the situation in which those who will be in financial trouble caused (or amplified) by a lack of financial literacy representing a **negative externality** for the financial system. People who become bankrupt will probably negatively affect the balance of their creditors and will ask for an intervention by public institutions (e.g. judgement courts, lawyers, solicitors, etc.). Nye and Hillyard (2013) reported data from the national statistics on financial choices of American consumers, showing how the US court data reveal that 1.3 million bankruptcies were filed from March 2011 to March 2012. In addition, according to the Federal Reserve, Americans' "revolving credit" debt totalled more than US$852 billion in August 2012, and, according to the Project on Student Debt, 67% of students graduating from college in 2011 had student loans with an average debt of $26,600.

All the aforementioned arguments highlight the relevance of financial literacy. In addition, a genuine interest about financial literacy seems to grow among policy makers. The European Parliament has taken a resolution[11] about the need to develop financial literacy of European consumers saying that "*raising the level of financial literacy of consumers should be a priority for policy-makers both at Member State and European level, not only because of the benefits for individuals but also because of the benefits for society and the economy, such as reducing the level of problem debt, increasing savings, increasing competition, making appropriate use of insurance products and making adequate provision for retirement*".

2.3 Financial literacy and financial behaviors: some evidence from previous studies

The assumption that financial literacy can play a relevant role in financial decision making processes and the magnitude of its renewed relevance in a dynamic socio-economic framework need to be confirmed by empirical analysis. A review of the literature about financial literacy will help to do it and will shed light on the relevance of financial literacy compared with other possible explanations of financial behaviors.

Keeping in mind that people financial literacy – as the knowledge and the ability to apply it – can change substantially when different area of knowledge and different financial decisions are taken into account, the analysis of the results of previous studies will be done referring to different areas of contents.

2.3.1 *Debt, borrowing, and loans*

Financial behaviors related with debt, loans, mortgages, and borrowing have been widely analyzed by previous studies. Moore (2003) used a sample of more than 1,400 residents of Washington state (US) to test how some risky behaviors in borrowing are related with financial literacy. The author referred to (1) the use of **payday loans**[12] and (2) taking **cash advance on credit cards** as risky behaviors, due to the fact that the high cost of borrowing usually required by these products suggests using them only when other options are not available. The measure of financial literacy used is the sum of correct answers to 12 multiple choice questions on different topics (money management, mortgages, bond pricing, diversification, etc.). Results of the study found that the willingness to use payday loans and to withdraw cash by credit cards is higher for individuals with lower financial literacy. These results are consistent even after controlling for variables such as age, gender, marital status, income, and education.

Robb (2011) used the information from a sample of American college students (1,354 obs.), collected in 2007, to check the role of financial literacy in the explanation of the **use of credit cards by college students**. Five different variables have been used for financial behaviors: (1) to have credit cards usually at their maximum credit limit, (2) to always pay off credit cards at the end of each month, (3) to often make only minimum payments on credit cards, (4) to be seldom delinquent in making payments on credit cards, and (5) to seldom take cash advances on credit cards. For all of these questions the respondents had the chance to agree or disagree using a one-to-five Likert scale. Financial literacy has been measured using six items, adopted in previous studies and related with the use of credit cards. The number of correct answers to the six questions has been used to develop three variables for financial literacy splitting the sample between low- (0–2 correct answers), middle- (3–4), and high-literate (5–6) individuals. As reported by the author, "*Results suggest that financial knowledge is a significant factor in the credit card decisions of college students. Students with higher scores on a measure of personal financial knowledge are more likely to engage in more responsible credit card use*" (p. 690). The use of different variables for financial literacy (low, middle, high) allowed the researcher to test different hypotheses and results to figure out whether low financial literacy or high financial literacy help to explain the use of credit cards. Negative behaviors such as "being late on payments" or "using credit cards for cash advances" are more frequent for people with low financial literacy. At the same time, positive behaviors – such as always paying off credit cards at the end of the month – are positively related with high-literate people.

The relationship between financial literacy and the **use of credit cards** in the US has been studied also by Allgood and Walstad (2011). The authors used a different database – the 2009 National Financial Capability Study (NFCS, by the FINRA Foundation) – with more than 28,000 observations of American adults. The financial outcomes used to assess the use of credit cards are quite similar to those of previous studies (being late on payments; always paying credit cards in full; exceeding the credit line limit; using credit cards for cash advances), while financial literacy has been assessed by two measures. The sum of correct answers to five questions on interest rates, inflation, risk diversification, bond pricing, and the use of mortgage[13] has been used as an objective measure of financial literacy, while a self-assessed measure (range 1 to 7) represented the subjective measure. The use of these two measures allowed the researchers to compare their different explanatory power on credit card use. Results show how perceived financial literacy better performed in explaining each of the five credit card behaviors considered, compared with the objective measures. However, the authors stressed that the perception of financial literacy "*is not the only measure that should be used to assess financial literacy because it depends on accurate self-assessment*".

In a similar study, Mottola (2013) used the same database (NFCS 2009) looking at the same financial behaviors on **credit cards** (being late on payments; always paying credit cards in full; exceeding the credit line limit; using credit cards for cash advances). In this study financial literacy has been assessed with a dummy variable equal to one if the respondents failed at least two of the five questions. That measure of low (and objective) financial literacy has been found positively related with faulty credit card behaviors. In the same study the author tried to connect financial literacy with the interest rates on credit cards, but no statistically significant evidence has been found.

Interest about the use of credit cards and financial literacy has been studied also outside the US. Disney and Gathergood (2012) used a sample of 3,041 residents in the UK to test if the **use of credit cards in the UK** is related with financial literacy. In this case it is not how people use credit cards that matters, but simply whether or not they use a credit card. Financial literacy has been measured by three questions on (1) interest rate calculation, (2) loan interest compounding, and (3) the effect of minimum balance payments on credit card debts. Answers to each question have been used as a separate financial literacy measure. The authors arrived at the conclusions that "*financial literacy is on average lower among who participates in the consumer credit markets, compared with who do not*" (p. 1). The robustness of this result is confirmed by the fact that the low likelihood of answering correctly a financial literacy question for credit card users is statistically significant for all the three measures (questions) of financial literacy, even if the marginal effect differs in magnitude across different measures. For instance, the likelihood of correctly answering the compound interest question for the credit card user (43%) is 13% lower than for the rest of the sample (56%). The difference for the question on simple interest is just 2% (84% credit card users vs. 86% non-users).

The same authors in a further study (Disney and Gathergood 2013) used the same database to analyze the relationship between financial literacy and either (1) the consumer credit portfolio weighted APRs of British residents and (2) the high-cost credit share on portfolios. In their analysis the authors took into account several financial products (credit cards, store cards, personal loans, overdrafts, hire purchases, payday loans, etc.) in order to estimate the portfolio APRs, while financial literacy has been assessed by two measures. In the first one, coherently with their previous study, the authors used the answer to three questions (about interest rate calculation, compound interest, and minimum balance payments) as different measures of financial literacy. The second one is a financial literacy index made by the number of correct answers to all three questions, which ranged from zero to three. The results from a multivariate analysis – that used as control variables socio-demographic characteristics such as age, homeownership, and income – confirmed the hypothesis that people with low financial literacy hold a greater fraction of high-cost credit products in their portfolios and have higher portfolio weighted average APRs. The effect of financial literacy seems to be impressive when people who correctly answered all three questions are compared with the ones who failed all. As reported by the authors, "*The difference between mean weighted averages APRs between households with respondents who answered all financial literacy questions correctly compared with households with respondents who answered all the financial literacy questions incorrectly is 9 percentage points (65%) and 7 percentage points (50%) against those who answered only one question correctly*", and "*one point higher financial literacy score on the scale of 0–3 is associated with a decline in the portfolio weighted average APR of 1.76 percentage points . . . [OMISSIS] . . . a one point improvement in financial literacy score is associated with a reduction in the share of a household's portfolio which is made up of high cost credit items of 86%*" (pp. 10–11).

High-cost of borrowing and the impact of financial literacy have been studied also in the US by Lusardi and de Bassa Scheresberg (2013). The authors used data from the 2009 National Financial Capability Study on more than 28,000 American adults using a dummy variable equal to one if the respondent engaged in at least one of five high-cost borrowing behaviors (auto title loans, payday loans, refund anticipation loans, pawn shops, and rent-to-own store) in the past five years. Financial literacy has been assessed by another dummy variable equal to one if the respondent correctly answered all three "Lusardi-Mitchell" questions on interest rates, inflation, and risk diversification. After using different regression models and controlling for age, gender, marital status, employment, income, and education, the authors found a strong (negative) relationship between financial literacy and the high-cost of borrowing. The magnitude of this relationship is so relevant that "*financial literacy accounts for 20 percent of the reduction in the use of high-cost borrowing*" (p. 22).

This result seems to be time consistent in the US, because in a previous study of Hilgert et al. (2003) the use of a credit management index that took into account several credit behaviors (having a credit card, paying credit card balances in full each month, reviewing credit reports, comparing offers before applying for a credit card) had been found to be related with a measure of financial literacy based on 28 true-or-false questions about credit, saving, investment, mortgages, and other financial issues. The study used data from a 2001 survey of consumers on around 1,000 American adults. Results show how people with low, medium, and high credit management indexes had financial literacy on credit respectively equal to 47%, 61%, and 66%, confirming a positive relationship between financial literacy and (positive) financial behaviors.

Within the studies on financial literacy and debt, borrowing, and loans, Lusardi and Tufano (2015) analyzed the role of financial literacy in explaining the **overindebtedness** and the use of other high-cost borrowing facilities (auto title loans, student loans, payday loans, pawn shops, salary advance loans) of Americans, using a sample of 1,000 observations collected in 2007. Overindebtedness has been self-assessed by the respondents who agree that they feel they have too much debt or may have difficulty paying it off. The use of high-cost borrowing has been directly asked about too. The answers to three questions on numeracy, credit cards, and compound interest have been used separately as measures of financial literacy. Each one of these three financial literacy measures is a dummy variable, equal to one if the respondent answered correctly (and zero otherwise). The results of the analysis confirm how low financial literacy is related with the use of high-cost transactions. In their conclusions the authors stress how "*as much as one-third of the charges and fees paid by less knowledgeable individuals can be attributed to ignorance*" (p. 332). In addition, a low level of financial literacy increases the chance that people feel their debt position is excessive. Even in this case a set of socio-demographic characteristics has been used for control variables (age, gender, ethnicity, marital status, income, employment, financial assets).

An analysis of **subprime mortgage delinquency** and financial literacy has been done by Gerardi et al. (2010), using a 2008 sample of American borrowers. An objective measure of delinquency on mortgage has been used together with different measures of financial literacy. If the respondents answered in a faulty way the first three of five numeracy questions[14] they were considered as "low-literate". They were included in the same category if they answered question 1 correctly, but got questions 2, 3, and 4 incorrect. A second index of financial literacy considered people who answered incorrectly at least one of the first four questions. A third index considered individuals who answered correctly the first four questions, but not the fifth. A last measure considered only people who correctly answered all five questions. In their conclusions the authors highlight how their "*results show a significant and quantitatively large association between one aspect of financial literacy, numerical ability, and mortgage delinquency. In addition, we find that foreclosure starts are two-thirds lower in the highest numerical ability group compared to the lowest group*" (p. 29).

2.3.2 Saving and investment

Interest about the role of financial literacy in explaining financial behavior related with saving and investment has grown with time and become very popular in recent years.

Within the studies on saving and investments, the connection between financial literacy and **stock market participation** represents one of the most analyzed topics. Kimball and Shumway (2006) analyzed data from a sample of 500 American adults (Survey of Consumer Attitudes), administrated in 2005 by the Survey Research Center of the University of Michigan. Stock market participation has been studied by five different measures. The first one was a dummy variable equal to one if the respondents (1) held stocks, (2) worked for a company with publicly traded stocks, but (3) did not hold stocks of the company they worked for. This measure should focus attention on individuals who intentionally decided to participate in the stock market and did not just invest their savings in the stock of their employer. The attitude about holding stock of an employer has been directly analyzed by a second variable, based on the answer to a specific question: "*whether employees should have the majority of their retirement funds in their current employer's stocks*", where the respondent could agree or disagree. A third measure tried to shed light on a possible "home bias" of American investors by looking at their propensity to hold investments located in foreign countries. The fourth and fifth measures took care of diversification of investment portfolios by looking at (1) the number of individual stocks held by an investor[15] and (2) the number of different asset types (stocks, bonds, real estate properties) held for investment purposes. These measures of stock market participation have been related with two measures of financial literacy. Starting from 15 multiple choice questions on stock market investment topics, the first index was the sum of correct answers, while the second index was the sum of "do not know" or "neither agree nor disagree" answers. Both the indices take into account the result of a principal component analysis used to check if different questions can be addressed to the same source of knowledge. The results of different regression models suggest that "*Sophistication [financial literacy] explains almost 24 percent of the participation variable, and about 15 percent of attitudes toward holding an employer's stock. . . . Sophistication explains about 15 percent of international asset holdings, but it has little explanatory power for respondents' attitudes about international assets. It also has economically significant explanatory power for diversification*" (p. 7).

The chance that investors' financial literacy matters in explaining their **portfolio diversification** has been studied also by Guiso and Jappelli (2009) on a sample of 1,686 clients of an Italian bank.[16] Portfolio diversification has been measured by an index (continuous variables that can range from zero to one) based on the relevance of single stock investment on the total financial wealth of the individual. Financial literacy has been measured by an objective and a subjective measure. The self-assessed financial literacy index (range 0–100) summarizes the self-assessment about the knowledge on different financial products. The objective measure is the sum of values from different dummy variables, where each of them is equal to one if the individuals correctly answer all the questions of a specific set. The authors found that (objective) financial literacy is strongly (positively) correlated with the degree of portfolio diversification. At the same time, the comparison between objective and subjective measures shows how they are weakly related. As reported by the authors, "*The evidence suggests that eliciting financial literacy by simply asking people if they know finance is bound to lead to serious mistakes: many self-confident investors will report that they know finance, while in fact their financial literacy is likely to be quite poor; pessimistic investors, on the other hand, might report knowing very little while in fact they have above average financial literacy*" (p. 21).

Yoong (2011) studied the relationship between stock market participation and financial literacy using a sample of 533 **American adults** (40+ years old) from the 2007 American Life Panel (ALP) survey. The ownership of any stock has been used as a measure of stock market participation, and it has been related with a measure of "financial illiteracy", constructed by a principal component analysis on seven binary indicators for "do not know" answers to questions on stock markets, mutual funds, diversification, and risk-returns on investments. Results highlight how ignorance about stock market investments significantly reduces the propensity to hold stocks. A decrease of one standard deviation above the mean level of financial literacy results in a decrease of stock market participation of 10%.

Almenberg and Dreber (2011) studied stock market participation in **Sweden**, using a sample of 1,300 observations of Swedish adults.[17] The ownership of either stocks or mutual funds has been used to develop a dummy variable that has been related with a financial literacy measure made by the sum of correct answers to 12 questions on numeracy, risk and return on investment, and other items, including the Lusardi-Mitchell questions replicated from other surveys.[18] Results from the Swedish sample confirm the positive role of financial literacy on stock market participation. At the same time, the authors analyzed the chance that financial literacy can help to explain the gender gap puzzle, where females are supposed to participate less in stock markets. In their analysis the authors show that even using a basic financial literacy measure the gap between genders in stock market participation is reduced, supporting the hypothesis that a lack of knowledge and familiarity with stock markets is the real cause of the differences in financial behaviors between genders. From a methodological perspective this paper has another source of interest, due to the fact that the authors tried to measure the effect of numeracy and financial knowledge separately, finding that "*numeracy and financial literacy are separated competencies, although strongly related*" (p. 4). Results show how both numeracy and financial knowledge are positively related with stock market participation.

Financial literacy and stock market participation in **the Netherlands** has been studied by van Rooij et al. (2011). Results of analysis on data from a survey administered by the Dutch national bank in 2005 on more than 1,300 Dutch adults are consistent with the results from other countries. A lack of financial literacy is addressed as a statistically relevant variable in explaining a lack of stock market participation. The authors show how their conclusion is substantially unchanged when different measures of financial literacy are used. Starting from 16 items on different financial topics[19] three measures of financial literacy were developed: (1) the sum of correct answers to each question, (2) the number of the quartile from the number of correct answers, and (3) the financial knowledge of peers. This last measure has been used as an instrumental variable to determine financial literacy of the respondents with the aim to check for endogeneity problems between financial literacy and stock market participation.[20]

But stock market participation does not represent the only financial behavior within saving and investment. Muller and Weber (2010) used a sample of 3,228 German adults from a survey of 2007 to test the hypothesis that, between investors, the more financially literate tend to rely more on passive **mutual funds** than low-literate people, who should be more prone to use active (and more expensive) mutual funds. Whether or not the latest fund purchased by the respondent was a passive fund has been used as the dependent variable in regression models, where financial literacy has been included in a set of control variables that included age, gender, income, education, and other socio-demographic characteristics. Both a subjective measure (self-assessment about financial knowledge in a zero to five scale) and an objective measure (sum of correct answers to eight multiple choice questions on stock market investment issues) have been used in the analysis. The authors established "*a significant positive relation between financial literacy and the likelihood of relying on passive funds, indicating that low financial expertise is indeed one explanation for the actively managed fund puzzle*" (p. 149). However, in the conclusions of the study, it seems that the relationship between the use of passive or active mutual funds and financial literacy is more sophisticated because "*even very sophisticated investors overwhelmingly select active funds despite being very aware of less expensive ETF and index fund alternatives . . . additionally, although more sophisticated investors are capable of giving more precise management fee estimates, they do not minimize fees*" (p. 149).

The **role of fees in investment products selection** and how much financial literacy matters in that process have been studied by Hastings and Tejeda-Ashton (2008) using data from the Mexican financial market.[21] Asking the respondents whether or not fees are the first-choice in selecting investment products, the authors analyzed how the answers to this question are related with a measure of financial literacy made by the sum of correct answers to three questions on interest rates, inflation, and risk diversification (the Lusardi-Mitchell questions). Controlling for socio-demographic characteristics (age, education, etc.) and other control variables (internet usage, presence of savings in equity/bond/foreign currencies) the authors found how very low levels of financial literacy as related with a decision path about investment products caused people to focus on the brand name of the issuer or manager, and the fees and returns seemed to not be considered as relevant. However, the authors highlight how by changing the format presentation of fees from an annual percentage rate to a cash amount, the relevance of this issue increases, and it did much more for low- (financially) literate people.

The role of financial literacy in **the analysis of information about investment products** is the aim of another study by Agnew and Szykman (2004). The authors used data on around 400 American adults – mostly employees of an American Southeast mid-size public university – involved in a research experiment. Providing different investment options to different groups, the authors found that the chance that individuals will choose the one proposed as the default option is much higher (20% vs. 2%) for the less financially literate[22] and motivates this result suggesting that individuals with below average knowledge are simply overwhelmed by the investment decision in general.

The **ability to make an investment decision** is the subject of a study of Deuflhard et al. (2014). The authors analyzed data from the 2005 De Nederlandsche Bank's Household Survey (DHS). The annual interest rates for saving accounts of 1,373 Dutch adults were related with different measures of financial literacy. The frequently used "sum of correct answers" index[23] was used together with two instrumental variables: (1) the financial experience of the oldest sibling and (2) the economic education of the respondents. After controlling for age, gender, education, income, employment, saving wealth, and net financial wealth, the authors found that the higher the financial literacy of individuals is, the higher the interest rate (APR) is they receive from their saving accounts. A one standard deviation increase in financial literacy is associated with a 13% increase compared to the median interest rate. Data about the use of new technologies (online banking usage) allowed the researchers to isolate one channel through which financial literacy positively affects interest rates.

Financial literacy seems to affect the investment behaviors not only by increasing interest rates on saving accounts. Arrondel et al. (2012) have shown how financial literacy positively affects the **propensity to plan**. Data from a sample of French adults[24] included a question where the respondents were asked whether or not they personally gathered financial information, reviewed it in detail, and formulated a specific financial plan for their household's long-term future. The results of the study stress how "*differences in financial knowledge across the population are correlated with differences in the propensity to plan: people with higher financial literacy are more likely to be engaged in the preparation of a clearly defined financial plan for the long-term future*" (p. 13). The risk that results could be affected by the methodology applied to measure financial literacy has been addressed by the use of three objective measures of financial literacy and an additional measure based on an instrumental variable. The researchers used (1) the sum of correct answers to the three Lusardi–Mitchell questions used in the survey (on interest rates, inflation, and diversification), (2) a dummy variable equal to one if the respondent correctly answered all three questions, and (3) the answers to each of these questions as three different variables, while the parents' financial knowledge was adopted as an instrumental variable in order to take into account endogeneity problems between financial knowledge and the propensity to plan.

The same Lusardi–Mitchell questions have been used in the Euro Survey of the Austrian central bank, and Beckman (2013) used the part of the survey about Romanian adults (1,030 obs.) to figure out how financial literacy affects the financial sophistication of Romanians, looking at the **number of saving instruments** that people hold in their investment portfolios.[25] Using the same financial literacy measures of Arrondel et al. (2012) and other previous studies (sum of correct answers, all correct answers, answers to each question as a separate measure) the author has found that individuals who are financially literate, especially with regard to inflation, are more likely to save using more than one interest-bearing saving instrument. However, Beckman pinpoints that results are not consistent between the different measures of financial literacy. While the financial literacy measure of the "sum of correct answers" seems to provide more clear results, the "all three questions correctly answered" index leads to results that are not statistically significant. Moreover, when financial literacy is addressed using the three questions as different measures, the explanatory power about the number of investment products in the investment portfolios is much higher for the question on inflation than the one on risk diversification.

In a similar study Klapper et al. (2013) used data from Russia[26] to assess how financial literacy is related with the **use of current accounts, deposit accounts, or plastic cards**. Results confirm what has been found in other countries: financial literacy is significantly related to greater participation in formal financial markets. However, about the likelihood to own a bank account, financial literacy seems to exert a moderate positive impact. This study confirms previous results from Hilgert and Hogarth (2002) that analyzed data on American adults[27] about the ownership of saving accounts, certificates of deposit, and other long-term saving products.

The work of Klapper, Lusardi, and Panos is even interesting for the variety of financial literacy measures used in their study. Starting from the number of correct answers to different questions, the authors measured financial literacy by a self-assessment measure (based on a one-to-seven Likert scale) and two instrumental variables: the total newspaper circulations in the region of the respondents and the total number of universities in the region.[28]

Hastings and Mitchell (2011) preferred as a measure the total amount of saving and investment in local currencies and used as a financial literacy measure the sum of correct answers to three basic questions and the sum of correct answers to a full set of six questions (the same three basic questions plus three more sophisticated ones). Regressions using data from **Chile**[29] confirm that financial literacy is associated with more (retirement) savings. An analysis of the data from the previous wave of the same survey[30] made by Behrman et al. (2012) confirms that financial literacy positively affects wealth, pension contribution, and retirement planning. In this case financial literacy has been assessed using a methodology that tries to take into account the difficulty of different questions by using a model of weights based on the number of correct answers to the questions, giving higher weights to questions where fewer respondents were able to correctly answer.[31]

The connection between saving and investment and financial literacy has been analyzed also looking at **saving plans for educational purposes**. Huang et al. (2013) used data from a research experiment on kids from the state of Oklahoma (US) in 2007[32] to assess if the ownership of college saving plans is related with financial literacy (measured by answers to the three Lusardi-Mitchel questions on interest rates, inflation, and risk diversification, summarized in two measures: "sum of correct answers" and "whether the respondents correctly answered all three questions"). Coherently with other studies on saving and investment behaviors, financial literacy has been found to play a significant role in having a college saving plan.

The connection between savings and financial literacy has been studied also looking at the **ability to save**. Klapper et al. (2013) paid attention to the effect of the financial crisis on the ability to save in Russia.[33] Referring to income adequacy to make ends needs,[34] the authors found that financial literacy[35] significantly increases the likelihood that the respondent reports greater unspent income, even after controlling for age, gender, education, employment, and income. This relationship seems to have been even more clear during the financial crisis.

Robb and Woodyard (2011) take into account several financial behaviors, including in their analysis (1) the presence of **emergency funds** and (2) the attitude to **overdraft from bank accounts**. In their results, from an analysis on a large sample of American adults,[36] the authors highlight how financial knowledge[37] is clearly an important component in financial decision making. At the same time their conclusion is that not only financial literacy matters, because other factors play a significant role as well, and "*knowledge alone is insufficient to ensure better financial behaviors*" (p. 66).

Almenberg and Widmark (2011) studied the impact of financial literacy outside financial investments, referring to the **real estate market**. Using data from Sweden[38] and addressing financial literacy by a sum of correct answers index based on 12 items,[39] the authors found that numeracy may be an important determinant of homeownership but financial literacy is not. The authors highlight how both numeracy and financial literacy seem to be relevant in explaining the homeownership of Swedish people when no other control variables are included in the analysis, but when other characteristics such as age, gender, education, income, and country of birth are included in a regression analysis, the coefficients on financial literacy approach zero and cease to be statistically significant. This is not the case for numeracy, where the coefficient of its measure is robust to the inclusion of the control variables. In the discussion of results the authors stressed how "*in the full specification of the model each additional point on the six-point numeracy score is associated with a four percent increase in the probability of participating in the housing market*" (p. 19).

2.3.3 Retirement and planning

The changes in the pension systems in several countries and the risk that people would not be prepared to go on retirement or even not be aware about the need to plan for retirement have been strong motivations to study the relationship between financial behaviors related with retirement and planning and financial literacy.

Gustman et al. (2010) studied **the preparedness for retirement** of Americans by analyzing data from the 2004 Health and Retirement Survey (HRS). The sample is made of American adults close to retirement (individuals from 51 to 56 years old) who should have already saved most of the wealth they need to retire. Their preparedness to go on retirement has been measured by (1) total **household wealth**, (2) the ratio of household wealth to household income, and (3) household wealth excluding pensions and Social Security benefits. Financial literacy has been assessed by the sum of correct answers to the Lusardi-Mitchell questions (interest rates, inflation, risk diversification). The results of the study show how there is a correlation between the wealth accumulated for retirement and financial literacy. However, the authors suggest that *"causality is more likely to run from pension wealth to pension knowledge, rather than the other way around"* (p. 2). They even arrive at the conclusion that financial literacy – measured by knowledge of compound interest, inflation, and diversification – is not a significant determinant of pension and Social Security knowledge. Finally, the lack of awareness about the pension system is proved also by the fact that wealth held outside of pensions is not influenced by knowledge of pensions. It seems that people's attitude to saving does not take into account wealth accumulated for retirement purpose (especially by the Social Security system). So, if the financial outcomes used to measure preparedness for retirement seems to be not related with financial literacy, the conclusions of the study are quite interesting: *"We thought that a part of the link between cognition and wealth reflected the fact that higher cognition leads to increased knowledge of retirement finances, which in turn leads to higher wealth . . . we have not succeeded in establishing these linkages. Although we find that more numerate individuals better understand their pensions or Social Security to be very fragile. Nor do we find evidence linking* [financial literacy] *to wealth accumulation in association with increased knowledge of pension and Social Security"* (p. 29).

The fact that people with better financial literacy are more aware about their fragile situation could be interpreted as a positive result, even if they seem to not take any action. The reasons why they do not show different financial outcomes can vary (e.g. financial "inertia" for long-term goals, lack of disposable income to be invested in retirement plans, etc.), but the awareness of financial need can be interpreted as the precondition for a behavioral change. It means that measuring the role of financial literacy on retirement planning by using a financial outcome such as retirement wealth risks being too optimistic about the potential effect of financial literacy on financial behaviors. This conclusion seems to be confirmed by the study of Song (2012), who studied **retirement planning in China** with a sample of 1,153 Chinese adults linking the contribution to a retirement saving plan (in local currency) with two measures of financial literacy.[40] Results show how a higher level of financial literacy is not a predictor of higher contributions to saving plans, but a low level of financial literacy is correlated with low contributions to pension plans.

The fact that people could be aware about their financial needs but other **external constraints** could affect the decision to save or not for retirement, or make decisions about how much to save and which investment vehicle to use to do it (e.g. pension funds, individual retirement accounts, real estate properties, etc.), suggests that it is important to analyze the role of financial literacy in retirement planning decisions by using different variables than monetary financial outcomes.

Under the assumption that financial literacy can help people **be aware of the need to save for retirement**, it follows that even if not all financially literate people will do it for sure, it is reasonable that financial literacy should be higher among savers as compared to the non savers. This hypothesis has been tested by Klapper et al. (2013) on a sample of more than 1,400 **Russian individuals**. They divided the sample into "private planners", "public planners", and "no planners" by asking the respondents what kind of income they expect to use for living after retirement. The first category (private planners) hosts people who rely on a privately owned retirement fund, on additional financial aid from an enterprise where they have been working, or other similar answers.[41] A "public planner" is a respondent who relies on a pension received from a publicly owned retirement fund. A subject is a "non planner" if he/she expects to live on retirement thanks to the financial support of children or relatives, by working after retirement, or by support from church and charitable organizations. In this category are included even respondents who simply said that they "do not know". The Lusardi-Mitchell questions are once more used to measure financial literacy by using a "sum of correct answers" index, an "all three correct answers" index, and each of the three questions (compound interest, inflation, risk diversification) as a separate measure of financial literacy. After controlling for age, gender, education, employment, number of household members, and whether the respondent lives in a urban area, the authors found that financial literacy is much higher among the private planners than the public planners and the non planners. At the same time, no significant differences concerning financial literacy have been found comparing public planners and non planners. Results are consistent with the different measures of financial literacy, but much more clear results are provided by taking into account people who correctly answered all three questions and the others.

The presence (or not) of a saving plan for retirement has been studied also by Sekita (2011) on a sample of more than 5,000 **Japanese**.[42] The use of the Lusardi-Mitchell questions makes the results of the study comparable with the ones from other studies. The "sum of correct answers" and the "all correct answers to the three questions" have been used to measure financial literacy, but the author used a self-assessment measure (scale 1 to 5) and instrumental variable too. Results from the Japanese database confirm that financial literacy increases the probability of having a saving plan for retirement, even after controlling for age, gender, education, and other socio-demographic variables. The instrument used for financial literacy is the answer to the question "*When you were 15 years old, where did your grades in Japanese rank among others in your* *grade?*", where respondents can answer choosing between a five grade scale.[43] The hypothesis is that having good knowledge of language (words and comprehension) is a good predictor of better financial literacy.[44] The use of such an instrument is supported by empirical analysis: Japanese skills increase the level of financial literacy with a very high statistical significance.[45]

Honekamp (2012) studied the relationship between financial literacy and retirement planning analyzing the relationship between the ownership of a voluntary pension plan and the answers to the Lusardi-Mitchell questions (compound interest, inflation, diversification) in a survey of **German adults**.[46] Results from analysis that used (1) the sum of correct answers, (2) "all correct answers", and (3) answers to each question separately as measures of financial literacy show how "*there is not a large difference between having zero, one or two questions right. . . . While about 40 percent of this group of respondents own a supplemental pension insurance, it is 59 percent of the respondents getting all three questions right*" (p. 15).

The use of Lusardi-Mitchell questions as a sort of "gold-standard" in the financial literacy surveys allows one to easily compare results from different studies. After the SLPS Japanese survey and the SAVE study from Germany, even the Euro Survey administrated by the Austrian central bank used the Lusardi-Mitchell questions to assess financial literacy. Beckmann (2013) used data from the Euro Survey to assess the connection between retirement planning and financial literacy in **Romania**. Using the number of saving instruments[47] and whether respondents have pension funds or not, the author used the same financial literacy measures of Honekamp (2012).[48] In this case the number of correct answers is positively and significantly related to savings, even if the magnitude of financial literacy seems to be marginal, due to the fact that "*correctly answering an additional financial literacy question raises the probability of saving in a pension fund by 1 percentage point*" (p. 16).

The study of Brown and Graf (2013), on a sample of more than 1,500 **Swiss adults**,[49] is quite similar to the studies of Beckmann (2013), Honekamp (2012), and Sekita (2011), due to the fact that the authors analyze the impact of financial literacy – measured by the Lusardi-Mitchell questions[50] – on a retirement account indicator that is equal to one for households that report having a voluntary retirement saving account (under the Swiss pension system), and zero otherwise. Results show how financial literacy is positively related to retirement planning and how "*respondents who answer all three financial literacy questions correctly are 9 percentage point more likely to have a voluntary retirement saving account than respondents who do not answer all questions correctly*" (p. 2).

Hence, financial literacy seems to be meaningful in the explanation of retirement planning behaviors. However, there is even the chance that financial literacy can play a positive role in retirement issues even without evidence of behavioral changes in financial outcomes (e.g. retirement wealth, having a pension plan, etc.). For instance, Bucher-Koenen and Lusardi (2011) used data from a sample of German adults[51] taking care of answers to the following question:

Have you and your partner ever tried to find out how much you would have to save today to reach a certain standard of living at old-age?.

Under the assumption that financial literacy helps consumers to be aware about the need to save for retirement, using items that are not affected by external constraints – such as the lack of disposable income to start saving or the use of saving tools that differ from pension funds or similar options – but that directly measure "the will to take care" for retirement, the role of financial literacy on retirement issues can be assessed more carefully. In their study, Bucher-Koenen and Lusardi used the Lusardi-Mitchell questions in (1) a sum-of-correct-answers index and (2) taking care of whether all the answers were correct or not. Two instrumental variables for financial literacy were used too. The first one measured the financial knowledge of parents, while the second concerned the residence of the respondents, whether they were in a region with a high share of left-wing voters (or not).

The authors support the hypothesis that political attitude plays an important role in financial decision making, and, according to results from previous studies, they assume that left-wing voters are less financially literate than others.

The rationale behind the use of political attitude as an instrument of financial literacy is that previous studies (van Rooij et al. 2011) have shown that those who do not participate in the stock market are less financially literate than those who do participate. At the same time left-wing voters seem to have lower stock market participation compared to right-wing voters (Kaustia and Torstila 2010). This seems to happen because of a different "taste for assets" that should be related to a different risk attitude and that should be independent of other preference parameters. So, if left-wing voters, on average, participate less in the stock markets, and participation in the stock market is related with more financial literacy, the assumption is that to be a left-wing voter can be used as an instrument of less financial literacy compared with right-wing voters. However, the authors do not have explicit measures of political attitude and used the residence in a country region as a proxy of political attitude referring to the results of the national election at the administrative district level. Doing so, the authors assume that living in an area where the majority of the population is right-wing voters (supposed to be more financially literate) will cause the rest of the population to increase their financial knowledge by social interaction.

Results support the hypothesis that people with more financial literacy pay more attention about retirement planning. The all-three-questions-correct measure of financial literacy seems to be more reliable than the sum-of-correct-answers measure. Referring to someone as "planner" if he/she tried to figure out how much savings are needed for going on retirement, and "non planner" for the others, the authors show how about 70% of the planners answered all three questions correctly versus only 54% of the non-planners. On the other hand, the non-planners are about twice as likely as the planners to have responded "do not know" to at least one question.

Results from analysis with instrumental variables confirm that financial literacy makes individuals be more aware about the need to save for retirement both when the instrument is the "left-wing voters attitude" and in the case of "financial knowledge of parents".

The attitude to save for retirement has been studied also by van Rooij et al. (2011). The key variable of the study is whether individuals have thought "a lot" or at least "some" about retirement. The data of the study are from a Dutch central bank survey[52] of 1,373 Dutch adults. The sum of correct answers to 16 financial literacy questions[53] has been used both as a measure of financial literacy itself and as an input for a measure where each individual has been ranked using the number of the quartile of the sum of correct answers distribution. The financial knowledge of peers has been adopted as an instrument for financial literacy in a separate analysis.

In their conclusions the authors stress how they "*find a strong and positive relationship between financial knowledge and retirement planning: those who are more financially knowledgeable are more likely to plan for retirement*" (p. 1).

The conclusion that financial literacy is higher and awareness is greater about people's need to plan for retirement is confirmed by the study of Lusardi and Mitchell (2011) for the US. The answers to the question "*Have you ever tried to figure out how much you need to save for retirement?*", included in the 2009 National Financial Capability Study of the FINRA Foundation, have been related with several measures of financial literacy,[54] and the findings are consistent with the hypothesis that financial literacy is positively linked to retirement planning.

These results are once more supported by another empirical analysis from **Australia**. Agnew et al. (2013) analyzed the answers to the question "*Have you ever tried to work out how much you need to save for retirement?*" in a sample of 2,014 Australians[55] finding that more financially literate individuals take more care about their retirement needs. The three Lusardi–Mitchell questions are once more the items used to assess financial literacy.[56] Results show how the probability of being a planner increases by 12.3 percentage points if individuals can answer all three questions correctly. In a second specification of the model, where financial literacy is measured by the number of correct answers, each question answered correctly raises the chances of planning by nearly 6 percentage points. The analysis controlled for other possible explanatory variables such as age, gender, education, employment, income, and homeownership.

If financial literacy helps people to be aware about the need to save for retirement, Hasting et al. (2011) have found that it is useful even when people **need to choose between different pension funds**. Using data from a large sample of Chileans,[57] the authors asked people why they have chosen a pension fund. The list of options included (1) friend recommendation, (2) profitability of the fund, (3) to help salesperson, (4) good service, (5) advertising, (6) gift offered, (7) low-fixed commission, (8) low-variable commission, and (9) employer recommendation. Results show how people with low financial literacy[58] rely more on employers and friends than on fundamentals, even after controlling for age, gender, marital status, education, and income.[59]

Finally, financial literacy seems to have a positive effect on people's financial behaviors even after the decision to buy a saving plan. A study of Utkus and Young (2011) has found that people with more financial literacy have more discipline and tend to **borrow from their saving plans** less likely than people with low financial literacy. Using data from a sample of 895 American saving plan participants[60] the authors found that low financial literacy[61] is associated with an increase in the probability of having a loan outstanding of 4–6 percentage points. In addition, *"a low literacy score raises the probability of having a 401(k) [saving plan] loan by 6 percentage points, and increase of 27 percent relative to 22 percent of participants in our sample who have a loan outstanding"* (p. 60).

2.4 Conclusions

The need to cope with different requirements of knowledge and to develop financial skills in order to make financial decisions, both in a long-term perspective and on a daily basis, makes financial literacy a relevant issue for a large part of the population (if not for the entire population). If the need to make financial decisions does not represent itself a new issue (due to the fact that people have always been required to manage their finances) the responsibility about critical decisions concerning, for instance, post-retirement life, coverage for healthcare related issues, and the decision about asset allocation of savings and wealth has been shifted to individuals as a consequence of changes in the regulatory and social framework (e.g. pension system reforms, growing complexity of financial markets, etc.). The greater responsibility about personal financial management and the growing number of decisions to be made on an individual basis have increased the need of financial literacy compared with just a few years ago.

The relevance of this knowledge about financial topics is probably great enough to include financial literacy, or at least the basics principle of finance, within the basic requirement of literacy in a modern society. If the need to treat financial literacy as a basic educational component in order to make people understand the consequences of their financial behaviors and be able to make a financial decision responsibly has been opposed by those who think that the hypothesis to make people aware about the consequences of their actions in finance is not just over-optimistic but even risky, there is a large consensus about the need to provide people with adequate financial literacy.

A review of the literature about financial literacy and financial behaviors has shown how knowledge on even very basic principles such as compound interest, inflation, and diversification positively affects different financial decisions and is related with positive financial outcomes. In addition, the impact of financial literacy on financial behaviors seems to be not great enough to look at it as the only or the main driver of a financial decision making process. Other relevant socio-demographic characteristics seem to play a relevant role in explaining different financial outcomes, but the high proportion of low financially literate individuals within the groups with not desirable outcomes (e.g. lack of saving for retirement, exclusion from the financial system, use of high-cost of borrowing products) highlights the need to take care about financial literacy.

The relevance of financial literacy has been stressed by the analysis of both an individual and a social perspective, and several warnings about the need to ensure people have an adequate level of financial literacy have been highlighted. A low level of financial literacy can represent itself an obstacle to improve financial literacy if some behavioral biases make the investment required to develop financial literacy be perceived as not worthy. At the same time, the motivation to learn can be related with more than previous financial experiences (usually "bad" experiences), because the chance that people will develop interest about a financial topic and will have the right motivation to learn, in order to avoid future mistakes or repair the consequences of previous wrong decisions, could not work, especially when awareness about the relevance of a financial issue arrives when it is too late to repair (e.g. the understanding about the need to save for retirement when it is time to go on retirement or the need to save for children's education when the children have grown).

The analysis of the relationship between financial literacy and financial behaviors suggested considering financial literacy as a key variable in the explanation of people's financial behaviors and stressed the need to address financial literacy as a pivotal tool in a consumer protection perspective. This conclusion paves the way to the need to measure financial literacy by collecting data and to study the determinants of financial literacy. About this, the analysis of the literature has shown how in some countries the study of financial literacy is supported by specific surveys which are available for research and systematically updated by the release of new waves, while in other countries the lack of data risks jeopardizing the effectiveness of any analysis of financial literacy.

Notes

1 The "stages of change" are part of a behavioral change model developed in the bigger framework of the TransTheoretical Model (TTM) of changes. In this model, developed studying the changes of addictive behaviors, five different stages of changes are summarized. The first one is the "Precontemplation" stage, where there is no intention to change behavior in the foreseeable future. The second stage is the "Contemplation" stage, in which people are aware that a problem exists and are seriously thinking about overcoming it, but have not yet made a commitment to take action. The next stage is "Preparation". Individuals in this stage are intending to take action in the near future and are in a decision making step, where they collect information and assess the available options to change. The fourth stage is called "Action" because in this stage individuals modify their behavior. The fifth and final stage is called "Maintenance" and is the stage in which people work to prevent relapse and consolidate the gains attained during action. (For further details see Prochaska et al. 1992.)

2 Data are from the 2001 University of Michigan Survey of Consumers.

3   Data used are an author's derivation from the RAND American Life Panel (ALP). The subsample used in the study is about 812 observations.

4   The study used data from the Dutch DNB Household Survey.

5   The old-age dependency ratio is calculated by the ratio of people on retirement and people in their working age (25–65 years old).

6   OECD (2013).

7   A 401(k) plan is "*a defined contribution plan where an employee can make contributions from his or her paycheck either before or after-tax, depending on the options offered in the plan. The contributions go into a 401(k) account, with the employee often choosing the investments based on options provided under the plan. In some plans, the employer also makes contributions such as matching the employee's contributions up to a certain percentage*" (Internal Revenue Service of the United States of America (www.irs.gov/Retirement-Plans/Plan-Participant,-Employee/ Definitions).

8   European Commission report (2014) "Special Eurobarometer 411 – Patient Safety and Quality of Care 2014".

9   "Permanent income" is defined as the expected long-term average income, which takes into account both present income and the expectation of future income and revenues, coherently with the studies of the Permanent Income Hypothesis (PIH) developed by Milton Friedman since the '50s.

10   From the "Presidential Proclamation – Financial Literacy Month". (www.whitehouse. gov/the-press-office/presidential-proclamation-financial-literacy-month)

11   European Parliament resolution of November 18, 2008 on protecting the consumer: improving consumer education and awareness on credit and finance (www. europarl.europa.eu/sides/getDoc.do?pubRef=-//EP//TEXT+TA+P6-TA-2008-0539 + 0+DOC+XML+V0//EN).

12   As reported by the Federal Deposit Insurance Corporation (FDIC 2003) "*Payday loans are small-dollar, short-term, unsecured loans that borrowers promise to repay out of their next paycheck or regular income payment. Payday loans are usually priced at a fixed-dollar fee, which represents the finance charge to the borrower. Because these loans have such short terms to maturity, the cost of borrowing, expressed as an annual percentage rate, can range from 300 percent to 1,000 percent, or more*" (www.fdic.gov/bank/analytical/fyi/2003/012903fyi.html, last accessed March 3, 2015).

13   The questions used by the NFCS to test financial literacy are the so called "Lusardi-Mitchell" questions, originally used in the 2004 Health and Retirement Study (HRS) and replicated by several other surveys.

14   The five numeracy questions are:

   1   *In a sale, a shop is selling all items at half price. Before the sale, a sofa costs $300. How much will it cost in the sale?*

   2   *If the chance of getting a disease is 10 per cent, how many people out of 1,000 would be expected to get the disease?*

   3   *A second hand car dealer is selling a car for $6,000. This is two-thirds of what it cost new. How much did the car cost new?*

   4   *If 5 people all have the winning numbers in the lottery and the prize is $2 million, how much will each of them get?*

   5   *Let's say you have $200 in a savings account. The account earns ten per cent interest per year. How much will you have in the account at the end of two years?*

15   The number of individual stocks "x" held has been used to calculate and index equal to $1 - (1/x)$. Such a measure makes the result range between zero and one.

16   Data are from the 2007 Unicredit Customers' Survey referred to the clients of Unicredit bank.

17   Data come from a survey commissioned by the Swedish Financial Supervision Authority in 2010.

18 The questions concern knowledge about compound interest, inflation, diversification, and bond pricing.

19 The questions of the survey on financial literacy investigate knowledge about linear interest, compound interest, inflation, time value of money, money illusion, risk, and diversification.

20 In their paper the authors take into account the hypothesis that financial literacy can be affected by participation in the stock market by a learn-by-doing process. Using knowledge of peers, which should not be related with the financial experiences of the respondents, is used as a proxy of their financial literacy.

21 The study relies on data from a survey on participants in Mexico's privatized Social Security system. The sample is made by 763 observations, and data have been collected during 2007.

22 The authors rely on a financial literacy index calculated as the sum of correct answers to ten questions on investment issues.

23 The index takes into account the correct answers to 16 questions on (1) linear interest, (2) compound interest, (3) inflation, (4) time value of money, (5) money illusion, and (6) risk and diversification.

24 Data are from the Patrimoines et Préférences face au Temps et au Risque (PATER) survey (3,616 obs.).

25 The 2011 Euro Survey includes data about the following investment products: cash, saving deposit, life insurance, mutual funds, stocks, pension funds, bonds, current account, other. The chances to answer by saying "I have no savings" or "Do not know" and not to answer at all are contemplated.

26 Data concern 1,240 Russian individuals and have been collected between 2008 and 2009. Financial literacy questions have been mutated by the Lusardi-Mitchell questions.

27 Data come from the 2001 survey of consumers, commissioned by the Federal Reserve system (1,000 obs.).

28 Using the number of newspapers as an instrument for financial literacy, the assumption is that financial literacy is related with education and more educated people tend to read newspapers more than others. At the same time the hypothesis that more financially literate people tend to use financial information more than others is coherent with the assumption that areas where more newspapers are read are the ones where people are more financially literate.

   About the second instrumental variable – the total number of universities in the region – in this case the choice can be justified by referring to a positive correlation between education and financial literacy and assuming that to be in touch and interact with very literate people causes a natural improvement of knowledge.

29 Data source is the 2009 Chilean EPS "Encuesta de Proteccion Social" (14,243 obs.).

30 Data come from the 2006 Chilean EPC "Encuesta de Proteccion Social" (13,054 obs.).

31 The methodology used is the PRIDIT model that takes into account the difficulty of the questions for both correct and wrong answers. If correct answers to an easy question (a question where most of the respondents were able to answer correctly) will contribute to financial literacy less than a correct answer to a difficult question (a question where just a few respondents answered correctly), even wrong answers will be differentiated taking into account the difficulty of the question. To be wrong on a question will negatively affect the assessment of financial literacy, and a wrong answer to an easy question will do it more than a mistake on a difficult item.

32 The SEED for Oklahoma Kids experiment involved 2,651 participants.

33 The authors used data from a 1,240 observation sample, collected between 2008 and 2009 in Russia.

34 The authors use two variables. The first one is a low-spending dummy variable, equal to one for the individuals who report not having money for more than food. The second one is a zero-to-five variable where the higher the value is, the higher the financial fragility of the respondents is (e.g. not being able to save at all).

35 Several measures of financial literacy have been used in the study, including objective measures, subjective measures, and instrumental variables (total newspaper circulation in the region and number of universities in the region).

36 Data are from the 2009 National Financial Capability Study (NFCS) administered by the FINRA Foundation. The sample size is 28,146 observations and includes data from all the states of the US.

37 The measure of financial literacy used is the sum of correct answers to five questions, included the widely used Lusardi-Mitchell questions.

38 The survey concerns 1,300 Swedish adults and has been commissioned by the Swedish Financial Supervision Authority) in 2010.

39 The survey includes questions on numeracy and financial literacy, including four questions from the Lusardi-Mitchell ones on (1) compound interest, (2) inflation, (3) diversification and (4) bond pricing.

40 Financial literacy is assessed by the sum of correct answers to eight questions on compound interest. The answers to each of these questions have been used as different financial literacy measures too.

41 Other possible answers related with "private planners" are "income from leasing and selling properties" and "private savings".

42 Data are from the 2010 Survey of Living Preferences and Statistics (SLPS) with 5,386 observations.

43 The five options are: "in lower rank", "in rather lower rank", "in the middle", "in rather higher rank", and "in higher rank". The variables used as an instrument of financial literacy are two dummy variables: the first is equal to one if the respondent answered that he/she has been "in rather higher rank", while the second is related to having been "in higher rank".

44 The author motivated the use of this variable saying, "*I take an instrumental variable approach that uses individual Japanese skills and average regional Japanese skills because individuals with a high level of knowledge of the meaning of words and a high level of sentence comprehension are likely to have a high degree of financial literacy and because when individuals live in the same prefectures as people with high Japanese skills, it is expected that individual Japanese skills become higher and the level of financial literacy also becomes higher*".

45 The coefficients of the two instrument variables are strongly significant at a 1% level.

46 Data are from the SAVE study ("Sparen und AltersVorsorgE"). The SAVE study is a survey administered since 2001 by the Munich Center for the Economics of Aging (MEA center) situated in Munich (Germany), which collects data about private households' saving behavior in Germany. After 2001, further waves of the survey have been released in 2003/04, 2005, 2006, 2007, 2008, 2009, 2010, 2011, and 2013.

47 The list of saving instruments monitored is the following: cash, saving deposit, life insurance, mutual funds, stocks, pension funds, bonds, current account, other.

48 The financial literacy measures of the study are (1) the sum of correct answers, (2) all correct answers or not, and (3) answers to each of the three questions as separate variables.

49 The study is based on a survey administered by the University of St. Gallen (Switzerland) in 2011.

50 The measures used were (1) the sum of correct answers and (2) the all-correct-answer measure.

51 Data are from the 2001 SAVE study, with 1,059 observations.

52 Data are from the 2005 wave of the De Nederlandsche Bank's Household Survey (DHS Survey), administered by the central bank of the Netherlands.

53 Questions on financial literacy concern (1) linear interest, (2) compound interest, (3) inflation, (4) time value of money, (5) money illusion, and (6) risk and diversification.

54 The 2009 NFCS includes the Lusardi-Mitchell questions on compound interest, inflation, and risk diversification. The authors used them in both a sum-of-correct-answers and an all-three-correct-answers measure. An instrumental variable approach has been

followed too by using the "length of time that financial education mandated benefits were in effect when the respondents were young" as an instrument of financial literacy.

55 Data have been collected in 2012.

56 The authors used four indices of financial literacy: (1) sum of correct answers, (2) all three answers correct, (3) number of "do not know" options, and (4) answers to each question as a separate measure of financial literacy – and used the financial experiences of respondents' siblings and parents as an instrument of financial literacy.

57 Data are from the "Encusta de Proteccion Social" (EPS), a survey about the pension system in Chile with 14,243 observations collected in 2009.

58 Financial literacy has been measured as the sum of correct answers to three plus three questions, where the first three have been used for a "basic financial literacy" measure (questions on numeracy) and the other three as "sophisticated financial literacy" (Lusardi-Mitchell questions on compound interest, inflation, and risk diversification).

59 Results of the analysis show how low levels of education and income are more correlated with decisions to choose a pension plan by referring to employers and friend recommendations too.

60 The saving plan analyzed in the study is a 401(k) plan, which is "*a defined contribution plan where an employee can make contributions from his or her paycheck either before or after-tax, depending on the options offered in the plan. The contributions go into a 401(k) account, with the employee often choosing the investments based on options provided under the plan. In some plans, the employer also makes contributions such as matching the employee's contributions up to a certain percentage*" (definition provided by the Internal Revenue Service of the US).

61 Financial literacy is measured by an all-correct-answers index on four questions about (1) compound interest, (2) debt, (3) risk in investment, and (4) risk and return in investment.

References

Agnew, J., Bateman, H., Thorp, S. (2013). Financial Literacy and Retirement Planning in Australia. *Numeracy Advancing Education in Quantitative Literacy*, 6(2), *article* 7. DOI: http://dx.doi.org/10.5038/1936-4660.6.2.7

Agnew, J., Szykman, L. (2004). Asset Allocation and Information Overload: The Influence of Information Display, Asset Choice and Investor Experience. *Center for Retirement Research at Boston College, CRR WP 2004–15.*

Allgood, S., Walstad, W. (2011). The Effects of Perceived and Actual Financial Knowledge on Credit Card Behavior. *Networks Financial Institute at Indiana State University Working Paper, 2011-WP-15.*

Almenberg, J., Dreber, A. (2011). Gender, Financial Literacy and Stock Market Participation. *SSE/EFI Working Paper Series in Economics and Finance, No 737.* http://ssrn.com/abstract=188090

Almenberg, J., Säve-Söderberg, J. (2011). Financial Literacy and Retirement Planning in Sweden. *NETSPAR Discussion Paper 01/2011–018.*

Almenberg, J., Widmark, O. (2011). Numeracy, Financial Literacy and Participation in Asset Markets. *SSRN.* DOI: http://dx.doi.org/10.2139/ssrn.1756674

Arrondel, L., Debbich, M., Savignac, F. (2012). Stockholding and Financial Literacy in the French Population. *International Journal of Social Sciences and Humanity Studies*, 4(2), 285–294.

Beckmann, E. (2013). Financial Literacy and Household Savings in Romania. *Numeracy Advancing Education in Quantitative Literacy*, 6(2), *article* 9. DOI: http://dx.doi.org/10.5038/1936-4660.6.2.9

Behrman, J., Mitchell, O.S., Soo, C., Bravo, D. (2012). Financial Literacy, Schooling, and Wealth Accumulation. *American Economic Review Paper and Proceedings*, 102(3), 300–304.

Bhattacharya, U., Hackethal, A., Kaesler, S., Loos, B., Meyer, S. (2014). Is Unbiased Financial Advice to Retail Investors Sufficient? Answers from a Large Field Study. *SSRN*. DOI: http://dx.doi.org/10.2139/ssrn.1669015

Björnberg, A. (2014). Health Consumer Powerhouse Euro Health Consumer Index 2014 Report. https://old.healthpowerhouse.com/wp-content/uploads/2015/01/EHCI_2014_report.pdf

Björnberg, A. (2015). Health Consumer Powerhouse Euro Health Consumer Index 2015 Report. https://old.healthpowerhouse.com/wp-content/uploads/2016/01/EHCI_2015_report.pdf

Brown, M., Graf, R. (2013). Financial Literacy and Retirement Planning in Switzerland. *Numeracy Advancing Education in Quantitative Literacy*, 6(2), *article* 6. DOI: http://dx.doi.org/10.5038/1936-4660.6.2.6

Bucher-Koenen, T., Lusardi, A. (2011). Financial Literacy and Retirement Planning in Germany. *Journal of Pension Economics and Finance*, 10(4), 565–584.

Bumcrot, C., Lin, J., Lusardi, A. (2013). The Geography of Financial Literacy. *Numeracy Advancing Education in Quantitative Literacy*, 6(2), *article* 2. DOI: http://dx.doi.org/10.5038/1936-4660.6.2.2

Carpena, F., Cole, S., Shapiro, J., Zia, B. (2011). Unpacking the Causal Chain of Financial Literacy. *World Bank – Policy Research Working Paper 5798*. World Bank, Washington DC. http://documents.worldbank.org/curated/en/329301468322465624/Unpacking-the-causal-chain-of-financial-literacy

Clark, R., Sandler, M., Mallen, S. (2010). The Role of Financial Literacy In Determining Retirement Plans. *NBER Working Paper, No. 16612*. www.nber.org/papers/w16612

Collins, J. (2012). Financial Advice: A Substitute for Financial Literacy? *Financial Service Review*, 24(4), 307–322.

Crossan, D., Feslier, D., Hurnabard, R. (2011). Financial Literacy and Retirement Planning in New Zealand. *Journal of Pension Economics and Finance*, 10(4), 619–635.

Deuflhard, F., Georgarakos, D., Inderst, R. (2014). Financial Literacy and Savings Account Returns. *MPRA (Munich Personal RePEc Archive)*. DOI: http://dx.doi.org/10.2139/ssrn.2358564

Disney, R., Gathergood, J. (2012). Financial Literacy and Consumer Credit Use. *CFCM – Centre for Finance and Credit Markets, Working Paper, 12/01*

Disney, R., Gathergood, J. (2013). Financial Literacy and Consumer Credit Portfolios. *Journal of Banking and Finance*, 37(7), 2246–2254.

European Commission (2014) European Commission report Special Eurobarometer 411 Patient Safety and Quality of Care 2014. https://ec.europa.eu/health/patient_safety/eurobarometers/ebs_411_en

FDIC (2003). Payday Lending. www.fdic.gov/bank/analytical/fyi/2003/012903fyi.html

Fernandes, D., Lynch, J., Netemeyer, R. (2013). The Effect of Financial Literacy and Financial Education on Downstream Financial Behaviors. *NEFE – National Endowment for Financial Education*.

Fornero, E., Monticone, C. (2011). Financial Literacy and Pension Plan Participation in Italy. *Journal of Pension Economics and Finance*, 10(4), 547–564.

FSA (2005). Measuring Financial Capability: An Exploratory Study. *Financial Service Authority, Consumer Research*, 37.

Gamble, K., Boyle, P., Bennett, D. (2013). Aging, Financial Literacy, and Fraud. *Netspar Discussion Paper No. 11/2013–066. Available at SSRN*. DOI: http://dx.doi.org/10.2139/ssrn.2361151

Gerardi, K., Goette, L., Meier, S. (2010). Financial Literacy and Subprime Mortgage Delinquency: Evidence from a Survey Matched to Administrative Data. *Federal Reserve Bank of Atlanta Working Paper, 2010–10*.

Guiso, L., Jappelli, T. (2009). Financial Literacy and Portfolio Diversification. *CSEF – Centre for Studies in Economics and Finance, Working Paper, No. 212.*

Gustman, A., Steinmeier, T., Tabatabai, N. (2010). Financial Knowledge and Financial Literacy at the Household Level. *Michigan Retirement Research Center, Working Paper, 2010–223.*

Hastings, J., Mitchell, O.S. (2011). How Financial Literacy and Impatience Shape Retirement Wealth and Investment Behaviors. *NBER Working Paper, No. 16740.*

Hastings, J., Mitchell, O.S., Chyn, E. (2011). Fees, Framing, and Financial Literacy in the Choice of Pension Manager. *Published in Financial Literacy – Implications for Retirement Security and the Financial Marketplace.* New York, NY: Oxford University Press, 101–115.

Hastings, J.S., Tejeda-Ashton, L. (2008). Financial Literacy, Information, and Demand Elasticity: Survey and Experimental Evidence from Mexico. *NBER Working Paper, No. 14538.* www.nber.org/papers/w1453

Hilgert, M., Hogarth, J.M. (2002). Financial Knowledge, Experience and Learning references: Preliminary Results from a New Survey on Financial Literacy. *Consumer Interest Annual*, 48

Hilgert, M., Hogarth, J.M., Beverly, S. (2003). Household Financial Management: The Connection Between Knowledge and Behavior. *Federal Reserve Bulletin*, July, 309–322.

Honekamp, I. (2012). Financial Literacy and Retirement Savings in Germany. *Networks Financial Institute at Indiana State University Working Paper, 2012-Wp-03.*

Huang, J., Nam, Y., Sherraden, M. (2013). Financial Knowledge and Child Development Account Policy a Test of Financial Capability. *Journal of Consumer Affairs*, 47(1), 1–26.

Kaustia, M., Torstila, S.(2010) Stock Market Aversion? Political Preferences and Stock Market Participation. Journal of Financial Economics, 100(1), 98–112

Kimball, M.S., Shumway, T. (2006). Investor Sophistication and the Home Bias, Diversification, and Employer Stock Puzzles. http://dx.doi.org/10.2139/ssrn.1572866

Klapper, L., Lusardi, A., Panos, G. (2013). Financial Literacy and its Consequences: Evidence from Russia During the Financial Crisis. *Journal of Banking and Finance*, 37(10), 3904–3923.

Korniotis, G., Kumar, A. (2011). Do Older Investors Make Better Investment Decisions? *Review of Economics and Statistics*, 93(1), 244–265.

Laibson, D. (1997). Golden Eggs and Hyperbolic Discounting. *Quarterly Journal of Economics*, 112(2), 443–477.

Lusardi, A., de Bassa Scheresberg, C. (2013). Financial Literacy and High-Cost Borrowing in the United States. *Global Financial Literacy Excellence Center (GFLEC) Research Paper.* www. usfinancialcapability.org/downloads/HighCostBorrowing.pdf?utm_source=

Lusardi, A., Mitchell, O.S. (2007). Financial Literacy and Retirement Planning: New Evidence from the Rand American Life Panel. *Michigan Retirement Research Center Research Paper No. WP 2007–157. Available at SSRN.* https://ssrn.com/abstract=1095869 or DOI: http://dx.doi.org/10.2139/ssrn.1095869

Lusardi, A., Mitchell, O.S. (2011). Financial Literacy and Retirement Planning in the United States. *Journal of Pension Economics and Finance*, 10(4), 509–525.

Lusardi, A., Mitchell, O.S. (2014). The Economic Importance of Financial Literacy: Theory and Evidence. *Journal of Economic Literature*, 52(1), 5–44.

Lusardi, A., Tufano, P. (2015). Debt Literacy, Financial Experiences, and Overindebtedness. *Journal of Pension Economics and Finance*, 14(04), 332–368.

Mak, V., Braspenning, J. (2012). Errare Humanum Est: Financial Literacy in European Consumer Credit Law. *Journal of Consumer Policy*, 35, 307–332.

Mason, C., Wilson, R. (2000). Conceptualising Financial Literacy. *Loughborough University Business School (UK), Research Series Paper 2000:7.* ISBN 1 85901 168 3.

Moore, D. (2003). Survey of Financial Literacy in Washington State: Knowledge, Behavior, Attitudes and Experiences. *Washington State University Social and Economic Sciences Research Center, Technical Report 03–39.*

Mottola, G. (2013). In Our Best Interest: Women, Financial Literacy, and Credit Card Behavior. *Numeracy Advancing Education in Quantitative Literacy*, 6(2), *article* 4. DOI: http://dx.doi.org/10.5038/1936-4660.6.2.4

Muller, S., Weber, M. (2010). Financial Literacy and Mutual Fund Investments: Who Buys Actively Managed Funds? *Schmalenbach Business Review*, 62, 126–153.

NFCS (2009). *National Financial Capability Study.* FINRA Financial Education Foundation. http://www.usfinancialcapability.org/

Nye, P., Hillyard, C. (2013). Personal Financial Behavior: The Influence of Quantitative Literacy and Material Values. *Numeracy Advancing Education in Quantitative Literacy*, 6(1), *article* 3. DOI: http://dx.doi.org/10.5038/1936-4660.6.1.3

Obama, B. (2010). Presidential Proclamation of the Financial Literacy Month. www.gpo.gov/fdsys/pkg/CFR-2011-title3-vol1/pdf/CFR-2011-title3-vol1-proc8493.pdf (last access October 2017)

OECD (2013). Financial Literacy Framework. *PISA 2012 Assessment and Analytical Framework: Mathematics, Reading, Science, Problem Solving and Financial Literacy. OECD Publishing.* www.oecd.org/pisa/pisaproducts/PISA%202012%20framework%20e-book_final.pdf

Pahnke, L., Honekamp, I. (2010). Different Effects of Financial Literacy and Financial Education in Germany. *MPRA, Paper No. 22900.* http://mpra.ub.uni-muenchen.de/22900/

Prochaska, J.O., Di Clemente, C., Norcross, J.C. (1992). In Search of How People Change Applications to Addictive Behaviors. *The American Psychologist*, 47(9), 1102–1114.

Robb, C.A., Woodyard, A. (2011). Financial Knowledge and Best Practice Behavior. *Journal of Financial Counseling and Planning*, 22(1), 60–70.

Robb, C.A. (2011). Financial Knowledge and Credit Card Behavior of College Students. *Journal of Family and Economic Issues*, 32(4), 690–698.

Rutledge, S.L. (2010). Consumer Protection and Financial Literacy Lesson from Nine Country Studies. *World Bank, Policy Research Working Paper, No. 5326.*

Schmeiser, M., Seligman, J. (2013). Using the Right Yardstick: Assessing Financial Literacy Measures by Way of Financial Well-Being. *Journal of Consumer Affairs*, 47(2), 191–374.

Sekita, S. (2011). Financial Literacy and Retirement Planning in Japan. *Journal of Pension Economics and Finance*, 10(4), 637–656.

Song, C. (2012). Financial Illiteracy and Pension Contributions: A Field Experiment on Compound Interest in China. http://dx.doi.org/10.2139/ssrn.2580856

Standard and Poor's (2017) Standard and Poor's Service Rating. www.standardandpoors.com

United Nations (2013). World Population Prospects: The 2012 Revision, DVD Edition. *United Nations, Department of Economic and Social Affairs, Population Division.* https://esa.un.org/unpd/wpp/publications/Files/WPP2012_Volume-II-Demographic-Profiles.pdf

Utkus, S.P., Young, J.A. (2011). Financial Literacy and 401(k) Loans. *Published in Financial Literacy Implications for Retirement Security and the Financial Marketplace.* New York, NY: Oxford University Press, 59–75.

van Rooij, M., Lusardi, A., Alessie, R. (2011). Financial Literacy and Retirement Planning in the Netherlands. *Journal of Economic Psychology*, 32, 593–608.

Willis, L.E. (2008). Against Financial Literacy Education. *Iowa Law Review*, 94, 197–285.

World Health Organization (1995). World Statistic Health Global indicator. www.who.int/healthinfo/indicators/1995/en/

World Health Organization (2000). World Statistic Health Global indicator. www.who.int/healthinfo/indicators/2000/en/

World Health Organization (2005). World Statistic Health Global indicator. www.who.int/healthinfo/indicators/2005/en/

World Health Organization (2010). World Statistic Health Global indicator. www.who.int/healthinfo/indicators/2010/en/

World Health Organization (2012). World Statistic Health Global indicator. www.who.int/healthinfo/indicators/2012/en/

Xiao, J., Chen, C., Chen, F. (2013). Consumer Financial Capability and Financial Satisfaction. *Social Indicators Research*, 118(1), 415–432.

Yoong, J. (2011). Financial Illiteracy and Stock Market Participation: Evidence from the RAND American Life Panel. *Published in Financial Literacy Implications for Retirement Security and the Financial Marketplace*. New York, NY: Oxford University Press, 76–10.

Part II

Financial literacy in Europe

3 Financial literacy in Europe

An overview

3.1 Introduction

The relevance of financial literacy in making financial decisions and the chance to use financial literacy as a key variable in consumer protection by regulators and policy makers have been already stressed in previous chapters. So, it is time to address financial literacy from an empirical perspective by measuring how much people know about finance, paying attention to the case of European countries. In recent years interest about the measurement of financial literacy has grown, as well as awareness about the need to compare results from different countries. In this chapter are reported results from different studies that tried to measure financial literacy with various approaches referring to different targets. In order to provide a big picture about financial literacy in Europe, results of two studies promoted by the OECD will be taken into account. The first study is the Programme for International Student Assessment (PISA) project; the second is the OECD-INFE International Survey of Adult Financial Literacy Competencies. These studies analyze respectively the financial literacy of young students and the financial literacy of adults. Both of them involve several countries. Comparing different countries, using the same items, allows us to compare different national contexts, stress the similarities, and highlight the basic differences between national populations.

The **PISA project** was done in 2015 and focused on 15 year-old students in 18 countries. Eight European countries were part of the study,[1] which included also non-European countries like the US, Russia, China,[2] Canada, Chile, and Brazil. The whole sample size is about 48,000 observations.

The measurement of financial literacy of adults is one of the aims of the **OECD-INFE** International Survey of Adult Financial Literacy Competencies. This study was released in 2016 on data collected in 2015 and follows the pilot study launched in 2012. It represents the most comprehensive international survey on financial literacy, with 32 participating countries. The target of recipients are individuals between 18 and 79 years old, and the total number of available observations is 51,650.

The need to replicate the same study in countries that could differ for several reasons – including differences in the structure of the financial system, the regulatory framework, etc. – is probably the main reason behind the decision to analyze – in both the PISA and the OECD-INFE cases – general financial principles and very basic scenarios, instead of specific products and services. This strategy is coherent with the need to establish a baseline with the aim to figure out the current degree of financial literacy, and identify the most critical areas of knowledge to be addressed. In the following paragraphs the results of these two surveys are summarized.

3.2 Financial literacy of young students: the PISA project

The Programme for International Student Assessment (PISA) is a triennial international survey, promoted by the OECD, which aims to evaluate education systems worldwide by testing the skills and knowledge of 15 year-old students. The first wave of the survey collected data in 2000, and from 2012 a module that assesses financial literacy was included. Other modules of the survey assess the students' knowledge in science, mathematics, reading, and collaborative problem solving. In 2015 more than half a million students, representing 28 million 15 year-old students from 72 countries and economies, took the internationally agreed two-hour test. In 14 of these 72 countries – Belgium, Brazil, Canada, Chile, China, Croatia, Italy, Lithuania, the Netherlands, Poland, Russia, the Slovak Republic, Spain, and the US – the financial literacy assessment module was included, collecting data of around 48,000 students.

The definition of financial literacy adopted by the OECD for this target of recipients is the following:

> *Financial literacy is knowledge and understanding of financial concepts and risks, and the skills, motivation and confidence to apply such knowledge and understanding in order to make effective decisions across a range of financial contexts, to improve the financial well-being of individuals and society, and to enable participation in economic life.*

(OECD 2017a p. 50)

The contents taken into account in the measurement of financial literacy are (1) money and transactions, (2) planning and managing finances, (3) risk and reward, and (4) the financial landscape (OECD 2017a).

The content category "**money and transactions**" is considered by the OECD as the first core content category of financial literacy. It includes awareness of the different forms and purposes of money, and handling simple monetary transactions (e.g. everyday payments, spending, value for money, bank cards, cheques, bank accounts, and currencies).

The content category "**planning and managing finances**" regards planning and managing income and wealth over both the short term and long term. Special attention has been paid to the knowledge and ability needed to monitor income and expenses, and to make use of income and other available resources to enhance financial well-being.

The third category, "**risk and reward**", incorporates the ability to identify ways of managing, balancing, and covering risks (including through insurance and saving products) and an understanding of the potential for financial gains or losses across a range of financial contexts and products, such as a credit agreement with a variable interest rate, and investment products.

The last category, "**financial landscape**", relates to the features of the financial world and covers the rights and responsibilities of consumers in the financial marketplace. It includes an analysis of the main implications of financial contracts and incorporates an understanding of the consequences of change in economic conditions and public policies, such as changes in interest rates, inflation, taxation, or welfare benefits.

These contents have been addressed in different processes that included the ability to (1) identify financial information, (2) analyze information in a financial context, (3) evaluate financial issues, and (4) apply financial knowledge and understanding to make a financial decision.

Data have been collected by using a one-hour, computer-based test composed of 43 question items. The common types of items are simple multiple choices (with four options, one of which is right) and complex multiple choices, where students respond to a series of yes/no questions. However, not all the questions were selected-response questions (e.g. yes/no or multiple choice questions); the test also included constructed-response items that required students to generate their own answers by reporting sentences or a worked calculation.

The full questionnaire of the financial literacy module is not available, but the OECD publications (OECD 2017a) show examples of the test (see Figures 3.1 and 3.2).

From the examples of tests provided by the OECD it is clear that the will to test financial literacy goes beyond basic knowledge of a topic (e.g. "what is a bank account?") trying to propose real scenarios that involve the application of such knowledge (e.g. knowledge that a bank account requires a user ID and a password to access and awareness that these private keys must never be shared by mail or telephone).

The test design for PISA was based on a variant of matrix sampling, which means that each student was administrated a subset of items from a more generous pool of items. The consequence of having different groups of students that answered different (overlapping) sets of items is that the use of any statistic based on the number of correct answers becomes inappropriate. In this case the sum of correct answers as a measure of financial literacy is biassed, for instance, by the chance that the set of items administered to different students can differ in term of difficulty, making any comparison between students based on the number of correct answers unfair.

Item response theory[3] (IRT) was used by the OECD in order to overcome the matrix sampling issues that exclude the chance to use the sum of correct answers as a standard measure of financial literacy. According to the IRT both the difficulty of the item and the ability of the respondents should be taken into account simultaneously to assess performance in a test. A statistical model

---

BANK ERROR

David banks with ZedBank. He receives this e-mail message.

Dear ZedBank member,

There has been an error on the ZedBank server and your Internet login details have been lost.

As a result, you have no access to Internet banking.

Most importantly your account is no longer secure.

Please click on the link below and follow the instructions to restore access. You will be asked to provide your Internet banking details.

https://ZedBank.com/

ZedBank

BANK ERROR – *QUESTION 1*

Which of these statements would be good advice for David?

Circle "Yes" or "No" for each statement.

Statement	Is this statement good advice for David?
Reply to the e-mail message and provide his Internet banking details.	Yes / No
Contact his bank to inquire about the e-mail message.	Yes / No
If the link is the same as his bank's website address, click on the link and follow the instructions.	Yes / No

Question type: *Complex multiple choice*
Description: *Respond appropriately to a financial scam e-mail message*
Content: *Financial landscape*
Process: *Evaluate financial issues*
Context: *Societal*
Difficulty: *797 (Level 5)*

Scoring

Full credit

Three correct responses: No, Yes, No in that order.

No credit

Fewer than three correct responses.

Missing.

Comment

This question asks students to evaluate a potential financial fraud in the context of Internet banking, which is part of the broader financial landscape in which students are likely to participate, either now or in the near future. The question investigates whether they know how to take appropriate precautions. Students are asked to respond appropriately to a financial scam e-mail message. They must evaluate the presented options and recognise which piece of advice can be considered as good advice. No numerical operations are required. The question is located at Level 5.

Figure 3.1 Examples of the financial literacy test from the OECD – PISA 2015: Bank Error

Source: OECD (2017b). "PISA 2015 Results (Volume IV): Students' Financial Literacy". PISA OECD Publishing, Paris (p. 57)

that combines the Rasch model and the Partial Credit Model with the Two Parameter-Logistic Model (2PLM) and the Generalized Partial Credit Model (GPCM) was developed by the OECD, dealing with the sampling issues.[4] The final score on financial literacy is a scale with a range from 0 (minimum) to 1,000 (maximum).

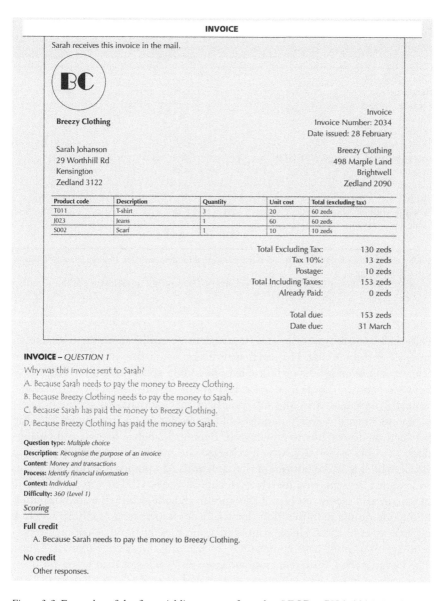

Figure 3.2 Examples of the financial literacy test from the OECD – PISA 2015: Invoice

Source: OECD (2017b). "PISA 2015 Results (Volume IV): Students' Financial Literacy". PISA OECD Publishing, Paris (p. 58)

Table 3.1 shows the average financial literacy scale for all the participating countries in the 2015 PISA.

The lack of details about the single items used in the questionnaire and the statistical sophistication required to deal with the use of different items

Table 3.1 Averages for 2015 PISA financial literacy scale, aged 15 years, by all students

Jurisdiction	All students	
	Average	Standard error
China (B-S-J-G)°	566	(6.0)
Belgium	541	(3.0)
Canada	533	(4.6)
Russia	512	(3.3)
Netherlands	509	(3.3)
United States	487	(3.8)
International average (OECD)	**487**	**(1.2)**
Poland	485	(3.0)
Italy	483	(2.8)
Spain	469	(3.2)
Slovak Republic	445	(4.5)
Chile	432	(3.7)
Brazil	393	(3.8)

° "China (B-S-J-G)" refers to the four PISA participating China provinces: Beijing, Shanghai, Jiangsu, and Guangdong

Source: OECD (2017b). PISA 2015 Results (Volume IV): Students' Financial Literacy, p. 71

with different groups of students restrict considerations about the results to an analysis of the ranking. However, even being aware that differences between countries exist and some technical reasons could explain part of the differences between countries' average scores, it is clear how the average score of the whole sample – represented by the 487 points of the international average score – is representative for some countries but is absolutely not for others. The gap between the four Chinese provinces of Beijing, Shanghai, Jiangsu, and Guangdong ("China B-S-J-G"), which achieved the top average score of 566, and Brazil, which is at the bottom of the rank with 393 points, is about 170 points and cannot be explained merely by technical issues. China's top performance in a financial literacy test is probably (positively) affected by the administration of the questionnaire in the most financially developed areas of China. The lack of rural areas in the Chinese sample (that are present in other national representative data) must have contributed in changing the average score in China. The fact that the US students' average score (487) is lower than scores from less financially sophisticated countries such as Belgium (541) and Russia (512) is an interesting result that suggests how financial knowledge and financial attitude in a life stage where individuals have limited financial experience are not affected by the financial framework of a country.

Looking at the European countries, we find a quite heterogeneous distribution, with countries that scored significantly above the average (e.g. Belgium 541, and the Netherlands 509), others that scored below the average (e.g. Spain 469, and the Slovak Republic 445), and others placed around the mean (e.g. Poland 485, and Italy 483).

The different standard errors of the national average scores remind us that the mean cannot represent itself the whole national distribution of the data. Analysis of the different financial literacy proficiency levels provided by the PISA results (Table 3.2) definitely improves understanding of financial literacy in the different countries.

Analysis of the top performers that achieved the proficiency level 5 shows a different ranking. If the Chinese provinces are still on top of the rank (695), Brazil is not anymore at the bottom (666), and scored better than Chile (659), Italy (662), Spain (662), Russia (665), and Poland (665). At the same time, looking

Table 3.2 Averages for 2015 PISA financial literacy scale, aged 15 years, by PISA financial literacy proficiency levels

Jurisdiction	Below level 1 (score < 326)	At level 1 (326 < score <400)	At level 2 (400 < score < 475)	At level 3 (475 > score > 550)	At level 4 (550 < score < 625)	At level 5 (score > 625)
	Average (s.e.)	Average (s.e.)	Average (s.e.)	Average (s.e.)	Average (s.e.)	Average (s.e.)
International average (OECD)	274 (1.5)	367 (0.4)	440 (0.3)	512 (0.3)	584 (0.3)	670 (0.8)
Belgium	281 (4.2)	367 (1.6)	441 (1.1)	515 (1.0)	587 (0.9)	676 (2.2)
Canada	273 (5.3)	368 (1.4)	441 (1.1)	514 (0.7)	586 (0.8)	685 (2.7)
Chile	269 (2.7)	366 (0.9)	437 (0.9)	10 (1.2)	581 (1.3)	659 (3.0)
Italy	282 (3.7)	368 (1.2)	440 (0.7)	512 (0.7)	582 (1.2)	662 (1.8)
Netherlands	271 (8.5)	367 (1.4)	440 (1.1)	514 (1.1)	586 (0.8)	678 (2.1)
Poland	277 (3.8)	368 (1.2)	440 (0.7)	512 (0.9)	583 (0.8)	665 (2.7)
Slovak Republic	257 (3.7)	365 (0.8)	438 (0.7)	511 (0.8)	583 (0.9)	670 (2.8)
Spain	273 (3.1)	367 (1.3)	440 (0.9)	511 (0.7)	582 (0.8)	662 (2.4)
United States	278 (2.8)	367 (1.1)	439 (1.0)	512 (0.8)	584 (0.9)	669 (2.8)
Brazil	257 (2.2)	363 (0.6)	436 (0.5)	509 (0.7)	582 (1.1)	666 (2.9)
China (B-S-J-G)	275 (6.2)	369 (1.4)	441 (1.1)	514 (1.0)	588 (0.9)	695 (4.0)
Russia	289 (3.7)	370 (1.5)	442 (0.9)	513 (0.8)	583 (0.9)	665 (2.0)

° "China (B-S-J-G)" refers to the four PISA participating China provinces: Beijing, Shanghai, Jiangsu, and Guangdong

Source: Organization for Economic Cooperation and Development (OECD), Programme for International Student Assessment (PISA), 2015 Financial Literacy Assessment

at the worst performers (below level 1), Brazil (257) and the Slovak Republic (257) represent the worst performers, while Russia is the country with the highest average score (289). Differences in single countries between students with the highest scores and students with the lowest scores can show how big is the gap between different groups of students. If on average (international average OECD) the difference between the average score in level 5 (670) and the average score in the group below level 1 (274) is around 400 points, in some countries the gap between the most and the least financially literate students is much smaller (380 in Italy, 376 in Russia), while in others there is evidence of bigger differences (420 in China, 413 in the Slovak Republic).

The differences between countries in average scores almost disappear in the middle levels (level 2 and level 3).

Interesting results are the ones from average scores by gender (Table 3.3). If a typical result of financial literacy studies is the presence of a gender gap – with males scoring better than females – the results of the PISA for 2015 seem to present a different scenario.

A comparison between males and females in the whole panel (the international average OECD) confirms the presence of an average 5 point gap.

Table 3.3 Averages for 2015 PISA financial literacy scale, aged 15 years, by all students, and gender

Jurisdiction	All students		Male		Female		Gender gap (male–female)			
	Average	Standard error	Average	Standard error	Average	Standard error	Average	Standard error	P-value	
China (B-S-J-G)	566	(6.0)	568	(6.1)	563	(6.7)	5	(4.2)	0.233	
Belgium	541	(3.0)	541	(3.8)	541	(4.3)	0	(5.6)	0.987	
Canada	533	(4.6)	531	(4.8)	536	(5.2)	−5	(3.9)	0.187	
Russia	512	(3.3)	510	(4.2)	514	(3.3)	−3	(3.6)	0.352	
Netherlands	509	(3.3)	507	(3.9)	512	(3.6)	−5	(3.6)	0.152	
United States	487	(3.8)	488	(4.4)	487	(4.1)	2	(3.8)	0.609	
International average (OECD)	**487**	**(1.2)**	**485**	**(1.4)**	**490**	**(1.4)**	**−5**	**(1.5)**	**0.002**	**
Poland	485	(3.0)	478	(3.6)	493	(3.2)	−15	(3.5)	0.000	***
Italy	483	(2.8)	489	(3.9)	478	(4.0)	11	(5.6)	0.044	**
Spain	469	(3.2)	464	(3.7)	474	(4.1)	−10	(4.4)	0.026	**
Slovak Republic	445	(4.5)	433	(4.9)	458	(5.6)	−25	(5.3)	0.000	***
Chile	432	(3.7)	430	(4.2)	434	(4.5)	4	(4.4)	0.327	
Brazil	393	(3.8)	389	(4.5)	397	(4.3)	−8	(4.4)	0.057	*

° *"China (B-S-J-G)" refers to the four PISA participating China provinces: Beijing, Shanghai, Jiangsu, and Guangdong.*

Note: * = *p-value* < 0.10; ** = *p-value* < 0.05; *** = *p-value* < 0.01 (differences in variables between male and female)

Source: Organization for Economic Cooperation and Development (OECD), Programme for International Student Assessment (PISA), 2015 Financial Literacy Assessment

If this result can be somehow interpreted as a marginal gap – and so deny the evidence of studies from other targets like adults, workers, etc. – the evidence from single countries is even more controversial. In almost half of the cases the differences between gender-based-average scores are not statistically significant (China, Belgium, Canada, Russia, the Netherlands, the US, and Chile). This result is coherent with the one from the whole sample, even if in the other half of the sample we have a gap between males and females, but the evidence is about an average score that is bigger for females than males. Moreover, in this case the differences between scores are statistically significant and support the hypothesis that in some countries female students have on average more financial literacy than their male colleagues. The gap is sometimes small, like in Brazil (8 points), but in some others is not (e.g. 10 points in Spain, and 15 points in Poland), with the female students in the Slovak Republic scoring on average 25 points more than males. The only exception is Italy, where the results for this young target (15-year-old students) confirm the typical results of adult samples, with male students scoring better than females for an average of 11 points.

The evidence that a gender gap does not exist between young students (and if it exists in some cases it is in favour of females) is coherent with the hypothesis that financial literacy is not itself caused by gender, but this is only a proxy of some other experience related differences. One of the possible interpretations of the gender gap in adults is that males score better than females because in the distribution of duties related with the organization of family management males are more frequently the ones who deal with banks and take care of financial issues, developing more knowledge and more confidence than females, and becoming more financially literate.

Another interesting result is that students who were born in the country perform on average better than students born abroad (Table 3.4). Data from the whole sample (international average OECD) show that students born outside the country where they took the test score on average 29 points lower than locally born students.

This result is confirmed by most of the countries in the sample. This country gap is close to the average in some cases (−28 in the US, −30 in Italy, −35 in Spain) and becomes wider in countries like the Netherlands (−51) and Belgium (−92), rising to more than 100 points in Brazil (−101) and China (−186. A small and not statistically significant difference in financial literacy between students born in the country and outside the country does exist in Canada, Russia, Poland, and the Slovak Republic. Like for the gender gap, the differences in financial literacy between students born in different countries cannot be related with the country of birth itself, but this variable is probably correlated with other explanatory factors like the financial literacy of the parents, their education, and their wealth that could inhibit the transmission of financial knowledge and the transmission of financial literacy at home.

Table 3.4 Averages for 2015 PISA financial literacy scale, aged 15 years, by all students, and students born in the country of the test (locals) and students born in another country (foreigners)

Jurisdiction	All students		Country of test (A)		Other country (B)		Country gap (B − A)		
	Average	Standard error	Average	Standard error	Average	Standard error	Average	Standard error	P-value
China (B-S-J-G)°	566	(6.0)	568	(6.0)	383	(33.6)	−186	(33.9)	0.000 ***
Belgium	541	(3.0)	550	(2.9)	458	(9.2)	−92	(9.4)	0.000 ***
Canada	533	(4.6)	536	(4.6)	541	(7.3)	5	(6.2)	0.417
Russia	512	(3.3)	514	(3.4)	514	(10.8)	0	(11.3)	0.987
Netherlands	509	(3.3)	513	(3.1)	462	(13.0)	51	(13.1)	0.000 ***
United States	487	(3.8)	492	(3.6)	465	(9.5)	−28	(8.7)	0.002 ***
International average (OECD)	**487**	**(1.2)**	**491**	**(1.2)**	**462**	**(4.9)**	**−29**	**(4.7)**	**0.000** ***
Poland	485	(3.0)	486	(2.9)	499	(21.7)	13	(21.6)	0.542
Italy	483	(2.8)	487	(2.8)	458	(7.0)	−30	(6.9)	0.000 ***
Spain	469	(3.2)	473	(3.1)	438	(8.0)	−35	(7.9)	0.000 ***
Slovak Republic	445	(4.5)	446	(4.4)	447	(25.7)	0	(24.8)	0.994
Chile	432	(3.7)	435	(3.7)	390	(16.0)	−45	(15.7)	0.005 ***
Brazil	393	(3.8)	396	(3.8)	295	(18.7)	−101	(19.0)	0.000 ***

° *"China (B-S-J-G)" refers to the four PISA participating China provinces: Beijing, Shanghai, Jiangsu, and Guangdong*

Note: * = p-value < 0.10; ** = p-value < 0.05; *** = p-value < 0.01 (differences in variables between male and female)

Source: Organization for Economic Cooperation and Development (OECD), Programme for International Student Assessment (PISA), 2015 Financial Literacy Assessment. OECD (2017b). PISA 2015 Results (Volume IV): Students' Financial Literacy, p. 71

3.3 Financial literacy of adults: the OECD–INFE study

According to the OECD definition, financial literacy is "*a combination of awareness, knowledge, skill, attitude and behaviour necessary to make sound financial decisions and ultimately achieve individual financial wellbeing*".[5] Coherently with this definition, the financial literacy score proposed by the OECD is made by using three separate scores related to financial knowledge, financial behavior, and financial attitude.

The **financial knowledge score** counts the number of correct responses across the seven questions reported in Table 3.5.

The fact that the underlying topics of the financial knowledge score are quite simple and are enough just to provide an overview of the person's basic knowledge is clearly stated in the OECD report containing the results of the survey.[6] In the same report the aim of these questions is also declared, which are used to test consumers' ability to autonomously manage their financial matters and react to news and events that may have implications for their financial well-being. Using the sum of correct answers to seven questions as a measure of financial knowledge, the score has a minimum of 0 and a maximum of 7.

Table 3.5 Financial knowledge questions

Topic	Question	Answer type
Inflation (1)	Imagine that five <brothers> are given a gift of <$>1,000 in total. If the <brothers> have to share the money equally ... [and] have to wait for one year to get their share of the $1,000 and inflation stays at <X> percent. In one year's time will they be able to buy ... a) More than they could buy today b) The same amount that they could buy today c) Less than they could buy today	Multiple choice
Inflation (2)	High inflation means that the cost of living is increasing rapidly	True/false
Interest (1)	You lend $25 to a friend one evening and he gives you $25 back the next day. How much interest has he paid on this loan?	Open answer
Interest (2)	Suppose you put $100 into a <no fee, tax free> savings account with a guaranteed interest rate of 2% per year. You don't make any further payments into this account and you don't withdraw any money. How much would be in the account at the end of the first year, once the interest payment is made?	Open answer
Interest (3)	[referring to previous question 'Interest(1)'] ... and how much would be in the account at the end of five years? Would it be ... a) More than $110 b) Exactly $110 c) Less than $110 d) Or is it impossible to tell from the information given	Multiple choice
Risk-return	An investment with a high return is likely to be high risk / or If someone offers you the chance to make a lot of money it is likely that there is also a chance that you will lose a lot of money	True/false
Diversification	It is usually possible to reduce the risk of investing in the stock market by buying a wide range of stocks and shares / or It is less likely that you will lose all of your money if you save it in more than one place.	True/false

Source: OECD (2016). OECD-INFE International Survey of Adult Financial Literacy Competencies, p. 20

The second score that contributes to the overall financial literacy score is the **financial behavior score**. This is based on a number of questions to explore the extent to which people are behaving in financially literate ways. Coherently with the financial knowledge score, the financial behavior score counts positive behaviors exhibited by respondents. It takes a minimum value of 0 and a maximum of 9. The items used for the financial behavior score are listed in Table 3.6.

Table 3.6 Financial behavior items

Topic	Question	Answer type
Budgeting	Are you responsible for making day-to-day decisions in your household?	1 if "Yes"
Budgeting	Does your household have a budget?	1 if "Yes"
Active savings	Active savings (back over a 12 month time period)	1 if "Yes"
Making a considered purchase	"Before I buy something I carefully consider whether I can afford it"	1 if "Agree"
Paying bills on time	"I pay my bills on time"	1 if "Agree"
Keeping watch of financial affairs	"I keep a close personal watch on my financial affairs"	1 if "Agree"
Striving to achieve long-term goals	"I set long-term financial goals and strive to achieve them"	1 if "Agree"
Avoiding borrowing to make ends meet	Did you borrow (in the last 12 months) to make ends meet?	1 if "No"
Planning for long-term goals	Do you strive to achieve long-term goals?	1 if "Yes"

Source: OECD (2016). OECD-INFE International Survey of Adult Financial Literacy Competencies

The **financial attitude score** draws on three questions designed to capture attitudes toward the long term. Each of the statements focuses on preferences for the short term through 'living for today' and spending money. The questions ask people to use a 1-to-5 scale to indicate whether they agree (= 1) or disagree (= 5) with particular statements. The minimum value of the financial attitude score is 1, the maximum is 5, and it is made by calculating the average of the three responses. The questions of the financial attitude score are reported in Table 3.7.

The **financial literacy score** summarizes the scores on financial knowledge, behavior, and attitude by their sum. Due to the differences of the maximum values of these scores, this financial literacy score gives more relevance to people's behavior (max 9) than knowledge (max 7) and attitude (max 5), and the result is a financial literacy score with a minimum of 1 and a maximum of 21.

The OECD-INFE study on financial literacy collected data on 16 European countries.[7] The values of the scores for these countries are reported in Figure 3.3.

The average financial literacy score in the sample of European countries is 13.42, which represents 63.93% of the maximum score. Looking at the geographical distribution, it seems that the Eastern European countries (e.g. Poland, Hungary, Latvia) are the less financially literate ones. On the other side, France is the country with the highest financial literacy score, followed by the Scandinavian countries (Finland and Norway).

From the break down of the financial literacy score to its basic components it can be seen how countries with similar financial literacy average scores differ for the contribution that knowledge, behavior, and attitude give to this result. For instance, the gap between the top score (France) and the bottom country

Table 3.7 Financial attitude questions

Topic	Question	Answer type
Attitudes towards the long term	"I tend to live for today and let tomorrow take care of itself"	[1 | 2 | 3 | 4 | 5] 1 = Completely agree 5 = Completely disagree
Attitudes towards the long term	"I find it more satisfying to spend money than to save it for the long term"	[1 | 2 | 3 | 4 | 5] 1 = Completely agree 5 = Completely disagree
Attitudes towards the long term	"Money is there to be spent"	[1 | 2 | 3 | 4 | 5] 1 = Completely agree 5 = Completely disagree

Source: OECD (2016). OECD-INFE International Survey of Adult Financial Literacy Competencies

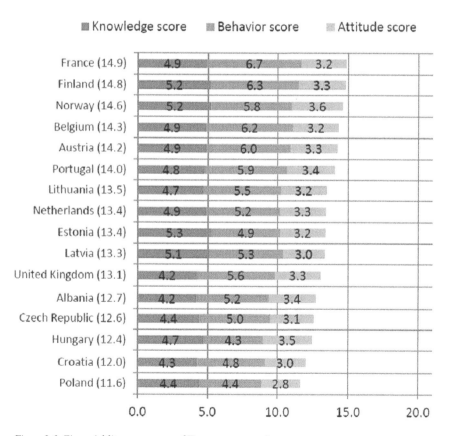

Figure 3.3 Financial literacy scores of European countries

Source: Author's analysis of OECD-INFE (2016) data

(Poland) is more than 3 points, but looking at the financial knowledge score the gap is just 0.5 (France 4.9 vs. Poland 4.4). The different composition of the financial literacy scores appears even with the comparison between France and Estonia, where the financial knowledge score of the first (4.9) is even lower than the second (5.3), but the big difference in the financial behavior score (France 6.7 vs. Estonia 4.9) is behind the overall scores' gap.

Paying attention to the financial knowledge score it is interesting how the UK and Albania scored on average at the same level, which is the lowest one in the sample (4.2 of 7). The fact that London represents one of the main financial hubs in Europe clashes with the low financial literacy of Britain's households. At the same time most of the countries in the sample fail to achieve the minimum target score on financial knowledge, fixed by the OECD as more than 4 of 7 correct answers. The percentage of people that achieved that level was 70% in Finland and Norway, 66% in Austria, 60% in Belgium and Portugal, 59% in France, and only 47% in the UK.

Analysis of the average response rates to the financial knowledge questions (see Table 3.8) provides additional elements to the discussion.

The third question on interest was clearly the most difficult question for people in Europe. Less than 1 of 2 (45%) of the whole sample provided the correct answer, despite the multiple choice structure of the question being technically less complicated than open answers – such as questions "interest (1)" and "interest (2)" – whose response rates were more than double compared with

Table 3.8 Financial knowledge questions: average of correct answers

	Inflation (1)	Inflation (2)	Interest (1)	Interest (2)	Interest (3)	Risk-return	Diversification
Albania	50%	75%	88%	48%	28%	77%	65%
Austria	66%	85%	86%	68%	44%	86%	62%
Belgium	73%	80%	91%	63%	50%	83%	56%
Croatia	54%	74%	80%	62%	33%	69%	66%
Czech Republic	68%	73%	83%	58%	34%	71%	69%
Estonia	83%	88%	89%	79%	43%	85%	65%
Finland	83%	58%	98%	79%	58%	89%	66%
France	59%	87%	94%	57%	54%	87%	75%
Hungary	67%	89%	91%	53%	33%	84%	65%
Latvia	75%	86%	89%	72%	48%	82%	64%
Lithuania	75%	67%	79%	68%	41%	75%	75%
The Netherlands	65%	74%	92%	76%	61%	73%	53%
Norway	76%	74%	91%	80%	65%	86%	59%
Poland	80%	69%	77%	61%	30%	77%	56%
Portugal	55%	87%	87%	61%	41%	82%	73%
UK	38%	80%	83%	57%	52%	74%	52%
Average	**67%**	**78%**	**87%**	**65%**	**45%**	**80%**	**64%**
St. dev.	*0.13*	*0.09*	*0.06*	*0.10*	*0.11*	*0.06*	*0.07*

Source: OECD (2016). OECD-INFE International Survey of Adult Financial Literacy Competencies, pp. 23–24

"interest (3)". This question is even the one with the biggest standard deviation, showing how the gap between countries is in this case quite clear. In fact, this question has been on average correctly answered by only 1 of 3 Czechs (34%), while 4 of 5 Norwegians did (65%). A more comfortable result comes from the risk-return question. On average 80% of the respondents in the whole European sample seem to be aware that an increase in the (expected) return of an investment product is related with an increase in the risk of the investment. This average is quite persistent within the sample, with the lowest value for Croatia around 70% (69%) and the top performance from Finland, where almost 9 of 10 (89%) are aware about the risk-return relationship in financial markets.

3.4 Conclusions

Results from the OECD studies on financial literacy are not positive. The scenario of the young generations provided by the PISA project is about European students who scored on average just a bit above the mid-scale value. The score system adopted by the PISA study has a range from 0 to 1,000, and the best European country performance is from Belgium, with a 541 average score. Other European countries such as the Netherlands (509), Poland (485), and Italy (483) did not score well. The lack of details about the structure of the questionnaire and single questions (topics, level of difficulty, wording, etc.) denies an analysis about the possible explanation of such results. However, comparing the European countries with the other countries of the sample it does not seem that European students performed differently from others. There are some countries in the top of the ranking, while others are below the average. An interesting result is the lack of a gender gap within the youth, keeping in mind that this is quite common when financial literacy studies target adults. In some cases there is even evidence that females scored significantly better than males (Poland, Spain, and Slovak Republic). The only exception is Italy, where there is a strong gender gap with males scoring on average 11 points better than females.

Looking at the big picture for adults (OECD-INFE study) it comes out that financial literacy is low even for this target group. The geographical differences in Europe suggest that Eastern Europe (Poland, Hungary, and Latvia) is less financially literate than Western Europe (France, Finland, and Norway). Another warning comes from the evidence that the minimum target score on financial knowledge – fixed by the OECD in at least four correct answers of the seven financial literacy questions – has not been achieved by large portions of the European sample. The percentage of who failed to reach that threshold was 30% in Finland and Norway, but was around 40% in France and more than 50% in the UK. So the average low financial literacy is not the only negative result, and the fact that part of the European population is below a minimum score is even more worrying.

Lack of access to the raw data used by the OECD in its reports does not give the chance to analyze in detail financial literacy in Europe. In order to do it the following chapters will use data provided by the Consumer Finance Research Center (CFRC) coming from a research project focused on the measurement of financial literacy. The availability of data on several European countries, the comparability of the data between countries, and the large number of items available to assess financial literacy are just some of the elements that make the CFRC data a unique database for researchers who want to go beyond general measures of financial literacy, investigating specific areas of knowledge on consumer finance.

Notes

1 Belgium, Croatia, Italy, Lithuania, the Netherlands, Poland, the Slovak Republic, and Spain.
2 In the case of China, data are related only to the four provinces of Beijing, Shanghai, Jiangsu, and Guangdong.
3 For details about the IRT methodologies see van der Linden and Hambleton (2016).
4 For more details about the statistical methodology details of the scale, see OECD (2017b) PISA 2015 Technical Report. Chapter 9 "Scaling PISA data". www.oecd.org/pisa/data/2015-technical-report/
5 OECD (2015). 2015 OECD-INFE Toolkit for Measuring Financial Literacy and Financial Inclusion.
6 OECD (2016). OECD-INFE International Survey of Adult Financial Literacy Competencies.
7 The European countries in the OECD-INFE study are: Albania, Austria, Belgium, Croatia, Czech Republic, Estonia, Finland, France, Hungary, Latvia, Lithuania, Netherlands, Norway, Poland, Portugal, and UK.

References

OECD (2015). Programme for International Student Assessment (PISA), 2015 Financial Literacy Assessment. www.oecd.org/education/pisa-2015-results-volume-iv-9789264270282-en.htm

OECD (2016). OECD-INFE International Survey of Adult Financial Literacy Competencies. www.oecd.org/daf/fin/financial-education/OECD-INFE-International-Survey-of-Adult-FInancial-Literacy-Competencies.pdf

OECD (2017a). *PISA 2015 Assessment and Analytical Framework.* Paris, France: PISA OECD Publishing. DOI: http://dx.doi.org/10.1787/9789264281820-en

OECD (2017b). *PISA 2015 Results (Volume IV): Students' Financial Literacy.* Paris, France: PISA OECD Publishing. DOI: http://dx.doi.org/10.1787/9789264270282-en

van der Linden, W.J., Hambleton, R.K. (1997). *Handbook of Modern Item Response Theory.* Springer. ISBN 978-1-4757-2691-6

4 Financial literacy in the UK

4.1 Introduction

This chapter analyzes financial literacy in the UK. The analysis is based on data provided by the Consumer Finance Research Center (CFRC). The CFRC is a research centre that gathers academics and NGOs from different countries with the aim to promote consumer finance studies. The analysis will start from several descriptive statistics with the aim to highlight differences between sub-groups of the population taking into account the gender and the age of the respondents. The analysis will be based on different measures of financial literacy that will take into account different areas of knowledge (e.g. stock investments, retirement and insurance, payments, etc.). In the second part a correlation between the financial literacy scores based on different topics will pave the way to a regression analysis that will try to shed light on the role of socio-demographic variables in explaining financial literacy in the UK.

4.2 Data

The analysis of financial literacy in the UK is based on a survey promoted by the CFRC in 2016 that targeted the adult population (18+ years old) in the UK. The survey was based on a questionnaire specifically developed to analyze financial literacy and financial behaviors of financial consumers in European countries. The structure and the contents of the questionnaire were released by the experts of the CFRC taking into account previous studies and customizing the questions to make them fit with the peculiarities of the specific country (e.g. financial products and services available, legal framework, features of the welfare system, etc.).

The questionnaire is organized in three sections.

The first section gathers information about the **socio-demographic characteristics** of the respondents. Questions concern the age, gender, education, marital status, income, and other personal information useful to identify the personal profile of the respondent.

The second section is made of **50 multiple choice questions on financial literacy**. Questions are organized in ten groups of five questions each.

Each group analyzes financial knowledge and financial behaviors on a specific area of contents. The ten areas are the following: interest rates, inflation, mortgages, investments, bonds, bank accounts, payments, savings and investments, loans and debts, and retirement and planning.

For every area, the five questions have been developed following the same principles. Questions are differentiated by the difficulty of the topic. The first two questions are the easiest ones. Questions three and four stress more advanced topics, while question five is the most difficult. Difficulty mainly refers to the sophistication of the financial content, while other technical sources of difficulty have been minimized. So, the length of the question (number of words) does not differ so much between questions, the need for mathematical skills has been reduced to basic operations, and the use of jargon has been limited. In that manner the chance that a respondent did not answer right, even being knowledgeable of the content, due to the additional difficulty related to the technicalities of the question should be avoided. The standardization of the test involved also the number of options in each question. With the only exception of the five questions frequently used in previous surveys (the "Lusardi-Mitchell" questions) – which are part of the questionnaire – all the questions have the same number of options, three. At the same time, two further options are available: "do not know" and "prefer not to say" options. As we stressed in the first part of this study, the will to avoid the risk of exchanging luck for knowledge recommends including a "do not know" option in order to give to the respondent the chance to admit his/her lack of knowledge. A question that does not have a "do not know" option represents an incentive to guess. At the same time, even if the respondent does not answer, because he/she does not know the answer, there is the risk of reading a blank answer as a lack of knowledge, when other possible explanations about this (blank) answer could be reasonable. A respondent could have simply unintentionally skipped the question, or the question could be related with a negative feeling[1] that pushes the respondent to react by not giving an answer. This latter case is managed by the option "prefer not to say". The second section of the questionnaire provides 50 items to be used to build financial literacy measures. A so generous number of items was intentionally included in the questionnaire in order to have the chance to develop and compare several measures of financial literacy. For instance, (1) a quite comprehensive measure made by the sum of correct answers to all 50 questions, (2) a measure that focuses on a specific area of contents and that uses only the five questions of a group, and (3) a measure that uses only the most difficult questions from each area are only a few of the available options to develop financial literacy scores.

The third section of the questionnaire investigates **financial behaviors and attitudes** in several financial areas. The use of banks accounts, preferences between different payments options (e.g. cash, credit cards, etc.) when different options are available, and preferences for bonds or stocks are a few of the financial behaviors discussed in the questionnaire.

The questions of the survey stress financial contents and do not rely on the functioning of specific products. In that manner the questionnaire should guarantee the chance to be immediately replicated in other studies and make data from different countries ready to be compared. However, starting from the standard questionnaire, when a question represented a potential source of mis-interpretation for a respondent of a particular country, it was rearranged so as not to affect the difficulty of the question and the focus on the financial topic.

Having a large number of items on financial literacy in the CFRC question-naire gives a chance to analyze in detail financial literacy in a single country and stress the differences between countries when specific areas of contents are taken into account. This database reach represents an opportunity to explore financial literacy more in depth than in international surveys – like the ones promoted by the OECD – that usually focus on analysis of basic financial principles. As has been argued in the first part of this study, if the chance that people are financially skilled in every area of knowledge (e.g. money manage-ment, debt, investment, retirement and planning, etc.) is not realistic, due to the different needs of knowledge of individuals, the CFRC data allow us to inves-tigate specific knowledge and examine some differences between the degree of financial literacy of individuals when different financial decisions have to be made (e.g. investment, borrowing, retirement, etc.).

4.3 The characteristics of financial literacy in the UK

Financial literacy in the UK has been measured by using data from the CFRC survey, collected in 2016 in the UK with around 600 observations of British households. These data show an average percentage of correct answers to the 50 questions on financial literacy equal to 43% (see Figure 4.1). It means that on average less than one question of two was correctly answered.

Looking at the scores for males and females we can find a gender gap, which is not unusual in financial literacy studies, that is equal to 7%, with males scoring on average at 47% and females at 40%. However, this score is a mean between the rate of correct answers to single areas of knowledge that are extremely different. The average percentage of correct answers about 'bonds' is only 19%, while the same rate in the case of 'payments' is 69%. The score on 'interest rates' is exactly 50%, and it means that for each correct answer another is wrong. The gender gap in this case is 11%, with males scoring at 56% and females at 45%. The results about 'inflation' are a bit more positive with an average score of 58%. In this case the gender gap is 13 percentage points, with males who answered right for 65% of questions (on average) and females who did it only for 52% of questions. The average score for 'mortgages' is quite representative of the overall means. Having correct answers in 45% of cases is a balance between 49% of right answers for males versus 41% for females. Knowledge about 'diversification' seems to be quite weak. Having correct answers in 31% of cases in the whole sample means that less than one question in three was known on average by the respondents. There is a

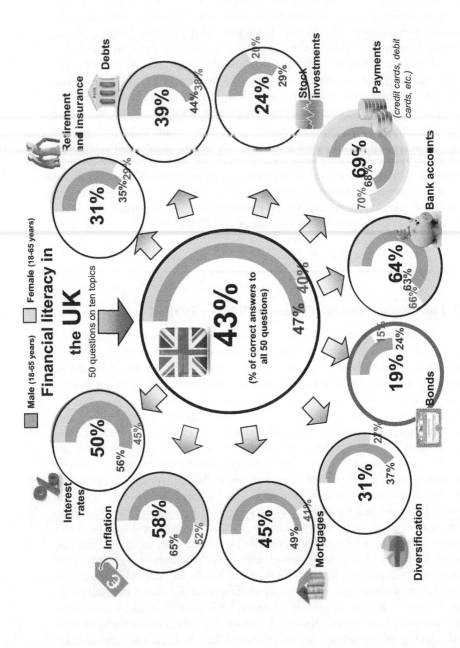

Figure 4.1 Financial literacy in the UK: break down and gender analysis

Source: Author's analysis of CFRC (2016) data

gender gap also in this case, and it is large, with males scoring at 37% and females at 27%. The area of knowledge where the respondents from the UK had the worst performance was the one about 'bonds'. The average score was only 19% (less than one correct answer to the five questions), with females' average score 15%, and men's score 24%. The evidence that financial topics related with saving and investments are the most difficult for the British is confirmed by the scores on 'stock investments', with an average score of 24%, and males giving a correct answer to less than one question of three (29% of correct answers) and females answering right only one of five (20%).

Results about knowledge on 'bank accounts' and 'payments' are quite interesting. In both cases the average response rate is absolutely different from the score about bonds and stocks. The average percentage of correct answers to questions on 'bank accounts' was 64%, and the score about 'payments' arrived almost to 70%. What is even more interesting is the evidence that females' knowledge on these financial topics seems to be higher than that of males. The female score on 'bank accounts' was 66% (men had 63%), and the financial literacy score about 'payments' for women was 70% (men scored 68%).

Answers to questions about 'debts' were right on average in 39% of the cases. The gender gap is about 6%, with males scoring at 44% and females at 38%. Results on 'retirement and insurance' are not promising, with less than one correct answer for every three questions (31% of right answers on average).

Financial literacy between age groups

Consider now the differences of financial literacy by age groups, making a distinction between the young, the adult, and the elderly respondents.

The overall score in different age groups seems to follow an upward trend with an increase of financial literacy with age (Figure 4.2). What is interesting is

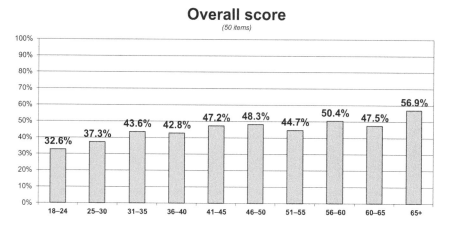

Figure 4.2 Overall score of financial literacy in the UK: break down by age

Source: Author's analysis of CFRC (2016) data

that the 65+-years-old group is the group with the overall highest average score (56.9%). This result is different from that of previous studies (most of them based on only a few items) where the "reverse U-shape" of the knowledge distribution by age – with the central age group being the most knowledgeable – sees the elderly less knowledgeable than younger groups. On the other hand, the first age group (18–24 years old) is the one with the lowest score (32.6%) with (on average) a correct answer every three questions.

To better understand the differences between age groups it is useful to break down the overall score in single topic-based scores. The 'interest rates' score, based on five questions on interest rates, shows an average score of 50%, which is above the overall average score of 43%. The 65+ age group is still the most knowledgeable group with 69.3% of correct answers, which means an average number of correct answers of 3.5 of five questions. Looking at Figure 4.3 it is evident that there is a gap of knowledge between those younger than 40 and those older than 40, with a gap that ranges from 5 to 33 points (depending on a one-to-one comparison between age groups). The big picture confirms the upward trend of financial literacy with age.

The upward trend in financial literacy of age groups is even more clear when the average scores about 'inflation' are taken into account (Figure 4.4). Those older than 65 are, one more time, the most knowledgeable, with four correct answers of five questions on average (79%). The gap with the lowest age group (18–24 years old), which is the least knowledgeable group, is evident, and shows a number of correct answers by those older than 65 (79%) that is double compared with those younger than 24 (40.7%). The scores for the other age groups increase systematically, and confirm a large gap between those younger than 35 and the others.

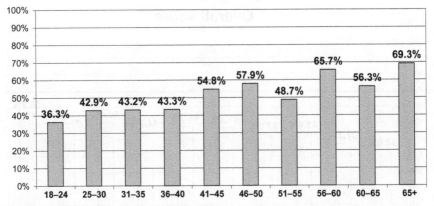

Figure 4.3 Financial literacy in the UK: knowledge on interest rates

Source: Author's analysis of CFRC (2016) data

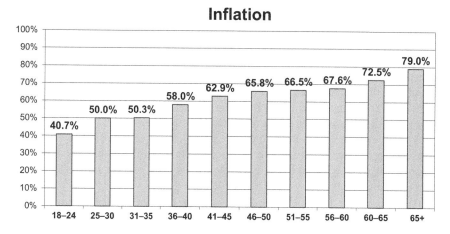

Figure 4.4 Financial literacy in the UK: knowledge on inflation

Source: Author's analysis of CFRC (2016) data

Figure 4.5 Financial literacy in the UK: knowledge on mortgages

Source: Author's analysis of CFRC (2016) data

In the case of 'mortgages' (Figure 4.5) the average score – equal to 45% – is in line with the overall average (43%) and shows less differences between age groups than the previous cases. Those older than 65 are the most knowledgeable also in this case, but the differences between other age groups, especially with those older than 40, are just a few percentage points. The response rate of the top performers (those older than 65 with 55.2%) is much lower than the best scores on 'interest rates' (69.3%) and 'inflation' (79%). This is evidence that financial literacy includes several topics that can be known with different degrees by the same individuals.

The average score on 'diversification' – equal to 31% of correct answers – shows how investment decisions are the most critical for British households (Figure 4.6). With respect to the overall score of 43% there is a 12 percentage point gap that seems to affect all the respondents in similar ways. In fact, there is still the tendency of adults to be more knowledgeable than youths, but this gap is based on average group scores that are quite below the overall averages. The top performers are those older than 65 with a score of 47.6% (around one correct answer for every two questions). The bottom performers are those younger than 24, with 20.6% of correct answers (one correct answer for every five questions).

Concern about financial knowledge on investments by British households that comes out from the 'diversification' scores is even more serious with financial literacy as measured by 'bonds' (Figure 4.7). This is the most critical area of knowledge of the sample. On average the respondents provided only 19% of correct answers (one of five), with a minimum score of 10.2% (51–55 years old group) and a maximum of 24.5%. The top performers are again those older than 65, but in this case those younger than 40 score on average better than those older than 40. However, this opposite result, as compared to the scores from the aforementioned areas of knowledge, is not due to a better performance of the younger groups, but is connected with the very poor score of the older groups, especially the 45–50s (15.0%) and the 51–55s (10.2%).

Similar results come from the financial literacy scores based on 'stock investments' (Figure 4.8). The average score of 24% is lifted up by an outstanding 58%

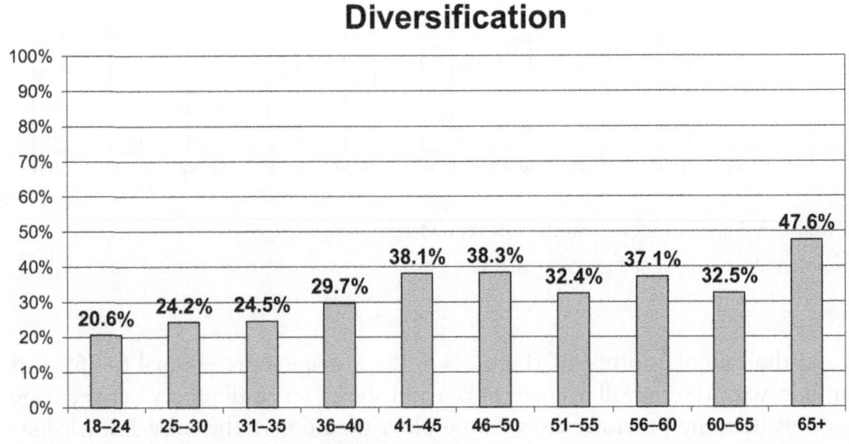

Diversification

Figure 4.6 Financial literacy in the UK: knowledge on diversification

Source: Author's analysis of CFRC (2016) data

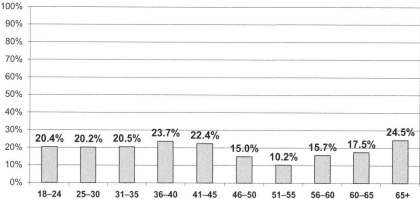

Figure 4.7 Financial literacy in the UK: knowledge on bonds

Source: Author's analysis of CFRC (2016) data

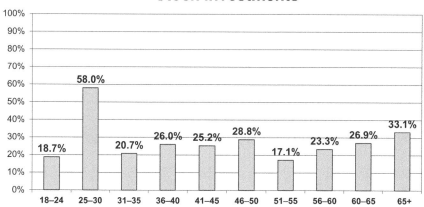

Figure 4.8 Financial literacy in the UK: knowledge on stock investments

Source: Author's analysis of CFRC (2016) data

of the 25–30 years-old group, which otherwise would be comparable with the results from the 'bonds' score.

The assessment of financial literacy in the UK completely changes when it is knowledge about 'bank accounts' to be considered (Figure 4.9). Correct answers in 64% of cases and a minimum score of 53.1% (25–30 and 31–35 years-old groups) are evidence that the British respondents of the survey are much

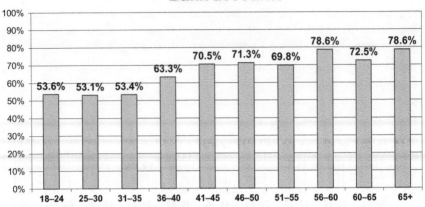

Figure 4.9 Financial literacy in the UK: knowledge on bank accounts

Source: Author's analysis of CFRC (2016) data

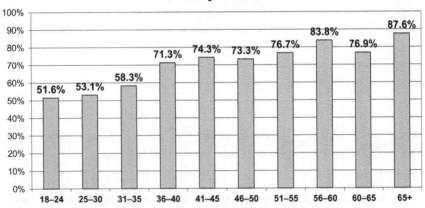

Figure 4.10 Financial literacy in the UK: knowledge on payments

Source: Author's analysis of CFRC (2016) data

more knowledgeable on banking products than on investment products. Those younger than 35 still fail on average half of the questions, but the big picture is quite a bit more positive in this area of knowledge compared with the investment related ones.

The good performance shown by financial literacy scores on 'payments' (see Figure 4.10), with an average score of 69%, supports the hypothesis that financial products with a high-frequency use, such as bank accounts and payments tools (e.g. credit cards, debit cards, etc.), tend to facilitate the development of financial literacy, with respect to financial decisions that are more rare. A possible explanation behind this hypothesis is that learning by doing is possible for high-frequency use products, while it is not with one shot decisions (e.g. investments).

Financial literacy scores based on knowledge about 'loans and debts' show some similarities with other topic-based scores (Figure 4.11). Those older than 65 are the most knowledgeable (49.3%), even if the differences with other adult groups are small (46–50 years-old group 47.9%; 56–60 years-old group 46.7%). On the other hand, the gap with the young is big, with more than 20 percentage points of difference with the 18–24 years-old group (average score 28.8%) and almost 30 percentage points with the 25–30 years-old group (33.9%). The differences between adults are less evident, even if they exist. Looking at the big picture about 'loans and debts', not even a single age group scored on average more than 50%, which means an ability to answer one correct answer for every two questions.

The evidence from financial literacy scores on 'retirement and insurance' is that British households find it difficult to approach long-term financial decisions. The average score of 31% is pretty close with the average scores on 'diversification' (31%) and 'stock investment' (24%). A comparison between scores on 'retirement and insurance' (Figure 4.12) stresses how the first age group (18–24) and the last one (65+) seem to differ from the others, which in most of cases shows financial literacy scores between a 30% and 35% range of values, which is far from being a good score.

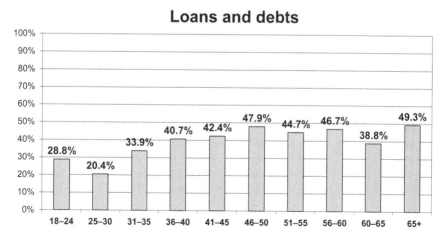

Figure 4.11 Financial literacy in the UK: knowledge on loans and debts

Source: Author's analysis of CFRC (2016) data

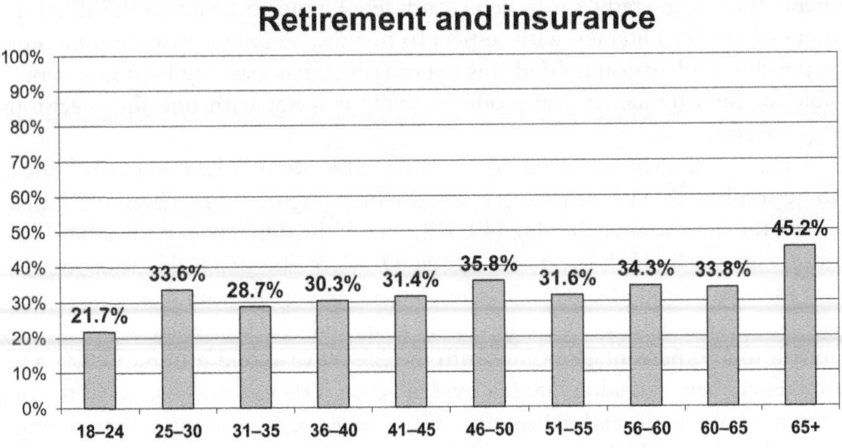

Retirement and insurance

Figure 4.12 Financial literacy in the UK: knowledge on retirement and insurance

Source: Author's analysis of CFRC (2016) data

The analysis of financial literacy scores based on questions on single topics (e.g. inflation, interest rates, bonds, etc.) highlighted how the same groups of individuals (e.g. males vs. females, or young vs. adults) can score quite differently when the tests are related to different issues. However, to better understand the relationship between financial knowledge on different topics the use of correlation is required. The results of a correlation analysis that takes into account both the overall financial literacy score (based on the full set of 50 items) and the specific scores (based on different subsets of five questions each) are reported in Table 4.1.

The first column shows the correlation of the overall score with the single topic-based scores. The fact that the overall score includes all the questions of each of the topic-based scores naturally increases the values of correlation. So, to understand if knowledge in some areas of finance is related with knowledge in other areas or, on the contrary, if being knowledgeable about some financial topic is not a good predictor of being knowledgeable also in others one must perform an analysis of correlation between single topic-based scores. Results show that correlations between scores on single topics are not high on average. Only in one of 45 the correlation is more than 0.60 ('payments' vs. 'bank accounts'), and in 15 cases of 45 (one of three) the correlation is less than 0.40. Inflation seems to be the most correlated knowledge. The fact that inflation is a financial phenomenon that affects several financial outcomes can be a reasonable explanation of this result. Financial literacy about 'bonds' is the least correlated one, with some values of the correlation index below 0.10. These results seem to suggest the need to address financial literacy in a broader sense than using single summary measures, and support the hypothesis of choosing

Table 4.1 Correlation between financial literacy scores (overall score, and the ten scores on single areas of knowledge)

	FL_OVERALL	FL_Interest rates	FL_Inflation	FL_Mortgages	FL_Diversification	FL_Bonds	FL_Bank accounts	FL_Payments	FL_Stocks and investments	FL_Loans and debts	FL_Retirement and insurance
FL_OVERALL	1										
FL_Interest rates	0.66	1									
FL_Inflation	0.76	0.50	1								
FL_Mortgages	0.72	0.42	0.49	1							
FL_Diversification	0.71	0.37	0.45	0.48	1						
FL_Bonds	0.40	0.12	0.13	0.26	0.35	1					
FL_Bank accounts	0.69	0.40	0.50	0.40	0.34	0.06	1				
FL_Payments	0.71	0.43	0.50	0.42	0.36	0.06	0.69	1			
FL_Stock investments	0.66	0.34	0.41	0.43	0.55	0.39	0.28	0.30	1		
FL_Loans and debts	0.72	0.42	0.51	0.49	0.44	0.22	0.47	0.48	0.42	1	
FL_Retirement and insurance	0.71	0.41	0.47	0.45	0.52	0.29	0.41	0.43	0.51	0.46	1

Source: Author's analysis of CFRC (2016) data

a financial literacy measure according to the financial behavior or the financial output that is being studied.

4.4 The determinants of financial literacy in the UK

The chance that financial literacy of individuals depends on which topic is being assessed and the assumption that people develop financial literacy according to their financial needs suggest it is useful to investigate if there are some sub-groups of the population that are more interested than others in some financial topics. To test this hypothesis a set of regression models have been applied to the British database using all 11 financial literacy scores (the overall score and each of the ten scores based on different topics) as dependent variables, using as independent variables a set of variables representing the main socio-demographic characteristics of the respondents, like age, gender, education, and income. If financial literacy cannot be completely explained by these variables, they are enough to identify the presence of sub-groups of the population that tend to develop their financial literacy differently or struggle to become financially literate at all.

The descriptive statistics of the socio-demographic variables are listed in Table 4.2.

Table 4.2 Descriptive statistics of the British sample

	#	%
Age		
18–24	107	17.7%
25–30	90	14.9%
31–35	71	11.7%
36–40	60	9.9%
41–45	42	6.9%
46–50	48	7.9%
51–55	55	9.1%
56–60	42	6.9%
60–65	32	5.3%
n.a.	50	9.6%
Gender		
Male	280	46.1%
Female	316	52.1%
n.a.	11	1.8%
Education		
Primary	2	0.3%
Some secondary	18	3.0%
GCSE	118	19.4%
A-level or equivalent	143	23.6%
Third level academic (e.g. university degree)	147	24.2%
Third level vocational (e.g. NVQ)	83	13.7%
Post-graduate degree (Master's, PhD, etc.)	88	14.5%
n.a.	8	1.3%
Income		
Less than £500 each month	94	14.0%
Between £500 and £750 each month	64	9.5%
Between £750 and £1,000 each month	57	8.5%
Between £1,000 and £1,500 each month	103	15.3%
Between £1,500 and £2,000 each month	74	11.0%
Between £2,000 and £3,000 each month	86	12.8%
Between £3,000 and £4,000 each month	35	5.2%
More than £4,000 each month	28	4.2%
n.a.	66	9.8%
Total	**607**	**100%**

Source: Author's analysis of CFRC (2016) data

Results from the 11 regression models (one for the overall score, plus one for each single topic score) are reported in Table 4.3. The 11 models use the same set of independent variables – age, gender, education, income – and differ from each other for the measure of financial literacy used as dependent variables.

For the overall score, whose range is between 0 and 50, a linear regression model has been used. For the single topic scores, which are integer values with a range between 0 and 5, an order logistic regression model has been preferred.

Table 4.3 Results from regression models on financial literacy scores

	Total (50 items)		Interest rates (1|2|3|4|5)		Inflation (1|2|3|4|5)		Mortgages (1|2|3|4|5)		Investments (1|2|3|4|5)		Bonds (1|2|3|4|5)		Bank accounts (1|2|3|4|5)		Payments (1|2|3|4|5)		Stock investments (1|2|3|4|5)		Loans and debts (1|2|3|4|5)		Retirement and insurance (1|2|3|4|5)	
	Coef.	p-value	Coef.	p-value	Coef.	p-value	Coef.	p-value	Coef.	p-value	Coef.	p-value	Coef.	p-value	Coef.	p-value	Coef.	p-value	Coef.	p-value	Coef.	p-value
Age (years)																						
18–24	(Ref. group)		(Ref. group)		(Ref. group)		(Ref. group)		(Ref. group)		(Ref. group)		(Ref. group)		(Ref. group)		(Ref. group)		(Ref. group)		(Ref. group)	
25–30	0.80	0.568	0.24	0.404	0.38	0.197	0.13	0.645	−0.08	0.796	−0.29	0.361	−0.20	0.505	0.41	0.172	0.01	0.964	0.18	0.538	0.16	0.606
31–35	4.42	*0.002***	0.74	*0.016***	0.39	0.212	0.53	*0.078**	0.54	*0.085**	−0.29	0.377	0.43	0.175	1.13	*0.000****	0.95	*0.003***	0.64	*0.040***	0.74	*0.018***
36–40	3.18	*0.040***	0.30	0.352	0.91	*0.007***	0.06	0.854	0.25	0.457	−0.35	0.325	0.30	0.348	1.11	*0.001**	0.30	0.374	0.60	*0.080**	0.50	0.136
41–45	5.86	*0.001***	0.97	*0.009**	1.19	*0.001***	0.75	*0.036***	1.04	*0.006***	−0.13	0.737	0.58	0.101	1.26	*0.001**	0.40	0.269	0.72	*0.041**	0.48	0.215
46–50	6.35	*0.000****	1.16	*0.002***	1.25	*0.000****	0.64	*0.072**	0.97	*0.005***	−1.01	*0.010***	0.99	*0.006***	1.40	*0.000****	0.55	0.131	1.37	*0.000****	0.69	*0.057**
51–55	6.15	*0.000****	0.83	*0.017**	1.38	*0.000****	0.77	*0.028***	0.86	*0.015***	−0.94	*0.016***	0.91	*0.009***	1.97	*0.000****	0.03	0.940	1.09	*0.001**	0.70	*0.054**
56–60	8.72	*0.000****	1.96	*0.000****	1.70	*0.000****	0.85	*0.021***	1.07	*0.004***	−0.65	0.105	1.50	*0.000****	2.01	*0.000****	0.39	0.296	1.39	*0.000****	1.03	*0.004***
60–65	8.04	*0.000****	1.56	*0.000****	2.26	*0.000****	0.88	*0.024***	0.82	*0.037***	−0.21	0.604	1.23	*0.002***	1.54	*0.000****	0.77	*0.073**	0.76	*0.049**	1.01	*0.011***
65+	12.34	*0.000****	2.25	*0.000****	2.07	*0.000****	1.02	*0.003***	1.76	*0.000****	−0.01	0.985	1.75	*0.000****	2.44	*0.000****	1.20	*0.001***	1.56	*0.000****	1.87	*0.000****
Gender																						
Female	(Ref. group)		(Ref. group)		(Ref. group)		(Ref. group)		(Ref. group)		(Ref. group)		(Ref. group)		(Ref. group)		(Ref. group)		(Ref. group)		(Ref. group)	
Male	1.79	*0.026***	0.69	*0.000****	0.66	*0.000****	0.35	*0.040***	0.33	*0.059**	0.56	*0.002***	−0.20	0.247	−0.20	0.246	0.46	*0.008***	0.00	0.988	0.15	0.386

(Continued)

Table 4.3 (Continued)

	Total (50 items)		Interest rates (1|2|3|4|5)		Inflation (1|2|3|4|5)		Mortgages (1|2|3|4|5)		Investments (1|2|3|4|5)		Bonds (1|2|3|4|5)		Bank accounts (1|2|3|4|5)		Payments (1|2|3|4|5)		Stock-investments (1|2|3|4|5)		Loans and debts (1|2|3|4|5)		Retirement and insurance (1|2|3|4|5)	
	Coef.	p-value	Coef.	p-value	Coef.	p-value	Coef.	p-value	Coef.	p-value	Coef.	p-value	Coef.	p-value	Coef.	p-value	Coef.	p-value	Coef.	p-value	Coef.	p-value
Education																						
Primary school																						
Some secondary	1.93	0.765	0.78	0.572	−0.25	0.878	−0.70	0.588	−1.05	0.502	−0.09	0.951	1.44	0.294	1.63	0.237	−2.17	0.065*	0.25	0.858	1.05	0.461
GCSE	6.14	0.317	1.74	0.185	0.35	0.827	−0.09	0.943	−0.32	0.830	0.79	0.540	1.87	0.147	1.96	0.131	−1.35	0.229	1.37	0.297	1.18	0.374
A-level or equivalent	9.90	0.104	2.40	0.065*	1.00	0.526	0.37	0.756	0.20	0.891	0.90	0.480	2.34	0.068*	2.63	0.041**	−0.53	0.636	1.69	0.193	1.63	0.217
Third level academic (e.g. university degree)	11.79	0.053*	2.81	0.031**	1.32	0.403	0.69	0.567	0.19	0.900	0.88	0.493	2.73	0.033**	2.88	0.025*	−0.40	0.719	1.91	0.143	1.99	0.133
Third level vocational (e.g. NVQ)	10.04	0.102	2.29	0.080*	0.97	0.540	0.51	0.670	0.24	0.872	1.02	0.430	2.36	0.068*	2.51	0.052*	−0.65	0.552	1.78	0.174	1.62	0.224
Post-graduate degree (Master's, PhD, etc.)	9.22	0.131	1.82	0.162	0.79	0.615	0.41	0.733	−0.05	0.972	1.08	0.403	2.13	0.097*	2.40	0.062*	−0.74	0.536	1.75	0.179	2.08	0.117

Income (monthly base)

Each cell shows the coefficient (top) and its p-value (bottom, italic). Columns (1)–(11) are separate models (Obs. = 527 each).

Income (monthly base)	(1)	(2)	(3)	(4)	(5)	(6)	(7)	(8)	(9)	(10)	(11)
Less than £500	(Ref. group)	(Ref. group)	(Ref. group)	(Ref. group)	(Ref. group)	(Ref. group)	(Ref. group)	(Ref. group)	(Ref. group)	(Ref. group)	(Ref. group)
£500 to < £750	−0.43 *0.757*	−0.25 *0.403*	−0.54 *0.078**	0.05 *0.869*	0.45 *0.147*	0.20 *0.558*	−0.01 *0.971*	−0.12 *0.691*	0.01 *0.975*	−0.08 *0.775*	−0.08 *0.787*
£750 to < £1,000	0.33 *0.821*	−0.22 *0.486*	−0.15 *0.630*	0.03 *0.935*	0.19 *0.557*	0.53 *0.129*	−0.25 *0.417*	0.14 *0.660*	0.29 *0.375*	−0.13 *0.680*	0.24 *0.444*
£1,000 to < £1,500	1.43 *0.271*	0.25 *0.361*	−0.03 *0.916*	0.38 *0.168*	0.55 *0.052**	0.42 *0.173*	0.09 *0.750*	−0.25 *0.374*	0.57 *0.050**	0.29 *0.288*	0.25 *0.376*
£1,500 to < £2,000	0.52 *0.712*	0.03 *0.909*	−0.39 *0.204*	0.09 *0.769*	0.47 *0.119*	0.50 *0.143*	−0.02 *0.938*	−0.47 *0.122*	0.43 *0.170*	0.29 *0.328*	0.33 *0.271*
£2,000 to < £3,000	2.11 *0.132*	−0.01 *0.961*	0.07 *0.829*	0.55 *0.070**	0.92 *0.003***	0.45 *0.175*	−0.02 *0.937*	0.02 *0.954*	0.43 *0.162*	0.30 *0.314*	0.63 *0.038***
£3,000 to < £4,000	5.28 *0.005***	0.07 *0.864*	0.19 *0.626*	0.42 *0.288*	1.63 *0.000****	1.29 *0.002***	0.41 *0.314*	0.32 *0.447*	1.56 *0.000****	0.61 *0.135*	1.06 *0.010***
£4,000+	7.77 *0.000****	0.62 *0.000****	0.33 *0.464*	0.97 *0.022***	2.49 *0.000****	1.64 *0.000****	1.10 *0.015***	0.47 *0.299*	1.23 *0.003***	1.03 *0.015***	1.47 *0.001***
Constant	5.70 *0.352*	0.152 *0.000****	0.464	0.022**	0.000***	0.000***	0.015**	0.299	0.003**	0.015**	0.001**
Obs.	527	527	527	527	527	527	527	527	527	527	527
Adj. R-squared	0.2186	0.0661	0.0609	0.0309	0.0644	0.0418	0.0441	0.0582	0.0573	0.0389	0.0548

* = *p-value* < .10; ** = *p-value* < .05; *** = *p-value* < .001

Source: Author's analysis of CFRC (2016) data

Starting from the overall score, we can see how age plays a positive role in financial literacy. Using the youngest group (18–24) as a reference point, except for the 25–30 years-old group, all the other groups are statistically more knowledgeable. Looking at the values of the coefficients this gap of knowledge with the 18–24s tends to increase with age. This positive relationship between age and financial literacy can be explained by the knowledge achieved thanks to financial experiences. The results from financial literacy measures based on single topics tend to confirm this result. Inflation, payments, and loans and debts are the areas of knowledge where the positive effect of age on financial literacy is more clear. On the other hand, there are areas such as bonds and savings and investment where age is most of the time not able to explain financial literacy in the sample.

Results about gender are coherent with previous studies and confirm the positive relationship between being male and being financially knowledgeable. Although this effect is clear in the case where all 50 items are used to assess financial literacy, it is no more significant in several cases where the analysis focuses on knowledge related to single topics. The gender effect is quite clear when financial literacy is measured on interest rates (.69) and inflation (.66), becomes less relevant in the cases of mortgages (.35) and investments (.33), and disappears when financial literacy is measured on bank accounts, payments, loans and debts, and retirement and planning.

Results about education are somewhat surprising. Looking at the overall score, only one group seems to score differently from the reference group. Even in this case, the results change a lot when single areas of knowledge are taken into account. When financial literacy is measured on interest rates, bank accounts, and payments the expected positive effect of education on financial literacy is confirmed, even if only for the most educated groups.

The role of income in explaining financial literacy is quite weak. Looking at the overall score, only the last two (highest) income groups (£3,000–£4,000, and £4,000+) show coefficients that are statistically significant in most of the cases, while in general terms it seems that financial literacy is not directly affected by household income. So the hypothesis that people with more money available are more knowledgeable than others about finance is not confirmed in the case of the UK.

4.5 Conclusions

The big picture that comes out from the analysis of financial literacy in the UK is not positive. **Financial literacy is on average low**. Referring to the whole set of financial literacy items, on average the British respondents answered correctly only 43% of the 50 questions. Such a low result probably would not be considered sufficient in any educational exam (e.g. high school or college test).

What is interesting is that the conclusions about financial literacy in the UK change a lot when financial literacy is assessed by a different set of items, related to different areas of knowledge. This seems to be the confirmation that an individual can be financially literate in some areas and not be ready at all in others. The **investment related topics are the most critical** (stock investments, bonds, and diversification) with average scores that do not reach 20% in the case of bonds. Looking at previous results from financial literacy studies, the **gender gap is confirmed**. But, if males score on average better than females, the chance to assess financial literacy on specific areas of knowledge allows one to note how in the case of bank accounts and payments females scored on average better than males. The fact that these two areas are related with financial products and services that are used daily supports the hypothesis that the gender gap can be explained by different financial experiences between males and females and that gender is only a proxy of another explanatory variable. A usual result of financial literacy studies concerns the attitude of middle-aged individuals to score better than the elderly and the young. It seems that it is not the case of the UK, where **the best performers in the financial literacy questions are those more than 65 years old**.

Comparing financial literacy on different topics it is interesting that **correlations between single topic scores are pretty low**. Only one of the 45 correlation indices between the ten topic-based financial literacy measures showed a correlation greater than .60, while in some cases the correlation was pretty close to zero.

Last, the statistical analysis that tried to relate financial literacy to the socio-demographic profile of British respondents confirmed the positive role of age on financial literacy and the presence of a gender effect. At the same time, no great differences exist in the financial literacy of people with different education or different income, with only few exceptions for the tails of the distributions (very high-educated, and high income individuals).

Note

1 People who experienced a default on their mortgage or a big loss on investment could be quite sensitive with regard to talking about, for instance, overindebtedness or diversification, and they could prefer to not answer questions on these topics.

Reference

CFRC – Consumer Finance Research Center (2016). Survey on Consumers' Financial Literacy in the UK. www.consumer-finance.org/

5 Financial literacy in Germany

5.1 Introduction

This chapter is based on the analysis of a 2017 survey on financial literacy in Germany. Data come from the Consumer Finance Research Center (CFRC), and they are part of a research project whose aim is to assess financial literacy in different countries in a common research framework and using the same questionnaire. The questionnaire hosts around 100 questions organized in three sections. The first one collects data on the socio-demographic profile of the respondents (e.g. age, gender, income, education, etc.). The second part proposes 50 questions with the aim to assess the respondents' financial literacy. In the third part there are questions on the financial behaviors and attitudes of the respondents.[1]

The survey was administrated in 2017 targeting German adults (18+ years old). After controlling for blank answers and incomplete questionnaires the final sample size is of 533 observations. In the remainder of this chapter the main descriptive statistics are presented and discussed. In the last part a correlation analysis between the different areas of knowledge and a set of regression analysis are used to highlight how financial literacy is influenced by the socio-demographics of the respondents. The main conclusions are summarized in the last section.

5.2 The characteristics of financial literacy in Germany

The data on the German survey provided 50 items on the financial literacy of the respondents. These items are organized in ten groups of five questions, where each set of questions includes questions with different levels of difficulty. The ten areas of financial knowledge in the survey are interest rates, inflation, mortgages, diversification, bonds, bank accounts, payments, stock investments, debts, and retirement and insurance. The sum of correct answers to these questions has been used as a measure of financial literacy. Taking into account the whole set of questions – made of 50 items – an overall financial literacy score was assessed. Using only questions on a specific topic allowed the building of topic-based scores, which count the number of correct answers to the five questions of each topic.

According to this methodology a big picture of the level of financial knowledge in Germany is summarized in Figure 5.1. The average percentage of

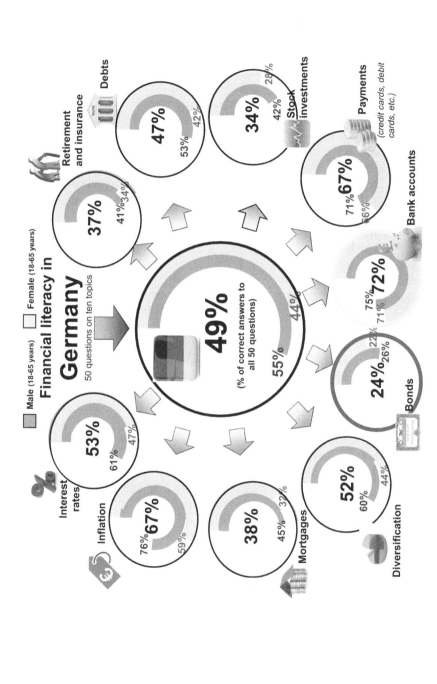

Figure 5.1 Financial literacy in Germany: break down and gender analysis

Source: Author's analysis of CFRC (2017) data

correct answers to the 50 financial knowledge questions was 49%. The analysis by gender highlights a better average score for males (55%) than females (44%), showing a "gender gap" that is typical of most of the financial literacy surveys.

However, the average score of the whole set of financial knowledge questions is just a starting point for an analysis of financial literacy. Awareness that individuals develop financial literacy on the topics they are more interested in (or they are more forced to deal with) recommends an analysis of the performance on the tests based on the knowledge of specific financial topics.

The high scores on 'bank accounts' (average score 72%) and 'payments' (67%) represent a similarity with other countries. At the same time, the low score on 'bonds' (24%) makes this area of knowledge critical, as it has been found for other countries too.

Knowledge on basic concepts like 'interest rates' (53%) and 'inflation' (67%) is above the average and, especially for males, seems to involve topics familiar to a good part of the respondents. Knowledge about indebtedness – related with the areas 'mortgages' (38%) and 'debts' (47%) – is not very high, but anyway better than knowledge on 'stock investments' (34%) and 'retirement and insurance' (37%), which represent, after bond pricing (24%), the most critical areas of knowledge.

Looking at the gender gap, we can see how the average 11 percentage point gap in the overall score (male 55% vs. female 44%) grows up to 17 points in the case of 'inflation' (male 76% vs. female 59%), and is shrunk to only 4 points when financial literacy is assessed by knowledge on 'bank accounts' (male 75% vs. female 71%). Even financial knowledge about 'payments' seems to be pretty similar between male (71%) and female (66%). Looking at the macro-area of knowledge about investments and long-term planning decisions (e.g. 'stock investments', 'bonds', 'retirement and insurance') this is for Germany – as for other countries – the less confident area of knowledge. The fact that the area related with money management (e.g. 'bank accounts' and 'payments') is the one where the German respondents have shown the highest knowledge is coherent with the assumption that financial literacy tends to grow more and faster in the case of short-term financial products, which are more related with daily use (e.g. credit cards, ATMs, etc.) and a learning by doing process.

Learning by doing and, generally speaking, previous financial experiences can be related with age. Results from analysis of the average overall score in the different age groups (Figure 5.2) seem to confirm a positive relationship between age and financial literacy.

If in previous studies the financial literacy distribution by age groups has shown a humped shape, with the middle-age groups the more knowledgeable and the older groups the more financially literate than the younger groups, in the case of Germany it seems that there is a clear linear trend between age and financial literacy, with financial literacy that tends to grow for individuals who belong to the older groups compared with others. The gap between the best performing age group (65+ with an average score of 56.6%) and the worst performers (18–24 year-old group with 40.8%) is not small (15.8 percentage

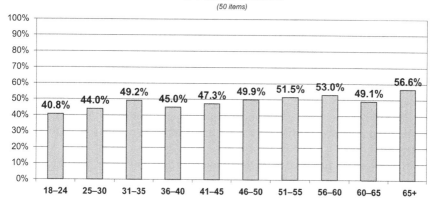

Figure 5.2 Overall score of financial literacy in Germany: break down by age

Source: Author's analysis of CFRC (2017) data

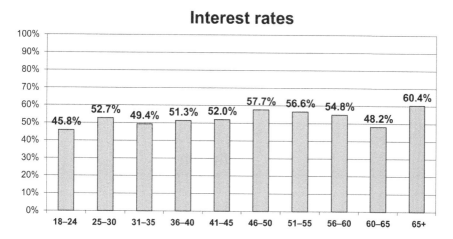

Figure 5.3 Financial literacy in Germany: knowledge on interest rates

Source: Author's analysis of CFRC (2017) data

points) but is mediated by the fact that the worst performers scored on average above the 40% threshold.

Results about the age group distribution of financial literacy, when it is assessed by questions on 'interest rates' (Figure 5.3), confirm the feeling from the overall score. The last age group is the one with the best score (65+, average score 60.4%), and the youngest group is the worst performer (18–24 year-old group, average score 45.8%). With respect to the overall score the linear increasing trend in the age distribution is less evident, with the slope of the trend line not very steep. The fact that in all age groups the average correct response rate is close to or above 50% means that a common basic knowledge of interest rates exists in Germany, even if a more advanced understanding does not.

Knowledge about inflation (Figure 5.4) confirms the good performance on the financial literacy test by those older than 65 (79.1% of correct answers) and the fact that Germans 18–24 years old are the least knowledgeable (52.1%). However, except for the 18–24s, all the other age groups scored on average beyond 60%, showing a good understanding about inflation. As in the overall score, even in this case there is a clear linear trend between age and financial literacy.

In the case of financial knowledge on mortgages (Figure 5.5) the correct response rate drops for all the age groups compared with the previous cases. If the 65+ are once more the ones with the best knowledge of the topic, their average score is below the 50% threshold. At the same time those 18–24 years old are not anymore the lowest knowledgeable age group. Those 41–45 years old are the ones who on average scored at the lowest with only a 28% average response rate. With the only exception of those older than 65 almost all the other age groups did not score above 40%.

Financial knowledge on diversification (Figure 5.6) provides some interesting results.

In this case those older than 65 are not anymore the best performers. Their average score (60.4%) is below the one of those 56–60 years old (61.3%) and pretty close to the one of those 45–50 years old (59.4%). Another interesting outcome is the gap between those younger than 30 and the rest of the sample.

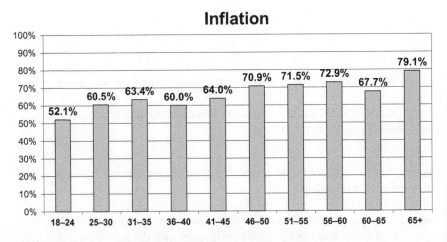

Figure 5.4 Financial literacy in Germany: knowledge on inflation

Source: Author's analysis of CFRC (2017) data

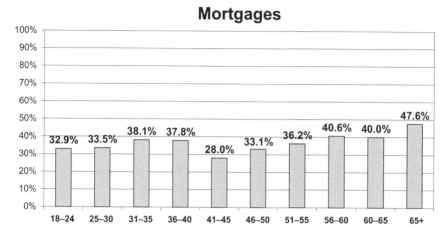

Figure 5.5 Financial literacy in Germany: knowledge on mortgages

Source: Author's analysis of CFRC (2017) data

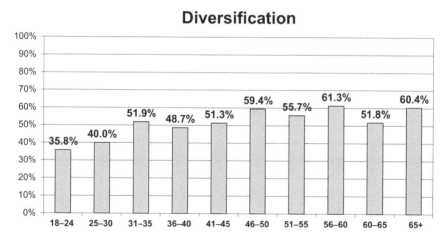

Figure 5.6 Financial literacy in Germany: knowledge on diversification

Source: Author's analysis of CFRC (2017) data

Those 18–24 years old scored on average 35.8%, and those 25–30 years old scored 40.0%. These data, when compared with the performance of the 31–35s (51.9%) and the 36–40s (48.7%), highlight a big gap that was not shown in the analysis of the previous cases ('interest rates', 'inflation', 'mortgages').

A somehow shocking result comes from the data on financial literacy related with 'bonds' (Figure 5.7).

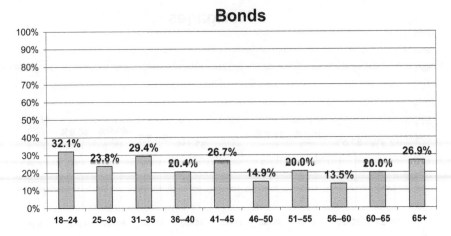

Figure 5.7 Financial literacy in Germany: knowledge on bonds

Source: Author's analysis of CFRC (2017) data

Those 18–24 years old become the most knowledgeable group about bonds, but a comparison between topic-based scores shows how this result can be probably explained by the high volatility of the topic-based scores for the other age groups, more than by good performance of the 18–24s. The average score of the 18–24s – equal to 32.1% – is not very far from the scores achieved in the case of 'diversification' (35.8%) and 'mortgages' (32.9%), while other age groups in the case of bonds scored even 30 percentage points less than other cases. For instance, those 56–60 years old scored only 13.5% in the case of bonds, while their average score on 'diversification' was 61.3% and on 'inflation' 72.9%.

Knowledge about 'stock investments' is summarized in Figure 5.8. The big picture is about a low level of knowledge for all the age groups. The best scores are the ones for those older than 65 (39.3%) and those 56–60 years old (38.7%), which are not so different from the scores of the other age groups.

If knowledge on 'bank accounts' is the area with the highest average score in the sample (72% of correct answers), results from the single age groups (Figure 5.9) provide additional insights.

Those 56–60 years old achieved the outstanding average score of 86.5%, showing a very deep knowledge and understanding of the functioning of this financial product. At the same time, there are four other groups that scored above the 75% threshold (which means almost four correct answers to the five questions of the test). They are the 46–50s (76.0%), the 51–55s (76.6%), the 60–65s (76.8%), and those older than 65 (77.5%). The worst performing age group is once more those 18–24 years old, which provided on average a correct answer to the five financial literacy questions only in 57.5% of the cases.

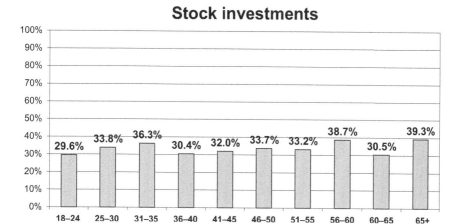

Figure 5.8 Financial literacy in Germany: knowledge on stock investments
Source: Author's analysis of CFRC (2017) data

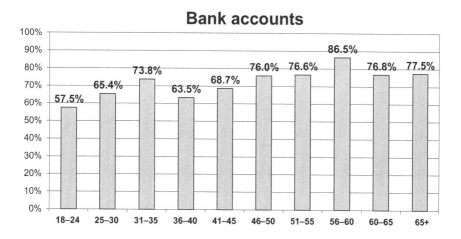

Figure 5.9 Financial literacy in Germany: knowledge on bank accounts
Source: Author's analysis of CFRC (2017) data

Also in the case of 'payments' results show a good understanding by the German sample (Figure 5.10). The flat trend across age groups highlights how on average there is not a substantial difference between age groups in term of knowledge on payments.

Age seems to matter when financial literacy is assessed on 'loans and debts' (Figure 5.11). From the 18–24 years-old group, which provided a correct answer on less than one of three questions (30.4%), there is a growing trend

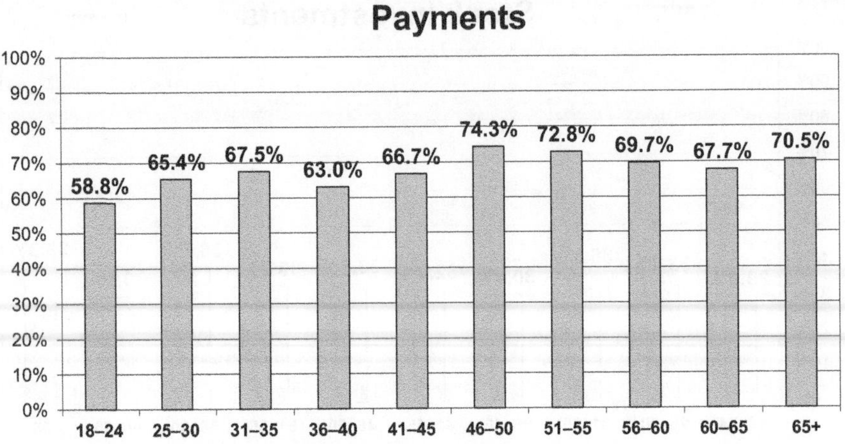

Payments

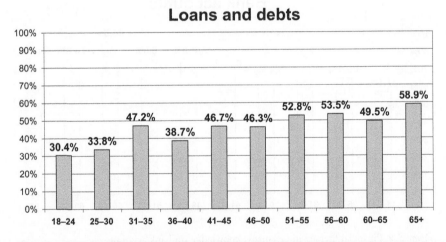

Figure 5.10 Financial literacy in Germany: knowledge on payments

Source: Author's analysis of CFRC (2017) data

Loans and debts

Figure 5.11 Financial literacy in Germany: knowledge on loans and debts

Source: Author's analysis of CFRC (2017) data

with the 25–30s that scored 33.8%, the 31–35s that scored 47.2%, up to those older than 65 that scored 58.9%.

Results from 'retirement and insurance' (Figure 5.12) show how low financial literacy on this topic is widespread across the age groups. The distance between the top score (45.1%) and the bottom score (32.5%) is about only 13 percentage points. This gap becomes even smaller if assessed using the second

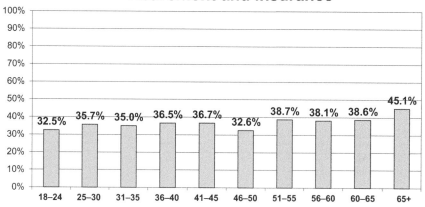

Figure 5.12 Financial literacy in Germany: knowledge on retirement and insurance

Source: Author's analysis of CFRC (2017) data

best score (38.7%). As in other countries, the fact that the youngest groups are not knowledgeable about retirement and insurance is alarming due to the long-term consequences of this lack of knowledge on their financial behaviors (e.g. retirement planning, retirement contributions, etc.).

The different scores on different financial topics can be evidence that individuals develop financial literacy according to their financial needs. An analysis of the correlation between the different financial literacy scores can shed light on this hypothesis (Table 5.1).

The first column shows the correlation index between the overall score and each of the ten groups of five questions used to build it. The intrinsic bias related to the fact that the five questions used to build a topic-based score are also part of the 50 items used to build the overall score tends to increase the value of the correlation index by definition. In any case, this measure can be used as a summary of the correlation between each set of five questions (each topic) and all the rest. If the correlation indices are on average high, it is evident how financial knowledge on 'bonds' is not so related with other financial knowledge. This evidence is confirmed by the analysis of the one-to-one correlation indices between topic-based scores. The lowest one is between 'bonds' and 'bank accounts' with a correlation pretty close to zero (0.07). Very low correlations are also between 'bonds' and 'interest rates' (0.11) and 'bonds' and 'payments' (0.02). This result can be interpreted as the fact that knowledge on financial markets (e.g. 'bonds') and knowledge about money management (e.g. 'bank accounts' and 'payments') can be developed separately and by different individuals who have to deal with different financial needs. However, even

Table 5.1 Correlation between financial literacy scores (overall score, and the ten scores on single areas of knowledge)

	FL_OVERALL	FL_Interest rates	FL_Inflation	FL_Mortgages	FL_Diversification	FL_Bonds	FL_Bank accounts	FL_Payments	FL_Stock investments	FL_Loans and debts	FL_Retirement and insurance
FL_OVERALL	1										
FL_Interest rates	0.60	1									
FL_Inflation	0.70	0.41	1								
FL_Mortgages	0.58	0.21	0.34	1							
FL_Diversification	0.73	0.39	0.49	0.31	1						
FL_Bonds	0.43	0.11	0.18	0.27	0.21	1					
FL_Bank accounts	0.60	0.32	0.34	0.26	0.33	0.07	1				
FL_Payments	0.59	0.36	0.39	0.17	0.36	0.02	0.50	1			
FL_Stock investments	0.70	0.31	0.38	0.36	0.53	0.30	0.29	0.31	1		
FL_Loans and debts	0.73	0.39	0.43	0.36	0.46	0.20	0.46	0.40	0.46	1	
FL_Retirement and insurance	0.62	0.26	0.32	0.32	0.43	0.27	0.22	0.24	0.45	0.41	1

Source: Author's analysis of CFRC (2017) data

when correlation is assessed on financial topics that share some similarities in term of application and time horizon, there are not very high values in the German sample. For instance, knowledge on 'bank accounts' and 'payments' should be quite correlated, due to the fact that they are both related with money management and short-term views, but the correlation is just 0.50. A similar result is the one for 'bonds', 'stocks and investments', and 'Diversification'. The correlations between these three financial literacy scores are 0.30 ('bonds' vs. 'stocks and investments'), 0.21 ('bonds' vs. 'diversification'), and 0.53 ('stocks and investments' vs. 'diversification'), which are not very high if we take into account that they are all related with portfolio management.

5.3 The determinants of financial literacy in Germany

So, the analysis of correlations suggests that those who show good financial knowledge on a topic cannot be considered skilled by definition on other topics. What can be interesting is the analysis that takes into account simultaneously the possible combinations of the socio-demographic characteristics of the respondents. The socio-demographic characteristics of the sample are reported in Table 5.2, while in Table 5.3 are listed the results of a set of regression models where each of the financial literacy scores has been related with the main socio-demographic variables of the sample (age, gender, education, income).

Table 5.2 Descriptive statistics of the German sample

	#	%
Age		
18–24	48	9.1%
25–30	74	14.0%
31–35	64	12.1%
36–40	46	8.7%
41–45	30	5.7%
46–50	35	6.6%
51–55	47	8.9%
56–60	31	5.9%
60–65	44	8.3%
65+	110	20.8%
Gender		
Male	244	45.8%
Female	275	51.6%
n.a.	14	2.6%
Education		
None	5	0.9%
(Kein Schulabschluss)		
Elementary/high school	66	12.4%
(Grundschul-/Hauptschulabschluss)		
College or equivalent	184	34.5%
(Realschulabschluss, Mittlere Reife oder gleichwertiger Abschluss)		
High school – university entrance qualification (Abitur)	119	22.3%
(Fachhochschulreife, Hochschulreife (Abitur))		
University of Applied Science ("Fachhochschule"): Bachelor, Diploma, Master	59	11.1%
(Fachhochschule: Bachelor, Diplom, Master)		
University: Bachelor, Diploma, Master	90	16.9%
(Universität: Bachelor, Diplom, Master)		
PhD	4	0.8%
(Promotion)		
n.a.	6	1.1%
Income		
Less than 500€ each month	47	8.4%
Between 500€ and 750€ each month	29	5.2%
Between 750€ and 1,000€ each month	84	14.9%
Between 1,000€ and 1,500€ each month	104	18.5%
Between 1,500€ and 2,000€ each month	70	12.5%
Between 2,000€ and 3,000€ each month	28	5.0%
Between 3,000€ and 4,000€ each month	118	21.0%
More than 4,000€ each month	24	4.3%
n.a.	29	5.2%
Total	533	100%

Source: Author's analysis of CFRC (2017) data

The statistical analysis on the explanatory power of socio-demographic characteristics of German adults on their financial knowledge provided interesting results. Looking at the regression model related with the overall score (the one based on 50 items), there is evidence of an age effect. Individuals more than

Table 5.3 Results from regression models on financial literacy scores

	Total (50 items)		Interest rates (1|2|3|4|5)		Inflation (1|2|3|4|5)		Mortgages (1|2|3|4|5)		Investments (1|2|3|4|5)		Bonds (1|2|3|4|5)		Bank accounts (1|2|3|4|5)		Payments (1|2|3|4|5)		Stock investments (1|2|3|4|5)		Loans and debts (1|2|3|4|5)		Retirement and insurance (1|2|3|4|5)	
	Coef.	p-value	Coef.	p-value	Coef.	p-value	Coef.	p-value	Coef.	p-value	Coef.	p-value	Coef.	p-value	Coef.	p-value	Coef.	p-value	Coef.	p-value	Coef.	p-value
Age (years)																						
18–24	(Ref. group)		(Ref. group)		(Ref. group)		(Ref. group)		(Ref. group)		(Ref. group)		(Ref. group)		(Ref. group)		(Ref. group)		(Ref. group)		(Ref. group)	
25–30	0.41	0.791	0.34	0.350	0.37	0.308	−0.06	0.864	0.02	0.954	−0.67	0.063*	0.38	0.329	0.18	0.645	−0.17	0.638	0.21	0.569	−0.30	0.410
31–35	2.63	0.105	0.01	0.980	0.46	0.245	0.11	0.772	0.61	0.100	−0.37	0.322	1.05	0.009**	0.46	0.255	0.04	0.909	1.22	0.002**	−0.29	0.450
36–40	2.06	0.248	0.41	0.339	0.62	0.158	0.26	0.529	0.74	0.071*	−0.92	0.030**	0.68	0.122	0.42	0.337	−0.19	0.639	0.47	0.272	0.12	0.778
41–45	3.26	0.088*	0.65	0.147	0.85	0.057*	−0.19	0.652	0.99	0.022**	−0.41	0.344	0.66	0.157	0.37	0.427	0.06	0.890	1.02	0.023**	0.11	0.815
46–50	3.90	0.034**	0.88	0.048**	1.27	0.003**	−0.06	0.888	1.29	0.002**	−1.46	0.002**	1.22	0.008**	0.86	0.056*	0.09	0.833	1.03	0.015**	−0.24	0.585
51–55	4.70	0.006**	0.82	0.038**	1.18	0.004**	0.18	0.648	1.17	0.003**	−0.93	0.024**	1.00	0.016**	0.62	0.130	0.01	0.979	1.48	0.000***	0.38	0.343
56–60	4.69	0.014**	0.49	0.269	1.25	0.006**	0.26	0.564	1.44	0.001**	−1.53	0.002**	1.77	0.000***	0.45	0.333	0.21	0.635	1.48	0.001**	0.20	0.643
60–65	3.12	0.078*	−0.05	0.900	0.91	0.031**	0.32	0.434	0.86	0.034**	−0.77	0.065*	0.97	0.022**	0.23	0.592	−0.28	0.494	1.16	0.004**	0.40	0.318
65+	6.81	0.000***	1.07	0.003**	1.72	0.000***	0.64	0.071*	1.37	0.000***	−0.55	0.120	1.04	0.006**	0.62	0.100	0.43	0.208	1.74	0.000***	0.81	0.022**
Gender																						
Female	(Ref. group)		(Ref. group)		(Ref. group)		(Ref. group)		(Ref. group)		(Ref. group)		(Ref. group)		(Ref. group)		(Ref. group)		(Ref. group)		(Ref. group)	
Male	3.56	0.000***	0.94	0.000***	0.84	0.000***	0.55	0.002**	0.76	0.000***	0.16	0.380	0.27	0.127	0.27	0.127	0.80	0.000***	0.52	0.003**	0.20	0.250

Education

Education											
None (Kein Schulabschluss)	(Ref. group)	(Ref. group)	(Ref. group)	(Ref. group)	(Ref. group)	(Ref. group)	(Ref. group)	(Ref. group)	(Ref. group)	(Ref. group)	(Ref. group)
Elementary/high school (Grundschul-/Hauptschulabschluss)	3.66 (0.367)	1.34 (0.126)	-0.43 (0.668)	-0.20 (0.844)	0.70 (0.467)	-0.02 (0.982)	1.20 (0.187)	1.83 (0.056*)	0.11 (0.907)	0.88 (0.433)	0.16 (0.888)
College or equivalent (Realschulabschluss, Mittlere Reife oder gleichwertiger Abschluss)	5.99 (0.134)	1.89 (0.027**)	-0.07 (0.945)	-0.30 (0.759)	1.26 (0.190)	0.07 (0.949)	1.72 (0.057*)	2.29 (0.016**)	1.01 (0.296)	1.07 (0.336)	0.38 (0.744)
High school – university entrance qualification (Abitur) (Fachhochschulreife, Hochschulreife (Abitur))	9.08 (0.024**)	2.75 (0.002**)	0.59 (0.555)	0.26 (0.794)	1.97 (0.040**)	0.30 (0.777)	1.63 (0.071*)	2.55 (0.007**)	1.33 (0.171)	1.13 (0.312)	0.77 (0.505)
University of Applied Science ("Fachhochschule"): Bachelor, Diploma, Master (Fachhochschule: Bachelor, Diplom, Master)	9.85 (0.017**)	2.62 (0.003**)	0.62 (0.541)	0.46 (0.651)	1.67 (0.091*)	0.27 (0.800)	2.38 (0.011**)	2.36 (0.015**)	1.78 (0.075*)	1.55 (0.174)	0.83 (0.480)
University: Bachelor, Diploma, Master (Universität: Bachelor, Diplom, Master)	8.93 (0.028**)	2.46 (0.005**)	0.47 (0.638)	0.35 (0.729)	1.77 (0.068*)	0.08 (0.937)	2.01 (0.028**)	2.46 (0.010**)	1.65 (0.094*)	1.35 (0.232)	0.73 (0.533)
PhD (promotion)	13.89 (0.022**)	3.39 (0.013**)	1.90 (0.229)	2.27 (0.173)	3.26 (0.019*)	-1.12 (0.479)	2.18 (0.103)	2.86 (0.044*)	2.86 (0.035**)	1.70 (0.239)	1.02 (0.491)

(Continued)

Table 5.3 (Continued)

	Total (50 items)		Interest rates (1|2|3|4|5)		Inflation (1|2|3|4|5)		Mortgages (1|2|3|4|5)		Investments (1|2|3|4|5)		Bonds (1|2|3|4|5)		Bank accounts (1|2|3|4|5)		Payments (1|2|3|4|5)		Stock investments (1|2|3|4|5)		Loans and debts (1|2|3|4|5)		Retirement and insurance (1|2|3|4|5)	
	Coef.	p-value	Coef.	p-value	Coef.	p-value	Coef.	p-value	Coef.	p-value	Coef.	p-value	Coef.	p-value	Coef.	p-value	Coef.	p-value	Coef.	p-value	Coef.	p-value
Income (monthly base)																						
Less than 500€	(Ref. group)		(Ref. group)		(Ref. group)		(Ref. group)		(Ref. group)		(Ref. group)		(Ref. group)		(Ref. group)		(Ref. group)		(Ref. group)		(Ref. group)	
500€ to < 750€	0.70	0.709	−0.08	0.862	0.10	0.816	−0.41	0.349	0.48	0.279	−0.84	0.096*	−0.10	0.827	0.60	0.172	0.22	0.617	0.52	0.227	0.05	0.904
750€ to < 1,000€	0.03	0.985	0.00	0.990	−0.39	0.254	−0.05	0.881	0.06	0.861	−0.31	0.379	0.49	0.176	0.46	0.191	−0.27	0.443	0.27	0.425	−0.30	0.387
1,000€ to < 1,500€	2.08	0.142	0.13	0.712	−0.13	0.678	0.12	0.696	0.56	0.082*	0.20	0.556	0.10	0.763	0.56	0.097*	0.31	0.355	0.66	0.046**	0.54	0.115
1,500€ to < 2,000€	0.14	0.924	−0.38	0.290	−0.13	0.711	−0.45	0.188	0.27	0.436	0.10	0.788	−0.08	0.828	0.11	0.762	0.20	0.575	0.29	0.412	0.05	0.880
2,000€ to < 3,000€	2.45	0.198	0.63	0.162	0.04	0.918	−0.08	0.844	0.89	0.043**	0.41	0.364	−0.14	0.764	0.27	0.544	0.68	0.134	0.07	0.874	0.77	0.097*
3,000€ to < 4,000€	2.20	0.117	0.25	0.446	0.20	0.544	−0.19	0.545	0.61	0.057*	0.28	0.385	−0.07	0.838	0.41	0.202	0.59	0.076*	0.32	0.316	0.60	0.074*
4,000€+	3.90	0.062*	−0.41	0.385	−0.24	0.652	0.87	0.086*	0.48	0.330	1.15	0.027**	0.05	0.925	0.64	0.197	0.45	0.338	1.37	0.006**	0.91	0.065*
Constant	11.31	0.005**																				
Obs.	488		488		488		488		488		488		488		488		488		488		488	
Adj. R-squared	0.1955		0.0615		0.0599		0.037		0.0592		0.0311		0.0343		0.0208		0.0572		0.0591		0.0381	

* = p-value < .10; ** = p-value < .05; *** = p-value < 0.001

Source: Author's analysis of CFRC (2017) data

40 years old tend to score better than the youngest (18–24 years old) group (used as a reference group). The effect of age is confirmed for each of the 40+ age groups with a value of the coefficients that tends to increase with age. The fact (already shown in the analysis of financial literacy by age) that those older than 65 are the most knowledgeable age group in the German sample is confirmed by the regression analysis.

This **age effect** and the evidence that the older groups are more knowledgeable than the younger groups is confirmed by the analysis of single topic measures of financial literacy, even if there are a few exceptions. This evidence is confirmed for 'inflation', 'stock investments', 'bank accounts', and 'loans and debts'. Less clear evidence exists in the case of 'interest rates', while the age effect does not exist in the case of 'mortgages' and 'retirement and insurance', where only those older than 65 seem to score differently (better) than the 18–24 years-old group. What is interesting is that in the case of 'bonds', the youngest group (18–24 years old) is statistically significantly more knowledgeable than other age groups. This result confirms the results of the correlation analysis, where the financial literacy scores on 'bonds' were systematically low correlated with the other financial literacy measures.

The analysis of gender on financial literacy in Germany confirms the **presence of a gender gap**, with the evidence that males score on average better than females. This result is quite clear in the overall score, and is confirmed in six out of ten cases when financial literacy is measured on single topics. The gender gap disappears in the case of 'bank accounts', 'payments', 'bonds' and 'retirement and insurance'. If in the first two cases the chance that a female knows these financial products and services as well as a male can be the logical explanation; in the case of 'bonds' the average very low scores in the sample (24%) and in the two genders (male 22%, female 24%) can be interpreted as evidence that there is not a difference because both genders are not very knowledgeable about bonds.

Education is another powerful explanatory power. The education effect on the overall score is significant for all the educational levels from the university entrance qualification level and above. The effect is quite strong, especially in the case of PhDs. However, this effect is not persistent when single areas of knowledge are considered to measure financial literacy. 'Interest rates', 'investments', 'bank accounts', and 'payments' are the financial topics where more educated people tend to score better than others. On the other hand, this educational effect is not confirmed in the case of 'inflation', 'mortgages', 'bonds', 'loans and debts', and 'retirement and insurance'. In all these cases none of the educational levels differs in a statistically significant way from the reference (low educated) group.

Results from **income** confirm the evidence from other countries. Financial literacy is not related with the income level of individuals, with the only exception being those who earn more than 4,000€ a month, who tend to be more knowledgeable than others. However, this effect is not always confirmed when the overall score of financial literacy is replaced by single topic-based scores. If there are some cases where a significant effect has been found for some income groups, the robustness of these results and the low level of the coefficients are not enough to support the hypothesis that income is a determinant to predict financial literacy of individuals.

5.4 Conclusions

The fact that on average the correct response rate of the respondents from the German sample to the 50 questions on financial literacy was 49% highlights how **financial literacy in Germany is low**. But this average score seems to be the mean between different scores on different topics. **More than in other countries the performances in a financial literacy test on a certain topic are not a good estimation about the performances in other areas**. In particular, even knowledge on related topics such as 'payments' and 'bank accounts' – which are supposed to be linked to money management – or 'bonds', 'stock investments', and 'diversification' – which all refer to investment decisions – does not show high correlation.

Another difference between the German sample and results from other countries is the distribution of financial literacy by age. Except for the investment related topics, **those older than 65 are the most knowledgeable group**. Results from previous studies tend to show a reverse U-shape (or "humped shape") in the distribution of financial literacy by age. What makes the German results similar to those from other countries is the presence of a gender gap, where males tend to systematically score better than females.

Education provides another interesting result. The analysis of the regression models suggests that for high-educated individuals (ones from the college entrance level – "*Fachhochschulreife, Hochschulreife (Abitur)*" – and above) there is a statistically significant difference from the low-educated groups, with an average better score on the financial literacy test for the high-educated.

Results about **income** confirm results from other countries, showing how this is not a pivotal variable in the explanation of financial literacy. Income seems to differentiate the financial literacy of individuals only a few times and only for very high income respondents.

Note

1 For details about the questionnaire and the CFRC research project see the description in the previous chapter presented in the §4.2 data.

Reference

CFRC- Consumer Finance Research Center (2017). Survey on Consumers' Financial Literacy in Germany. www.consumer-finance.org/

6 Financial literacy in France

6.1 Introduction

The analysis of financial literacy in France presented in this chapter is based on data from a survey organized in the summer of 2017 by the Consumer Finance Research Center (CFRC). The structure of the questionnaire used in the survey is the same as the surveys presented in the previous chapters on the UK and Germany.[1] The questionnaire is made of around 100 questions organized in three sections. The first set of questions collects data on age, gender, income, education, and other socio-demographic characteristics of the participants. The mid part hosts 50 multiple choice questions in order to assess their financial literacy, while the last part of the questionnaire is about the financial behaviors and attitudes of the respondents.

The target of the survey is the French adult population (18+ years old). The final sample size, after controlling for blank or incomplete answers, is 519 observations. The chance to assess financial literacy by using a large set of items on several financial topics allowed the assessment of both the average knowledge of French adults on quite different financial topics and the measurement of how financial literacy of French adults changes when specific financial issues are taken into account. The results of this analysis are presented in the following paragraphs, where differences between genders and age groups are stressed before a more comprehensive analysis of the determinants of financial literacy in France is presented.

6.2 The characteristics of financial literacy in France

In order to analyze financial literacy in France, it is useful to start from the big picture provided by the overall score that measures the number of correct answers to all 50 questions related to financial literacy of the sample. These questions are organized in groups of five questions, where each group concerns a different financial topic (e.g. inflation, stocks, payments, retirement and insurance, etc.), and the questions in the groups were designed to have different levels of difficulty.

The result from this overall score on the French sample is that on average a respondent provided a correct answer only in 39% of the cases, which is equal to around 19 right answers to the 50 questions (Figure 6.1). This score

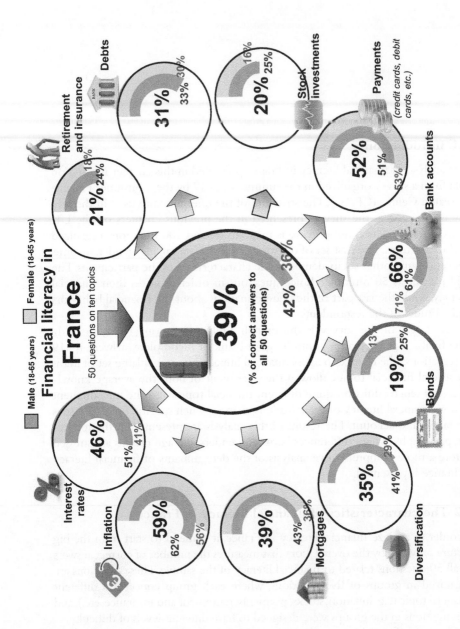

Figure 6.1 Financial literacy in France: break down and gender analysis

Source: Author's analysis of CFBC (2017) data

is evidence of a lack of knowledge on finance, and confirms the low level of financial literacy of individuals already found in other countries. Still looking at the overall score, there is a clear gap between males (42%) and females (36%), which represents another similarity between countries on an international basis.

Going beyond the summary score, it can be noted how the degree of financial knowledge of French people changes a lot when different areas of knowledge are considered. The extreme values of the topic-based scores distribution show how 'bank accounts' is the area of knowledge where the French scored the best, with an average correct response rate of 66%. On the other hand, knowledge about bonds is the most critical topic with an average score of 19%, which means less than one correct answer of five. From the big picture it seems that all the investment related topics are not familiar to the French. The average score in 'stock investments' is only 20% (one on five), and the 'retirement and insurance' score is 21%. A bit better result is the one on 'diversification' (35%), which represents an average correct answer rate of one of three. Like in other countries, even in France people are more knowledgeable about the use of 'bank accounts' (66%) and 'payments' (52%). A possible explanation is that these financial products and services are used more frequently than others and are related to basic financial needs, so both a stronger incentive to learn and a learning by doing process can support the development of financial knowledge and confidence by individuals.

'Inflation' is another area of knowledge with an above average mean score (59%), which cannot be considered common knowledge in the population, due to the fact that there is almost (on average) one wrong answer for every correct one. A similar situation is about 'interest rates' (46%), while it is worst in the case of 'debts'. The average correct answer rate in the case of 'mortgages' is only 39%, and when the use of debt in a broad sense is assessed ('debts') the average score drops to 31%.

Analysis of the **gender gap** offers other interesting results. If on average there are 6 percentage points of difference between males (42%) and females (36%), this gap differs a lot when it is measured taking account of single areas of knowledge. The biggest gaps exist in the case of 'bonds' (females scored on average 12 percentage points less than males) and 'diversification' (also in this case the gap is equal to −12%), but, in the case of 'bonds' it is not only the gender gap that represents a critical point, but there is also the fact that females were on average able to provide a correct answer only in 13% of the cases. Very low levels of financial knowledge for females are also evident in the case of 'stock investments' (16%) and 'retirement and insurance' (18%). In addition, there are areas of knowledge where the gender gap almost disappears ('debts' score is 33% for males and 30% for females) or areas where females scored on average better than males – 'payments' (males 51%, females 53%) and 'bank accounts' (males 61%, females 71%).

The analysis of the average overall score in the different **age groups** (Figure 6.2) shows another interesting result. Unlike other countries, where a reverse U-shape is frequent when financial literacy is assessed for different

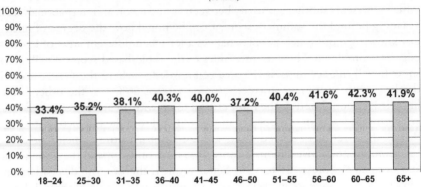

Figure 6.2 Overall score of financial literacy in France: break down by age

Source: Author's analysis of CFRC (2017) data

age groups, in the case of France there is a linear trend line with a very smooth slope.

There are only around 9 percentage points between the top performers (60–65 years-old group with 42.3% of correct answers) and the lowest score (33.4% of correct answers in the case of 18–24 years-old group). The trend line becomes flat in the middle groups (36–40, 41–45, 46–50, 50–55), which scored on average around 40%.

Homogeneous scores between age groups on the overall 50 items tend to remain when single areas of knowledge are taken into account separately, even if not in every case. Looking at the financial knowledge score on 'interest rates' (Figure 6.3) the linear trend in the distribution of results by age groups is still clear, even if the 30–40 years-old groups are a bit above the average (31–35 years old 48.8%, 36–40 years old 52.1%) and the 46–55 years-old respondents scored less than average (46–50 years old 40.0%, 51–55 years old 43.2%).

A more clear distinction between age groups appears in the case of 'inflation' (Figure 6.4). The three last age groups, which represent those older than 55 of the sample, scored around 15 to 20 percentage points better than those younger than 30.

The fact that the young generations never experienced a high inflation rate scenario can be a possible explanation for their lower scores. The evidence that knowledge on a basic financial concept – such as inflation – is so low to barely achieve a 50% level of correct answers for several age groups confirms the need to develop and implement financial education strategies even in developed countries, like France.

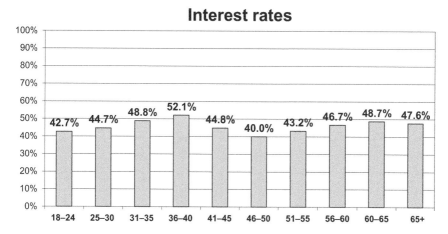

Figure 6.3 Financial literacy in France: knowledge on interest rates
Source: Author's analysis of CFRC (2017) data

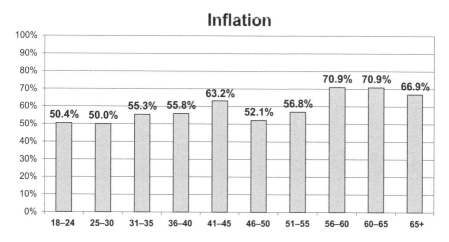

Figure 6.4 Financial literacy in France: knowledge on inflation
Source: Author's analysis of CFRC (2017) data

Financial knowledge on 'mortgages' (Figure 6.5) does not show relevant differences between age groups, with the only exception being those older than 65, who scored on average 46.2%, compared with the 39% average of the whole sample, which is around a 7 percentage point difference. Comparing the other age groups there is a very light increasing trend by age, which is not free of exceptions like the 46–50 age group that shows the lowest score (33.9%) of the sample.

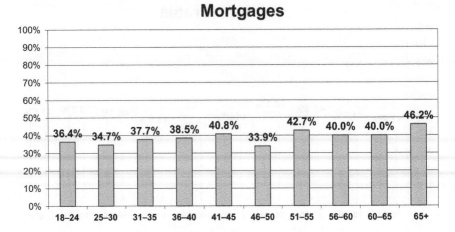

Figure 6.5 Financial literacy in France: knowledge on mortgages

Source: Author's analysis of CFRC (2017) data

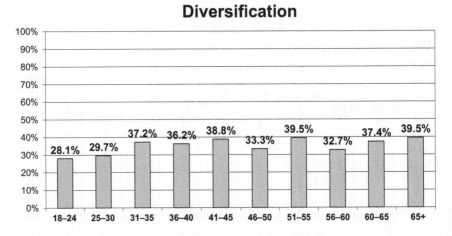

Figure 6.6 Financial literacy in France: knowledge on diversification

Source: Author's analysis of CFRC (2017) data

Results of the analysis of financial knowledge on 'diversification' (Figure 6.6) are not so different from what was observed in the case of 'mortgages', with the only difference that the average score is a bit lower (39% 'mortgages', 35% 'diversification').

The two youngest age groups (18–24 and 25–30 years old) present the biggest lack of knowledge and do not achieve an average correct response rate of 30%. As in the case of 'mortgages', those older than 65 are the ones who achieve the best score (together with the 51–55s: 39.5%). However, none of the age group scored on average more than 40%.

The fact that financial markets and investment related topics are the most critical to understand and to deal with for individuals is confirmed by the results of financial literacy about 'bonds' (Figure 6.7). If the average score of the sample is itself alarming (19% of correct answers) the break down by age groups is even more shocking. Unlike the previous case, now the older age groups are the ones that scored on average worse than others. The 51–55 years-old group provided on average correct answers only in 13% of the cases (which means not even one correct answer of five).

The fact that the top score within the age groups is 22.3% (36–40 and 51–55 years old) is clear evidence about the general lack of financial knowledge about bonds.

The flat trend across different age groups is a feature of the financial literacy score on 'stock investments' too (Figure 6.8). At the same time, the evidence that the last age groups are less knowledgeable about financial markets and investments is confirmed. The worst score is 14.8% (60–65 years-old group). The best one is 24.4%, by the 41–45 years-old group.

The scenario is completely different when financial literacy is measured on 'bank accounts' knowledge (Figure 6.9). The mean score in the whole sample – equal to 66% of correct answers – is the average between different scores across age groups.

The slope of the trend line is clearly positive. It can be seen that the lowest score is the one of the youngest age group (18–24 years old, 51.9%) and the highest score is the one of the 60–65 years-old group (77.8%). The gap between these two groups is about 25 percentage points and stresses how financial knowledge about bank accounts tends to increase with age. As in other

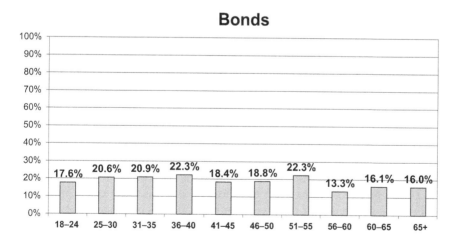

Figure 6.7 Financial literacy in France: knowledge on bonds

Source: Author's analysis of CFRC (2017) data

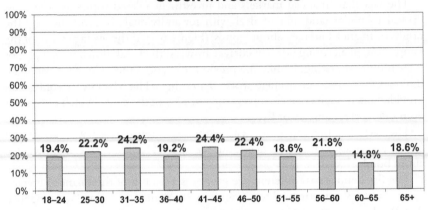

Figure 6.8 Financial literacy in France: knowledge on stock investments

Source: Author's analysis of CFRC (2017) data

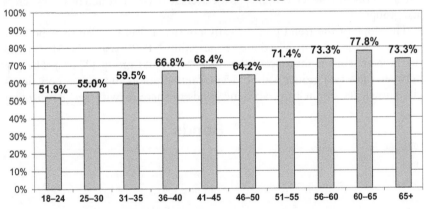

Figure 6.9 Financial literacy in France: knowledge on bank accounts

Source: Author's analysis of CFRC (2017) data

cases, a possible explanation is that bank accounts are used (almost) daily among financial products, which makes their users benefit in terms of a learning by doing process. Even if for those younger than 30 a response rate – not far from 50% – suggests that there is not still a deep understanding about the functioning and the use of this (essential) financial product, the results are much more encouraging than the ones presented before. In the case of those older than 50 the scores above 70% of correct answers can be considered a more than reasonable level of financial literacy about bank accounts.

Results from the financial literacy scores about 'payments' in the different age groups (Figure 6.10) show some similarities with the ones on 'bank accounts'. Knowledge about payment tools and services increases from the young to the older age groups, even if the trend is not so positive as in the previous case. The gap between the lowest score (41.5% 18–24 years-old group) and the highest (59.6% 60–65 years-old group) is not small, but the differences between other age groups are not big enough to support any relevant issue across age groups.

With the analysis of financial literacy on 'loans and debts' (Figure 6.11) a positive trend between age groups comes out, as in the case of 'bank accounts' and

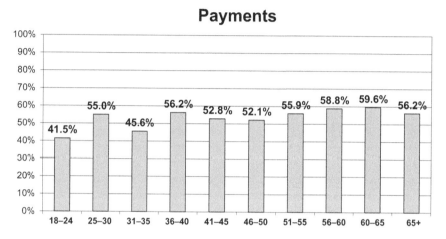

Figure 6.10 Financial literacy in France: knowledge on payments

Source: Author's analysis of CFRC (2017) data

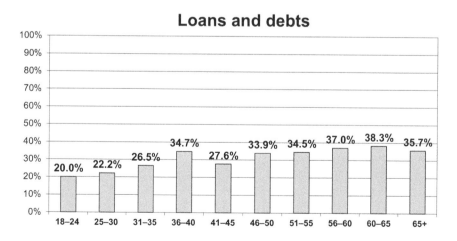

Figure 6.11 Financial literacy in France: knowledge on loans and debts

Source: Author's analysis of CFRC (2017) data

'inflation'. The 56–60 and 60–65 year-olds are the most knowledgeable groups, while those younger than 30s are once more the group with the lowest scores. In particular those 18–24 years old were able to answer correctly (on average) only one question of five. A similar score is the one of the 25–30 years old (22.2%). As in other areas of knowledge, none of the age group scored above 40%.

An interesting result is the one about financial literacy on 'retirement and insurance' (Figure 6.12). In this area of knowledge the youngest scored better than the rest of the sample. The top performers are the 25–30 years-old group (27.2%) and the 18–24 years-old group (25.7%), while the last two age groups scored 19.6% (60–65 years old) and 19.3% (65+), which is just a bit more than the lowest score of 19.1% achieved by those aged 51–55. It could be noted that the lower volatility of the financial literacy scores for the youngest age groups compared with the volatility of the oldest ones can explain part of the story. The fact that the average score for the whole sample in the 'retirement and insurance' area is only 21% and the evidence that there are only 6 percentage points between the extreme scores should probably stop any additional comment and stress how this area of knowledge represents a critical issue in the case of France.

The great volatility of the financial literacy scores between age groups, especially for the oldest groups, makes an analysis of the correlation between scores related to different areas of knowledge quite interesting (Table 6.1).

Keeping in mind that the scores from each area of knowledge are based on five questions, and that the sum of these questions creates the overall score, the positive but sometimes not really high correlation indices between the topic-based scores and the overall score suggest the presence of sharp differences about how much people know in various financial areas. This hypothesis is confirmed by the analysis of the one-to-one correlation between the single topic based scores in the ten areas of knowledge. The most correlated topics are the ones related with the financial markets. Financial literacy on 'stock Investments'

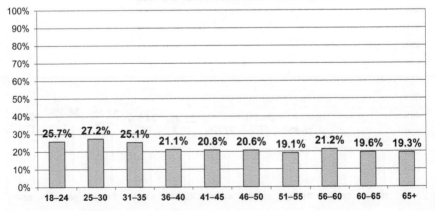

Figure 6.12 Financial literacy in France: knowledge on retirement and insurance

Source: Author's analysis of CFRC (2017) data

Table 6.1 Correlation between financial literacy scores (overall score, and the ten scores on single areas of knowledge)

	FL_OVERALL	FL_Interest rates	FL_Inflation	FL_Mortgages	FL_Diversification	FL_Bonds	FL_Bank accounts	FL_Payments	FL_Stock investments	FL_Loans and debts	FL_Retirement and insurance
FL_OVERALL	1										
FL_Interest rates	0.57	1									
FL_Inflation	0.69	0.42	1								
FL_Mortgages	0.56	0.26	0.34	1							
FL_Diversification	0.70	0.26	0.38	0.31	1						
FL_Bonds	0.43	0.09	0.10	0.15	0.37	1					
FL_Bank accounts	0.55	0.30	0.40	0.22	0.23	−0.07	1				
FL_Payments	0.51	0.20	0.33	0.15	0.22	0.10	0.38	1			
FL_Stock investments	0.54	0.21	0.22	0.23	0.44	0.38	0.05	0.09	1		
FL_Loans and debts	0.61	0.27	0.30	0.31	0.35	0.18	0.35	0.27	0.28	1	
FL_Retirement and insurance	0.44	0.07	0.09	0.21	0.36	0.33	0.03	0.09	0.35	0.20	1

Source: Author's analysis of CFRC (2017) data

has a correlation of 0.44 with the financial literacy on 'diversification'. Knowledge on 'stock investments' is correlated with knowledge on 'bonds' (0.38). These areas of knowledge seem to be not correlated with knowledge about 'bank accounts' and 'payments', which are instead correlated with each other (0.38). In the case of financial literacy on 'bank accounts' and 'bonds' the correlation is not only pretty close to zero, but shows even a negative sign (−0.07).

The correlation analysis suggests that French adults do not show the same level of knowledge on different financial topics. These results confirm the need to address financial literacy by stressing the content of the item used to assess financial literacy as well as the need to deal with a reasonable number of items.

6.3 The determinants of financial literacy in France

The hypothesis that financial literacy on different topics is not equally distributed among the population was tested by a set of regression models where a set of socio-demographic characteristics (age, gender, education, income) has been used to regress each financial literacy score of the study (the overall score and each of the ten topic-based scores).

Table 6.2 shows some descriptive statistics of the socio-demographic variables, while in the next table (Table 6.3) the results of the regression models are summarized.

Table 6.2 Descriptive statistics of the French sample

	#	%
Age		
18–24	67	13.0%
25–30	64	12.4%
31–35	43	8.3%
36–40	53	10.3%
41–45	50	9.7%
46–50	33	6.4%
51–55	44	8.5%
56–60	33	6.4%
60–65	46	8.9%
65+	84	16.2%
Gender		
Male	243	47.0%
Female	263	50.9%
n.a.	11	2.1%
Education		
Primary (or less)	37	7.1%
High school ("Collège BEPC")	112	21.6%
High school ("Lycée BAC")	116	22.4%
High school ("Études supérieures BTS")	72	13.9%
University ("Diplôme universitaire – Licence, M1")	89	17.1%
University ("Diplôme de troisième cycle – M2, Doctorat")	71	13.7%
"Grandes Ecoles"	16	3.1%
n.a.	6	1.2%
Income		
Less than 500€ each month	48	9.1%
Between 500€ and 750€ each month	45	8.5%
Between 750€ and 1,000€ each month	67	12.6%
Between 1,000€ and 1,500€ each month	126	23.8%
Between 1,500€ and 2,000€ each month	86	16.2%
Between 2,000€ and 3,000€ each month	74	14.0%
Between 3,000€ and 4,000€ each month	44	8.3%
More than 4,000€ each month	18	3.4%
n.a.	11	2.1%
Total	**519**	**100%**

Source: Author's analysis of CFRC (2017) data

The results from the regression model where the overall score (the one based on 50 items) was used as a measure of financial literacy show that financial literacy in France differs when the respondents belong to different **age groups**. Using the youngest group (18–24 years old) as a reference point, all the 35+ groups show statistically significant differences from the reference group. This is true for all of the seven 35+ age groups, and the value of the coefficients tends to increase when the age of the group increases. The (positive) effect of age on the financial literacy score is quite consistent when the overall score is replaced

Table 6.3 Results from regression models on financial literacy scores

	Total (50 items)		Interest rates (1|2|3|4|5)		Inflation (1|2|3|4|5)		Mortgages (1|2|3|4|5)		Investments (1|2|3|4|5)		Bonds (1|2|3|4|5)		Bank accounts (1|2|3|4|5)		Payments (1|2|3|4|5)		Savings and investments (1|2|3|4|5)		Loans and debts (1|2|3|4|5)		Retirement and insurance (1|2|3|4|5)	
	Coef.	p-value	Coef.	p-value	Coef.	p-value	Coef.	p-value	Coef.	p-value	Coef.	p-value	Coef.	p-value	Coef.	p-value	Coef.	p-value	Coef.	p-value	Coef.	p-value
Age (years)																						
18–24	(Ref. group)		(Ref. group)		(Ref. group)		(Ref. group)		(Ref. group)		(Ref. group)		(Ref. group)		(Ref. group)		(Ref. group)		(Ref. group)		(Ref. group)	
25–30	0.88	0.505	0.23	0.495	0.04	0.901	−0.13	0.707	0.10	0.760	0.04	0.909	0.25	0.459	0.52	0.125	0.04	0.913	0.35	0.297	−0.35	0.304
31–35	1.33	0.369	0.45	0.248	0.00	0.994	−0.23	0.535	0.20	0.599	−0.39	0.339	0.69	*0.066**	0.34	0.363	−0.14	0.723	0.36	0.351	−0.19	0.621
36–40	**3.57**	**0.010****	**0.73**	**0.036****	0.39	0.264	0.06	0.861	0.53	0.133	0.08	0.833	**0.93**	**0.008****	**1.20**	**0.001****	−0.18	0.633	**0.90**	**0.013****	−0.31	0.385
41–45	**3.46**	**0.014****	0.23	0.521	**0.82**	**0.021****	0.20	0.580	**0.60**	**0.087***	−0.26	0.507	**1.18**	**0.001****	**1.06**	**0.004****	0.26	0.468	0.56	0.125	−0.56	0.131
46–50	**3.27**	**0.040***	0.19	0.637	0.37	0.361	−0.21	0.608	0.52	0.196	−0.12	0.783	**1.05**	**0.011****	**0.98**	**0.020****	0.35	0.386	**1.21**	**0.003****	−0.50	0.242
51–55	**4.73**	**0.001****	0.37	0.328	**0.66**	**0.071***	0.50	0.186	**0.89**	**0.018****	0.33	0.400	**1.31**	**0.001****	**1.17**	**0.002****	0.04	0.922	**1.16**	**0.001****	−0.38	0.322
56–60	**6.19**	**0.000*****	**1.08**	**0.010****	**1.63**	**0.000*****	0.39	0.348	0.70	0.107	−0.70	0.155	**1.73**	**0.000*****	**1.56**	**0.000*****	0.61	0.148	**1.22**	**0.005****	−0.25	0.559
60–65	**5.75**	**0.000*****	**1.06**	**0.008****	**1.39**	**0.000*****	0.14	0.720	**1.02**	**0.008****	−0.21	0.607	**1.54**	**0.000*****	**1.35**	**0.000*****	−0.65	0.117	**1.50**	**0.000*****	−0.57	0.157
65+	**6.55**	**0.000*****	**0.86**	**0.014****	**1.30**	**0.000*****	**0.73**	**0.035***	**1.47**	**0.000*****	−0.16	0.661	**1.45**	**0.000*****	**1.24**	**0.000*****	−0.02	0.948	**1.24**	**0.000*****	−0.29	0.404
Gender																						
Female	(Ref. group)		(Ref. group)		(Ref. group)		(Ref. group)		(Ref. group)		(Ref. group)		(Ref. group)		(Ref. group)		(Ref. group)		(Ref. group)		(Ref. group)	
Male	**1.89**	**0.006****	**0.65**	**0.000*****	**0.30**	*0.088**	**0.37**	*0.033**	**0.51**	**0.004****	**0.70**	**0.000*****	**−0.41**	**0.019****	0.02	0.890	**0.54**	**0.003****	0.00	0.989	**0.35**	**0.053***

(Continued)

Table 6.3 (Continued)

	Total (50 items)		Interest rates (1|2|3|4|5)		Inflation (1|2|3|4|5)		Mortgages (1|2|3|4|5)		Investments (1|2|3|4|5)		Bonds (1|2|3|4|5)		Bank accounts (1|2|3|4|5)		Payments (1|2|3|4|5)		Savings and investments (1|2|3|4|5)		Loans and debts (1|2|3|4|5)		Retirement and insurance (1|2|3|4|5)	
	Coef.	p-value	Coef.	p-value	Coef.	p-value	Coef.	p-value	Coef.	p-value	Coef.	p-value	Coef.	p-value	Coef.	p-value	Coef.	p-value	Coef.	p-value	Coef.	p-value
Education																						
Primary (or less)	2.28	(Ref. group)	0.37	(Ref. group)	0.57	(Ref. group)	0.13	(Ref. group)	0.26	(Ref. group)	−0.32	(Ref. group)	0.90	(Ref. group)	0.63	(Ref. group)	0.51	(Ref. group)	−0.02	(Ref. group)	−0.20	(Ref. group)
High school ("Collège BEPC")	3.85	0.099*	0.76	0.296	0.90	0.105	0.11	0.710	0.99	0.453	0.01	0.417	0.98	0.012**	0.49	0.086*	0.44	0.202	0.03	0.961	−0.07	0.581
High school ("Lycée BAC")	6.31	0.008**	0.97	0.036**	1.47	0.015**	0.62	0.758	1.65	0.007**	0.42	0.971	0.78	0.009**	0.49	0.202	1.17	0.291	0.71	0.946	0.10	0.860
University ("Études supérieures" BTS)	6.80	0.000***	1.54	0.015**	1.36	0.000***	0.44	0.111	1.54	0.000***	0.27	0.329	1.20	0.054*	0.89	0.232	1.33	0.007**	0.13	0.076*	0.37	0.796
University ("Diplôme universitaire – Licence, M1")	6.65	0.000***	1.39	0.000***	1.42	0.001**	0.18	0.249	1.72	0.000***	0.03	0.525	1.23	0.002**	0.63	0.026**	1.25	0.002**	0.62	0.742	0.40	0.350
University ("Diplôme de troisième cycle – M2, Doctorat")	8.72	0.000***	1.42	0.001**	1.48	0.000***	0.12	0.659	1.98	0.000***	0.52	0.952	0.95	0.004**	0.81	0.137	1.82	0.006**	1.77	0.139	0.71	0.339
"Grandes Écoles"		0.000***		0.016**		0.012**		0.831		0.001**		0.407		0.101		0.189		0.002**		0.001**		0.214

Income (monthly base)

In each cell the regression coefficient is given first and the (italic) p-value below it. All eleven models use "Less than 500€" as the reference category.

Income (monthly base)	(Ref. group)	(Ref. group)	(Ref. group)	(Ref. group)	(Ref. group)	(Ref. group)	(Ref. group)	(Ref. group)	(Ref. group)	(Ref. group)	(Ref. group)
Less than 500€	(Ref. group)	(Ref. group)	(Ref. group)	(Ref. group)	(Ref. group)	(Ref. group)	(Ref. group)	(Ref. group)	(Ref. group)	(Ref. group)	(Ref. group)
500€ to <750€	-0.38 / *0.799*	0.27 / *0.468*	0.18 / *0.635*	0.07 / *0.858*	-0.53 / *0.171*	-0.23 / *0.599*	-0.06 / *0.870*	-0.14 / *0.720*	-0.01 / *0.983*	-0.20 / *0.590*	-0.31 / *0.447*
750€ to <1,000€	-0.04 / *0.980*	0.02 / *0.945*	0.22 / *0.530*	0.07 / *0.847*	-0.22 / *0.531*	-0.12 / *0.969*	-0.47 / *0.709*	0.07 / *0.708*	-0.13 / *0.739*	-0.12 / *0.772*	-0.32 / *0.384*
1,000€ to <1,500€	-0.86 / *0.499*	-0.24 / *0.446*	0.00 / *0.997*	0.20 / *0.542*	0.00 / *0.483*	0.01 / *0.731*	-0.30 / *0.149*	0.12 / *0.834*	0.13 / *0.702*	-0.16 / *0.720*	-0.15 / *0.649*
1,500€ to <2,000€	0.54 / *0.692*	-0.10 / *0.764*	0.48 / *0.177*	0.57 / *0.100*	-0.38 / *0.998*	0.43 / *0.972*	-0.34 / *0.393*	-0.05 / *0.727*	0.52 / *0.714*	0.20 / *0.659*	-0.15 / *0.671*
2,000€ to <3,000€	0.75 / *0.590*	-0.23 / *0.517*	0.47 / *0.192*	0.67 / ***0.059***	0.38 / *0.268*	/ *0.252*	/ *0.354*	-0.05 / *0.887*	0.37 / *0.161*	-0.19 / *0.586*	0.03 / *0.935*
3,000€ to <4,000€	1.29 / *0.425*	-0.66 / *0.116*	0.36 / *0.392*	0.94 / *0.024*	0.70 / *0.348*	**0.81** / ***0.064****	**-0.73** / ***0.089****	0.30 / *0.913*	/ *0.398*	0.71 / *0.655*	0.61 / *0.152*
4,000€+	**4.10** / ***0.058****	0.08 / *0.888*	0.59 / *0.347*	**1.10** / ***0.040*****	/ *0.225*	**1.12** / ***0.058****	0.19 / *0.746*	/ *0.586*	**1.42** / ***0.015*****	/ *0.217*	0.44 / *0.461*
Constant	**10.24** / ***0.000******										
Obs.	493	493	493	493	493	493	493	493	493	493	493
Adj. R-squared	0.1407	0.0332	0.0387	0.0254	0.0535	0.0459	0.0336	0.024	0.0593	0.0341	0.0284

* = p-value < .10; ** = p-value < .05; *** = p-value < 0.001

Source: Author's analysis of CFRC (2017) data

by the topic-based scores. That is true in the case of 'payments' and 'loans and debts', while in the case of 'bank accounts' an age effect exists even for the 31–35 years-old group. When financial literacy is assessed by items related to other areas of knowledge (e.g. 'interest rates', and 'inflation') the role of age in explaining financial literacy is not significant for all the age groups, even if results are quite persistent for those older than 55. The fact that none of the age group is relevant in explaining financial knowledge on 'savings and investments' and 'retirement and planning' reminds us that financial literacy can change a lot when it is assessed using items related to different topics.

The **gender effect** is quite clear. Males in France tend to know more about finance than females. This result is evident when financial literacy is assessed by a broad measure such as the overall score, but remains true even for seven out of ten topic-based financial literacy scores. What is interesting is that the common gender effect in favour of males in France becomes a "reverse gender effect" when financial knowledge is measured on 'bank accounts'. At the same time, the coefficients for the variable 'gender (= male)' for 'payments' and 'loans and debts' are both close to zero and not statistically significant.

Results on education are quite interesting. If in other countries the role of **education** in explaining financial literacy was very poor, in the case of France it seems that education matters. The overall score is affected by the educational level. Using the lowest group (primary school) as reference point, all the other educational levels increase the estimation of the financial literacy score. Looking at the value of the coefficients it is easy to note how university levels are related with values of coefficients that are almost double those of the lower educational levels. What is interesting is that the explanatory power of education remains even when single topics are used to assess financial literacy. With the only exceptions of 'bonds', 'loans and debts', and 'retirements and insurance', in all the other cases most of the educational levels make a difference in explaining financial literacy.

Results from **income** confirm results from other countries. Income is far from representing an explanatory variable of the financial literacy of individuals, with the only exception being the above 4,000€ income group, whose respondents tend to show more financial knowledge than others. However, even for this income group, results remain valid only in three out of ten cases when financial literacy is assessed on specific topics.

6.4 Conclusions

The average correct response rate of 39% for the 50 items on financial literacy highlights how financial literacy in France is low. A comparison with other countries (the UK 43%, Italy 47%, Germany 49%) stresses how the lack of financial knowledge in France is even bigger than in others. The fact that 'bonds' and 'stock investments' are the two areas of knowledge with the lowest scores represents a similarity with other countries, but the average scores equal to 19% ('bonds') and 20% ('stock investments') show a gap of financial literacy compared with other countries (e.g. the scores on 'bonds' and 'stock investments' in Germany are equal to 24% and 34%, while in Italy are 26% and 36%). The fact that only in three cases out of ten the topic-based scores are on average above 50% (one correct answer for every wrong answer) is other evidence that financial literacy in France is particularly low.

The differences between France and other countries exist even when the gender effect is taken into account. If in France, as in other countries, males tend to score better than females, in France the gender gap is smaller than in other countries. When one looks at the overall score, males scored on average at 42% and females at 36%.

Data on financial literacy in different age groups show how in most of the cases there is a flat trend, with individuals who belong to different age groups scoring in a pretty similar way (e.g. 'interest rates', 'mortgages', 'diversification', 'bonds', 'stock investments', 'retirement and insurance'). In other cases a positive trend that suggests how financial literacy tends to increase by age was found (e.g. 'bank accounts', 'loans and debts').

The fragmentation of financial literacy between different areas of knowledge is shown by the correlation analysis, with the highest value equal to 0.44 (correlation between 'stock investments' and 'diversification'), and cases with correlation indices close to zero (e.g. correlations between 'bank accounts' and 'bonds', 'bank accounts' and 'retirement and insurance', and correlation between 'interest rates' and 'bonds').

Results from the regression analysis confirm that financial literacy tends to increase by age – especially for those older than 50 – and that males usually are more financially literate than females. If the evidence that education is positively related with financial literacy (more than in other countries) is an interesting result, the fact that income fails to be related with financial literacy confirms results from other countries.

Note

1 For details about the questionnaire and the CFRC research project see the description presented in the §4.2 Data.

Reference

CFRC- Consumer Finance Research Center (2017). Survey on Consumers' Financial Literacy in France. www.consumer-finance.org/

7 Financial literacy in Italy

7.1 Introduction

This chapter analyzes financial literacy in Italy. Using data from a survey of the Consumer Finance Research Center (CFRC) the answers to a set of 50 multiple choice questions will be used to develop various measures of financial literacy that will differ from each other in the number of items and the financial topics taken into account. Because the structure of the questionnaire and the contents of the questions are the same used by the CFRC to collect data in other countries, some comparisons between the Italian results and the others will be possible.

The target of the survey is the Italian adult population (18+ years old), and the sample size, after controlling for blank or incomplete answers, is 500 observations. The analysis of financial literacy in Italy will start from the presentation of several descriptive statistics that will take into account the differences between genders and age groups. In the second part a set of regression models will help to figure out how financial literacy changes according to the socio-demographic profile of the individuals.

7.2 The characteristics of financial literacy in Italy

The analysis of financial literacy in Italy is based on data from a survey organized in 2015 by the CFRC that collected data on 500 Italian residents with the support of a survey sampling institute.[1]

The structure of the questionnaire used by the CFRC follows the standards adopted in other countries and presented in §4.2 of this study.

The average financial literacy score, based on the sum of correct answers to the whole set of available items (50 questions), is equal to 47% on a 0–100 scale.[2] So, on average, the respondents failed more than one question of two on the questionnaire. In Figure 7.1 a summary of the response rate to the full set of questions (the overall score), and to the subset of questions related to single topics, is provided. Break down of the data according to the gender of the respondents is available too. Looking at the response rates for men and women, there is confirmation of previous studies on financial literacy about the presence of

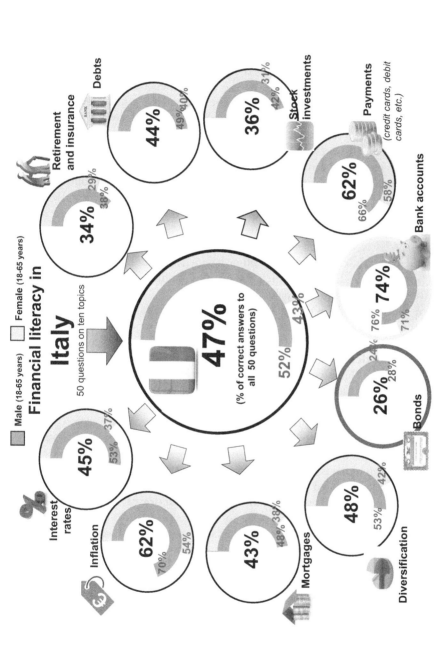

Figure 7.1 Financial literacy in Italy: break down and gender analysis

Source: Author analysis of CFRC data (2015)

a gender gap. Men scored on average 9 (percentage) points better than women (men 52% vs. women 43%). However, this overall result needs to be interpreted looking at the single areas of knowledge.

The scores, based on the sum of correct answers to the 50 financial literacy questions, have been standardized on a 0–100 scale both for the general score (based on all 50 questions) and for each single area's score (based on five questions each). Looking at the scores – the general one and the ones from single areas of knowledge – it is clear how the average general score (47%) is not representative of the financial literacy of the respondents when specific topics are taken into account. The area of knowledge on 'bank accounts' is the one with the highest average score, with 74% of correct answers on average. This means that the Italian residents gave on average a correct answer three times of four, which represents a much better score than the overall average. The gender gap remains, but there is only a 5% difference between male (76%) and female (71%). The hypothesis that financial products that are more frequently used by consumers are the ones where financial literacy is high, thanks to daily use and learning by doing, is confirmed. If we refer to the 'payments' area, the average score of 62% is still much more than the general score of 47%. Knowledge about debit cards, credit cards, and other payment facilities seems to be better than in other areas. In this case the gender gap is confirmed, with males scoring on average 8% better than females.

On the other side, when knowledge about 'diversification' in saving and investments and knowledge about 'stock investments' and 'bonds' are tested, the average scores fall down with results that are much lower than the overall average. **Knowledge about 'bonds' seems to be the most critical area of knowledge.** The average score of 26% means that the respondents have chosen a correct answer only one of four times. The average score for 'stock investments' is 36%, and it is only when the analysis involved 'diversification' of investments the average score approaches the overall mean, with a score of 48%.

Knowledge about 'debts' and 'mortgages' is almost in line with the mean score, with respectively an average score of 44% and 43%. Even in this case the gender gap remains, and it is easy to check how in each of the ten areas of knowledge males scored better than females. **'Retirement and insurance' is another source of worry, with an average score of 34%.** This lack of knowledge is particularly relevant due to the pension reforms that completely changed the Italian pension system in the last 15 years. The chance that people did not develop a (basic) knowledge on retirement needs because they are still referring to the generous Italian welfare state of the past (which does not represent anymore a reliable source of income in retirement age) risks negatively affecting the future quality of life in retirement age for an entire generation. As with other financial needs that are based on long-term planning, the retirement saving needs risk being underestimated by individuals, and their lack of savings risks being exacerbated by ignorance about the functioning of the new system.

A break down of financial literacy by age represents another interesting perspective. The average overall score for each of the age ranges is reported in Figure 7.2.

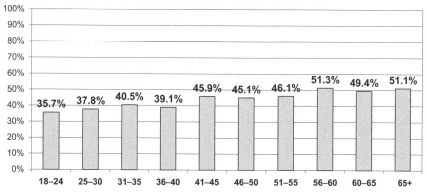

Figure 7.2 Overall score of financial literacy in Italy: break down by age

Source: Author analysis of CFRC data (2015)

Analysis of the response rate between different age groups shows a positive relationship between age and financial literacy. While in previous studies on financial literacy results show declining financial literacy for the last age groups (elderly), this is not the case of Italy. People older than 60 seems to show financial literacy that is comparable with that of other age groups. At the same time, the better financial literacy of middle-aged groups compared with the younger ones confirms results from previous studies. This result is coherent with the hypothesis that financial literacy develops with experience, with the consequence that young people are less knowledgeable than others because they have not had the chance to learn from previous financial events.

The analysis of the overall score deserves to be completed by an analysis of financial literacy in single areas of knowledge. Knowledge on 'interest rates' by different age groups is reported in Figure 7.3.

The last age groups (more than 55 years old) show the highest financial literacy scores. This result is coherent with the overall score and highlights the knowledge gap of Italians. On the other hand, the gap between young groups (18–24 and 25–30) and the others is less evident when financial literacy is measured referring to interest rates. If a gap with the last groups remains, the young respondents do not differ so much from the middle-aged groups, and in some cases perform even better (e.g. 31–35 and 36–40).

Financial literacy about 'inflation' (Figure 7.4) is more in line with the overall score, with a positive relationship between age and financial literacy.

The average response rate (62%) shows that knowledge about inflation is more developed than in other areas.

The differences by age almost disappear when financial literacy refers to 'mortgages' (Figure 7.5)

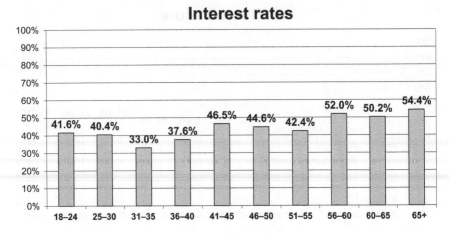

Figure 7.3 Financial literacy in Italy: knowledge on interest rates

Source: Author analysis of CFRC data (2015)

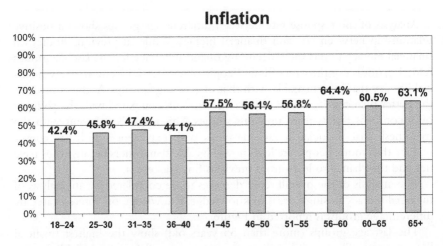

Figure 7.4 Financial literacy in Italy: knowledge on inflation

Source: Author analysis of CFRC data (2015)

All the age groups scored within a range of 10% with the lowest response rate 38.1% (31–35 years-old group) and the highest 47.5% (65+ years-old group). The fact that a mortgage is a financial product related with housing needs and that there is a high homeownership rate in Italy[3] helps to explain this small gap between the financial literacy scores of the age groups. The evidence that even young respondents answer on average like adults about mortgages can be explained by a transmission of knowledge from parents and other

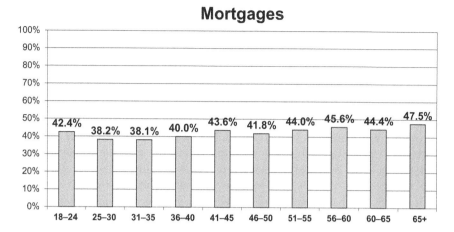

Figure 7.5 Financial literacy in Italy: knowledge on mortgages

Source: Author analysis of CFRC data (2015)

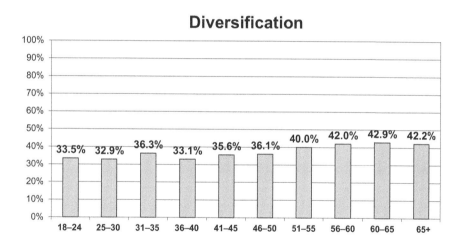

Figure 7.6 Financial literacy in Italy: knowledge on diversification

Source: Author analysis of CFRC data (2015)

family members, when (for instance) the need to pay instalments on a current mortgage or the recommendation to plan to buy a house or another real estate property is part of family conversations.

Financial knowledge on 'diversification', referring to contents like the diversification of investments, the functioning of mutual funds, and the role of the time horizon in the selection of investment products (Figure 7.6), is below the average ('diversification' 36% vs. overall score 47%), and confirms the better knowledge of the last age groups (older than 50s) compared with the others. For those younger than 30 the response rate falls to one (correct answer) of three. That means a lack of knowledge on diversification that is more serious than the average overall score, which is not even all that exciting itself.

The evidence that investment related issues are the most critical topics for the Italian respondents is confirmed by the questions on 'bonds' (Figure 7.7), where the average response rate is 26%, with some age groups that scored below 23% (the 51–55 years-old group scored 22.0%, the 65+ 22.5%). Against the trend of other areas' scores, knowledge on bonds sees the young groups score better than the elderly, even if the differences in the response rates are not significant.

Looking at the results of financial literacy on 'stock investments' (Figure 7.8), the average score of 36% confirms the difficulty of Italians with investment related topics. What is interesting is the wide gap between age groups, with the 18–24 year-old respondents achieving an average score of 22%, which is just half of the score for other categories (e.g. 56–60 and 65+). If the lack of knowledge on stock market investment products in youths can be explained by a lack of experience (due to the lack of capital to be invested), an average score of one of five can be critical even in a long-term planning perspective, because a lack of knowledge on financial risks, risk measures (e.g. ratings), and the main differences between bonds and stocks is not just related to investment of savings.

The need to differentiate the assessment of financial literacy in different measures that address different topics is evident when the results on bonds, stocks, and investments are compared with the results based on the functioning of 'bank accounts' (Figure 7.9).

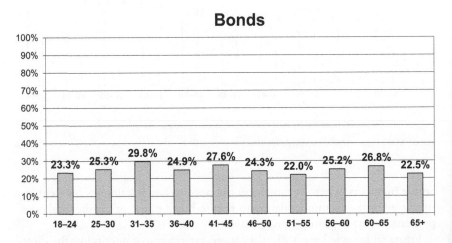

Figure 7.7 Financial literacy in Italy: knowledge on bonds

Source: Author analysis of CFRC data (2015)

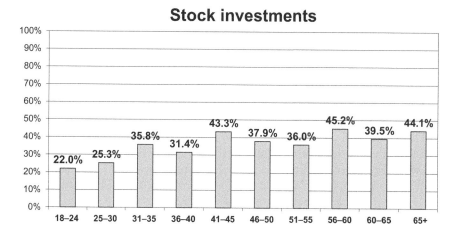

Figure 7.8 Financial literacy in Italy: knowledge on stock investments

Source: Author analysis of CFRC data (2015)

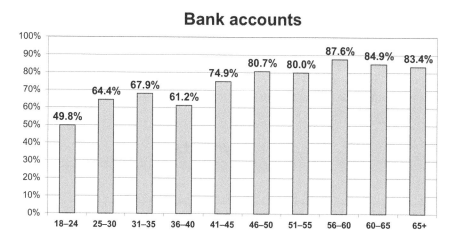

Figure 7.9 Financial literacy in Italy: knowledge on bank accounts

Source: Author analysis of CFRC data (2015)

The scores are above 80% in five age groups of ten. The positive relationship between age and financial literacy is confirmed. According to the World Bank statistics of 2014,[4] the percentage of 15+ year-old Italian residents with a bank account at a financial institution (e.g. banks or other financial institutions) is 87.3%.[5] This rate of financial inclusion changes when different age groups are taken into account. Only 60% of 15–24 year-olds have a bank account in Italy,[6] while this percentage grows to 91.5% for those older than 25. The low banking rate of youths can explain the gap of knowledge about the functioning of bank accounts.

Data about financial literacy on 'payments' (Figure 7.10) show some similarities with other scores related with frequent use financial products (e.g. bank accounts). The response rate does not go beyond the value of 60.6% (65+ group), with some age groups that scored between 40% and 45% (e.g. 15–24 years-old group 43.7%, 25–30 years-old group 42.2%). The positive correlation between age and financial literacy is confirmed one more time.

Financial literacy on 'loans and debt' (Figure 7.11) not only confirms the financial literacy trend of increasing with age, but the slope of this trend line seems to be higher than in previous cases. From 31.4% of the first age group (18–24 years old), financial knowledge on borrowing increases up to the last age group (65+), which scored on average at 55.9%.

The last area of knowledge concerns 'retirement and insurance' (Figure 7.12). The questions on pension funds, long-term planning, and insurance policies seem to be another critical area of knowledge for the respondents. The 34% average score is the second lowest score, after the bond area (26%). The possible long-term negative consequences of low financial literacy on retirement and insurance have been already stressed. The evidence that this gap of knowledge is bigger for the younger age groups represents an additional source of concern.

The break down of the overall financial literacy score into ten scores based on the ten financial topics of the survey has shown how there are substantial differences in the financial literacy scores of individuals when different topics are taken into account. The evidence that people develop more financial literacy in some areas of knowledge than others is interesting and suggests that we

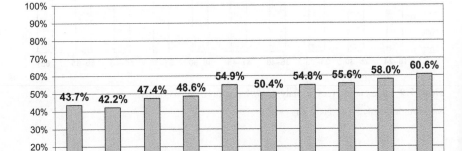

Figure 7.10 Financial literacy in Italy: knowledge on payments

Source: Author analysis of CFRC data (2015)

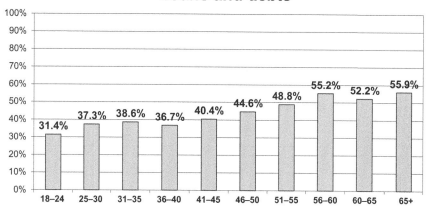

Figure 7.11 Financial literacy in Italy: knowledge on loans and debts
Source: Author analysis of CFRC data (2015)

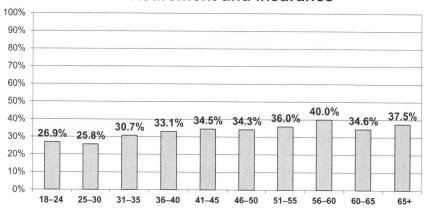

Figure 7.12 Financial literacy in Italy: knowledge on retirement and insurance
Source: Author analysis of CFRC data (2015)

can better understand the connection between these different financial topics by an analysis of correlation.

Table 7.1 summarizes the correlation between the financial literacy scores.

The correlation between the overall score and the single area scores (column one) is obviously affected by the fact that the five questions of each area are part of the 50 questions of the overall score. However, a low correlation between a

Table 7.1 Correlation between financial literacy scores (overall score, and the ten scores on single areas of knowledge)

	FL_OVERALL	FL_Interest rates	FL_Inflation	FL_Mortgages	FL_Diversification	FL_Bonds	FL_Bank accounts	FL_Payments	FL_Stock investments	FL_Loans and debts	FL_Retirement and insurance
FL_OVERALL	1										
FL_Interest rates	0.55	1									
FL_Inflation	0.70	0.35	1								
FL_Mortgages	0.55	0.27	0.32	1							
FL_Diversification	0.65	0.27	0.43	0.25	1						
FL_Bonds	0.46	0.14	0.21	0.24	0.28	1					
FL_Bank accounts	0.66	0.25	0.43	0.25	0.33	0.15	1				
FL_Payments	0.58	0.23	0.36	0.25	0.31	0.17	0.42	1			
FL_Stock investments	0.70	0.29	0.42	0.29	0.41	0.30	0.35	0.32	1		
FL_Loans and debts	0.73	0.33	0.44	0.37	0.44	0.24	0.52	0.29	0.47	1	
FL_Retirement and insurance	0.64	0.26	0.37	0.21	0.43	0.31	0.26	0.31	0.50	0.40	1

Source: Author analysis of CFRC data (2015)

subset of questions and the full set of financial literacy questions can be useful to identify some areas that could be out of the common knowledge of individuals. Analysis of the correlation between the ten topic-based financial literacy scores can shed more light on the presence of some macro-areas of knowledge that could overlap, or, on the contrary, the analysis could show that these ten areas are not correlated and refer to quite different financial needs.

The maximum correlation is 0.52 and concerns the financial literacy scores on 'bank accounts' and 'loans and debts'. The fact that these are both bank products, and that access to credit is usually connected with the presence of a bank account, can be reasonable explanations behind this high correlation. At the same time, a 0.50 correlation exists between 'retirement and insurance' and 'stock investments'. In this case it is the common long-term perspective of both retirement and investment needs that can be an explanation. The fact that 'stock investments' and 'loans and debts' represent two different areas of knowledge, related with two different kinds of financial needs, would support the hypothesis of a low correlation between these two financial literacy measures. Instead, the 0.47 correlation supports the hypothesis that there is an attitude to develop financial literacy across different topics and not in single 'niches' of competences.

If we look at the big picture, we cannot arrive to the conclusion that there is a common basis for financial literacy and that those who are skilled in some areas can be considered skilled even in others. For instance, knowledge on payment tools (e.g. credit cards, debit cards, bank transfers, etc.) is on average low correlated with other financial literacy areas, with the only exception of 'bank accounts' (0.42). The lowest correlation between single topic scores is between 'payments' and 'bonds' (0.17).

7.3 The determinants of financial literacy in Italy

To test the hypothesis that people develop financial literacy in different areas of knowledge according to their need of knowledge, their attitudes, and their socio-demographic characteristics, a set of statistical analysis has been generated. For each measure of financial literacy – the overall score and the ten topic-based scores – a regression model has estimated the connections between financial literacy and the main socio-demographic characteristics of individuals like age, gender, education, and income. If financial literacy cannot be explained merely by these variables, they are useful to test whether financial literacy in single areas of knowledge is developed more by single groups of the population or if there are no differences between groups.

Table 7.2 shows some descriptive statistics of the sample variables.

Table 7.2 Descriptive statistics of the Italian sample

	#	%
Age		
18–24 years	49	9.7%
25–30 years	45	8.9%
31–35 years	43	8.5%
36–40 years	49	9.7%
41–45 years	55	10.9%
46–50 years	56	11.1%
51–55 years	51	10.1%
56–60 years	50	9.9%
60–65 years	41	8.2%
65+ years	64	12.7%
Gender		
Male	247	49.2%
Female	255	50.8%
Education		
Primary school	2	0.4%
Secondary school	58	11.5%
High school	211	41.9%
University (attendance – no degree)	80	15.9%
University (degree)	112	22.3%
Master or PhD	38	7.6%
n.a.	2	0.4%

(Continued)

Table 7.2 (Continued)

	#	%
Income		
Less than 500€ a month	65	12.9%
500€–749€ a month	25	5.0%
750€–1,000€ a month	42	8.3%
1,000€–1,499€ a month	108	21.5%
1,500€–1,999€ a month	84	16.7%
2,000€–2,999€ a month	65	12.9%
3,000€–3,999€ a month	1	0.2%
More than 4,000€ a month	39	7.8%
n.a.	74	14.7%
Total	**503**	**100%**

Source: Author analysis of CFRC data (2015)

Table 7.3 summarizes the results of 11 regression models (one for the overall score, plus one for each of the ten topic-based scores), where the financial literacy scores represent the dependent variables, and age, gender, education, and income work as independent variables.

For the overall score, which ranges between zero and 50, a linear regression model has been used. For the single topic scores, which are integer values with a range between zero and five, an order logistic regression model has been preferred.

Results about **age** in the case of the overall score show how there is **a clear difference between those younger than 40 and older than 40** in the sample. The younger age groups, which include the reference group (18–24 years old), are not statistically different in terms of financial literacy. On the contrary all those older than 40 (41–45, 46–50, 51–55, 55–60, 60–65, and 65+) seem to know more than the young groups. The values of the coefficients are pretty similar with only a small (positive) difference for the last groups of the sample. However, when financial literacy is addressed by single areas of knowledge, this result is confirmed only in the cases of 'inflation' and 'loans and debts', while in other cases there are only some age groups that scored differently from the 18–24 years-old reference group ('investments' and 'retirement and insurance'). In other cases there is no evidence that any group is statistically more knowledgeable than others ('interest rates', 'mortgages', and 'bonds').

The **gender effect** is a typical result in financial literacy studies. In the case of Italy too there is evidence that males score better than females. However, if in other countries there are some exceptions when single topics are taken into account, this is not the case of Italy, where males score better than females in every single case. This is confirmed both by the value of the coefficient for "male" in the case of the overall score (3.31) and by the evidence that the gender effect persists in all the regressions based on financial knowledge on single topics, except the case of 'bonds' and 'payments'.

Table 7.3 Results from regression models on financial literacy scores

	Total (50 items) (1|2|3|4|5)		Interest rates (1|2|3|4|5)		Inflation (1|2|3|4|5)		Mortgages (1|2|3|4|5)		Investments (1|2|3|4|5)		Bonds (1|2|3|4|5)		Bank accounts (1|2|3|4|5)		Payments (1|2|3|4|5)		Stock investments (1|2|3|4|5)		Loans and debts (1|2|3|4|5)		Retirement and insurance (1|2|3|4|5)	
	Coef.	p-value	Coef.	p-value	Coef.	p-value	Coef.	p-value	Coef.	p-value	Coef.	p-value	Coef.	p-value	Coef.	p-value	Coef.	p-value	Coef.	p-value	Coef.	p-value
Age (years)																						
18–24	(Ref. group)		(Ref. group)		(Ref. group)		(Ref. group)		(Ref. group)		(Ref. group)		(Ref. group)		(Ref. group)		(Ref. group)		(Ref. group)		(Ref. group)	
25–30	1.35	0.398	−0.13	0.751	0.72	0.085*	−0.06	0.879	0.03	0.944	0.12	0.774	.	.	−0.34	0.414	−0.10	0.815	0.58	0.177	−0.22	0.599
31–35	2.05	0.228	−0.99	0.026**	0.69	0.130	−0.41	0.349	0.36	0.423	0.37	0.398	.	.	0.21	0.637	0.52	0.252	0.87	0.051*	0.22	0.617
36–40	1.16	0.458	−0.50	0.229	0.43	0.309	−0.16	0.700	0.15	0.725	0.08	0.856	.	.	0.13	0.750	0.26	0.524	0.43	0.299	0.23	0.574
41–45	5.07	0.001**	0.21	0.597	1.44	0.001**	0.19	0.654	0.28	0.495	0.32	0.452	.	.	0.68	0.099*	1.11	0.007**	0.74	0.070*	0.50	0.218
46–50	5.69	0.000***	0.32	0.443	1.50	0.001**	−0.08	0.858	0.65	0.115	0.18	0.663	.	.	0.39	0.360	0.90	0.037**	1.34	0.001**	0.65	0.112
51–55	5.89	0.000***	−0.06	0.891	1.51	0.001**	0.24	0.568	1.01	0.020	0.29	0.498	.	.	0.55	0.198	0.67	0.119	1.58	0.000***	0.70	0.095*
56–60	6.81	0.000***	0.36	0.378	1.69	0.000***	−0.06	0.888	0.84	0.047**	0.09	0.835	.	.	0.72	0.084*	1.00	0.014**	1.87	0.000***	0.93	0.023**
60–65	5.48	0.001**	0.11	0.802	1.61	0.001**	−0.21	0.635	0.87	0.059*	0.17	0.698	.	.	1.00	0.029**	0.53	0.249	1.66	0.000***	0.27	0.540
65+	6.21	0.000***	0.10	0.809	1.70	0.000***	0.11	0.798	0.60	0.152	−0.15	0.718	.	.	1.24	0.005**	0.86	0.037**	2.01	0.000***	0.72	0.083*
Gender																						
Female	(Ref. group)		(Ref. group)		(Ref. group)		(Ref. group)		(Ref. group)		(Ref. group)		(Ref. group)		(Ref. group)		(Ref. group)		(Ref. group)		(Ref. group)	
Male	3.31	0.000***	0.77	0.000***	0.84	0.000***	0.46	0.014**	0.89	0.000***	0.29	0.127	.	.	0.13	0.494	0.48	0.011**	0.49	0.011**	0.61	0.001**

(Continued)

Table 7.3 (Continued)

	Total (50 items) (1|2|3|4|5)		Interest rates (1|2|3|4|5)		Inflation (1|2|3|4|5)		Mortgages (1|2|3|4|5)		Investments (1|2|3|4|5)		Bonds (1|2|3|4|5)		Bank accounts (1|2|3|4|5)		Payments (1|2|3|4|5)		Stock investments (1|2|3|4|5)		Loans and debts (1|2|3|4|5)		Retirement and insurance (1|2|3|4|5)	
	Coef.	p-value	Coef.	p-value	Coef.	p-value	Coef.	p-value	Coef.	p-value	Coef.	p-value	Coef.	p-value	Coef.	p-value	Coef.	p-value	Coef.	p-value	Coef.	p-value
Education																						
Primary school	(Ref. group)		(Ref. group)		(Ref. group)		(Ref. group)		(Ref. group)		(Ref. group)		(Ref. group)	.	(Ref. group)		(Ref. group)		(Ref. group)		(Ref. group)	
Secondary school	−3.98	0.572	−2.51	0.170	−1.09	0.556	−2.09	0.216	0.07	0.964	−3.50	0.038**	.	.	3.31	0.038**	−1.00	0.523	−0.24	0.882	1.40	0.384
High school	−0.95	0.892	−1.77	0.328	−0.71	0.701	−1.96	0.244	0.73	0.641	−3.02	0.072*	.	.	3.55	0.025*	−0.53	0.731	0.39	0.806	2.07	0.194
University (attendance – no degree)	0.43	0.951	−1.82	0.316	−0.54	0.771	−1.83	0.280	1.16	0.465	−2.69	0.110	.	.	4.02	0.012**	−0.18	0.908	0.55	0.729	2.20	0.171
University (degree)	1.46	0.835	−1.62	0.371	−0.57	0.757	−1.43	0.396	1.20	0.447	−2.64	0.116	.	.	4.00	0.012**	−0.06	0.969	0.83	0.605	2.54	0.113
Master or PhD	−2.47	0.727	−2.03	0.269	−1.17	0.530	−1.66	0.331	0.13	0.933	−2.52	0.137	.	.	3.54	0.027*	−0.64	0.684	0.36	0.823	2.01	0.217
Income (monthly base)																						
Less than 500€	(Ref. group)		(Ref. group)		(Ref. group)		(Ref. group)		(Ref. group)		(Ref. group)		(Ref. group)	.	(Ref. group)		(Ref. group)		(Ref. group)		(Ref. group)	
500€ to < 750€	−0.38	0.816	0.52	0.238	−0.24	0.567	−0.10	0.810	−0.29	0.518	−0.67	0.146	.	.	−0.34	0.453	0.46	0.290	0.14	0.751	0.05	0.907
750€ to < 1,000€	−2.22	0.118	0.04	0.904	−0.44	0.241	0.36	0.350	−0.73	0.056*	−0.42	0.256	.	.	−0.19	0.612	0.10	0.798	−0.58	0.118	−0.59	0.115

	(1)	(2)	(3)	(4)	(5)	(6)	(7)	(8)	(9)	(10)	(11)
1,000€ to <1,500€	-0.31	**0.57**	-0.03	0.39	-0.43	-0.11	.	0.18	0.47	**-0.51**	**-0.65**
1,500€ to <2,000€	*0.791* 0.83	***0.066***** **0.85**	*0.920* -0.04	*0.198* 0.36	*0.173* -0.32	*0.722* -0.03	.	*0.567* 0.02	*0.118* **0.68**	***0.092***** -0.14	***0.032***** -0.02
2,000€ to <3,000€	*0.510* 1.95	***0.012***** **1.20**	*0.913* -0.18	*0.270* **0.88**	*0.354* -0.08	*0.925* 0.10	.	*0.955* 0.55	***0.042***** **0.74**	*0.680* -0.30	*0.959* -0.14
3,000€ to <4,000€	*0.146* 1.94	***0.001***** **2.75**	*0.622* 0.91	***0.013***** -0.16	*0.826* -1.11	*0.783* -0.44	.	*0.126* **2.30**	***0.038***** **3.22**	*0.401* -1.96	*0.690* -1.90
4,000€+	*0.782* **3.37**	*0.130* **0.93**	*0.622* 0.37	*0.919* **1.08**	*0.485* 0.05	*0.773* 0.06	.	*0.364* 0.51	***0.087***** **0.90**	*0.201* -0.02	*0.234* 0.29
Constant	***0.028***** **17.10** ***0.016****	***0.024*****	*0.371*	***0.006****	*0.901*	*0.887*	.	*0.203*	***0.028*****	*0.966*	*0.471*
Obs.	428	428	428	428	428	428	428	428	428	428	428
Adj. R-squared	0.216	0.0545	0.058	0.0297	0.0451	0.0225	0.0672	0.0403	0.0467	0.0478	0.0393

* = p-value < .10; ** = p-value < .05; *** = p-value < 0.001

Source: Author analysis of CFRC data (2015)

Results about **education** support the hypothesis that this variable **is not related with financial knowledge**. For all the education levels there is not a statistically significant difference when financial literacy is measured by the overall score. This result is confirmed in all the regressions that used specific financial literacy measures, except the case of 'payments', where education is positively related with financial knowledge.

The need to differentiate the analysis of financial literacy by taking into account the chance that individuals can be more knowledgeable on some financial topics than others is quite clear looking at the results about income in the Italian sample. **Income is not a relevant variable**[7] when financial literacy is assessed by the overall score that summarizes knowledge on several topics, but it plays a relevant role in explaining financial literacy of individuals in the case of 'stock investments', and 'interest rates'. In these cases the income groups above 1,500€ seem to be more knowledgeable than others. At the same time, the level of income is not relevant in explaining financial literacy in the cases of 'inflation', 'bonds', and 'payments'.

Looking at the big picture it can be noted how the explanatory power of the socio-demographic variables changes from time to time, when financial literacy is measured by using a different set of items. If knowledge on 'payments' is explained by age and education, knowledge about 'loans and debts' is related to age and gender, and knowledge on 'bonds' is not related at all with the households' income, gender, and age.

Results from Italy support the hypothesis that different groups of people tend to develop different financial literacy according to their needs. It follows that one needs to differentiate the measures of financial literacy to better understand the financial literacy of specific target groups, and keep in mind that financial literacy should be assessed referring to specific financial knowledge needs.

7.4 Conclusions

The big picture that comes out from the analysis of financial literacy in Italy shows how the average **financial knowledge of Italians is low**. The average score for the whole set of questions is 47%. This result is pretty close to the case of Germany and better than France (39%) and the UK (43%).[8] This low level of financial knowledge is combined with a **gender gap**, with males scoring on average 9 percentage points better than females. If this is a result already found in other countries, in the case of Italy there are not exceptions when single areas of knowledge related to single topics are taken into account.

The **most critical areas** of knowledge concern the investment decision areas. 'Bonds' (26%), 'stock investments' (36%), and 'retirement and insurance' (34%) are the knowledge areas with the lowest scores. The top score areas are the ones on 'bank accounts' (74%) and 'payments' (62%). These results are in line with the evidence from other countries.

The **correlation** between scores on different areas of knowledge is low. The areas that show the highest correlation are 'bank accounts' and 'loans and debts'

(0.52), while the lowest correlations concern 'bank accounts' and 'bonds' (0.15) and 'bonds' and 'inflation' (0.14). However, there are not null correlations as in the results from other countries. This result can be interpreted as a more homogeneous distribution of financial literacy between individuals in Italy compared with other countries.

Results from the **empirical analysis** based on regression models show how age matters in explaining financial literacy only for those older than 40 (and not for all the topic-based scores). The gender gap is confirmed and supports the hypothesis that males score better than females. The educational level is not a pivotal variable, and it seems to positively affect financial literacy only in the case of 'payments'. The results for the 'income' level are not clear, showing an explanatory power only in a few cases.

Notes

1 The sample of respondents has been organized by IPSOS (www.ipsos.it/).
2 The sum of correct answers to the 50 questions naturally has a range of 0–50. This score has been normalized on a 0–100 scale in order to be more easily interpreted as a percentage. This standardization of the score has been applied to all the financial literacy measures in order to facilitate comparison between scores.
3 According to the Eurostat data (2014) the homeownership rate in Italy in 2014 was 73.1%. This value is much higher than in other European countries such as France (65.0%), the UK (64.4), and Germany (52.5%), and even higher than the average of the European Union (70.0%). Source: http://ec.europa.eu/eurostat (last accessed March 2017).
4 World Bank website: http://databank.worldbank.org/data/reports.aspx?source=1228 (last accessed October 2017).
5 The rates of residents between 15 and 24 years old with a bank account for other European countries are the following: Germany (98.8%), France (96.6%), Spain (97.6), Sweden (99.7%), the UK (98.9%). The Euro area rate is 94.8%. Source: World Bank (http://databank.worldbank.org/data/reports.aspx?source=1228).
6 The rates of residents older than 25 with a bank account for other European countries are the following: Germany (93.7%), France (78.9%), Spain (84.7%), Sweden (98.6%), UK (90.8%). The Euro area rate is 80.5%. Source: World Bank (http://databank.worldbank.org/data/reports.aspx?source=1228).
7 The only exception is the 4,000€+ income group, with a significance level at 5%.
8 For details see the previous chapters.

Reference

CFRC- Consumer Finance Research Center (2015). Survey on Consumers' Financial Literacy in Italy. www.consumer-finance.org/

8 Financial literacy in Spain

8.1 Introduction

This chapter presents the results from a survey promoted by the Consumer Finance Research Center (CFRC) in 2015 with the aim to assess financial literacy in Spain. Data have been collected with the support of the Instituto de Estudios Financieros (IEF)[1] using the questionnaire developed by the CFRC whose full description is available in §4.2 of this study. In the first part of the chapter there is an overview of financial literacy based on the financial literacy scores of the whole sample, with a different analysis of the results based on the full set of items on financial literacy and analysis of financial literacy on specific areas of knowledge. In the second part of the chapter are reported the results of a set of regression analysis based on different measures of financial literacy.

8.2 The characteristics of financial literacy in Spain

The data collected by the survey of the CFRC in Spain amount to 148 observations. Data were collected by an online platform from Spanish adults (18+ years old). The small sample size and the overrepresentation of respondents from the city of Barcelona or the surrounding area represent two potential sources of bias that have to be taken into account in the analysis of the data. At the same time, the big percentage of high-educated people[2] can be another limitation on the chance to generalize the results from the sample.

Looking at the big picture of financial literacy in Spain, reported in Figure 8.1, the average overall score based on the 50 financial literacy questions in the questionnaire is quite a bit bigger than in other countries. On average the respondents provided a correct answer in 62% of the questions (Germany 49%, Italy 47%, the UK 43%, France 39%). If the chance that the sample does not represent the whole Spanish population affects the comparability with other countries, an analysis of financial literacy among different areas of knowledge is still feasible.

Still referring to the average score to the full set of 50 financial literacy questions, it can be noted how the presence of a gender gap, which represents a feature of other countries, is confirmed also in Spain. Males scored on average

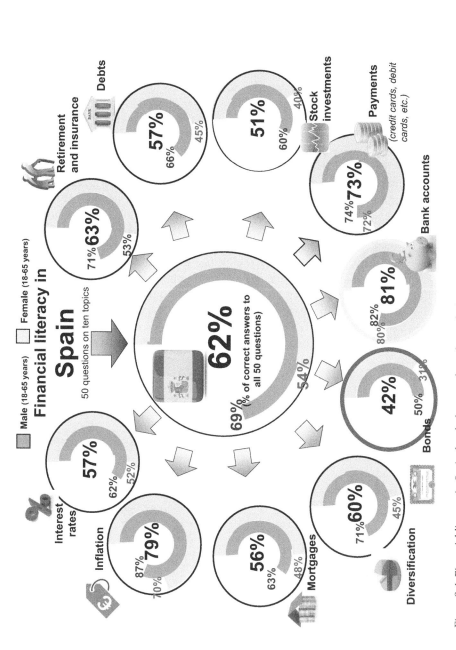

Figure 8.1 Financial literacy in Spain: break down and gender analysis

Source: Author analysis of CFRC data (2015)

15 percentage points better than females. While the average score for males is 69% of correct answers, the score for females is just 54%.

The volatility of the topic-based scores around the overall scores (62%) shows how financial literacy in the Spanish sample reaches an outstanding 81% score in the case of 'bank accounts', and drops to 42% in the case of 'bonds'. Even in this case, the fact that the best performing area is the one on 'bank accounts', and the worst performing area concerns 'bonds', confirms the similarities with other countries. 'Diversification' and 'stock investments' are the two areas where the gender gap is even stronger than the average. The mean score for 'diversification' (60%) is the average between 71% of correct answers for males and a 45% score for females. This 26 percentage point difference is the biggest one. However, also for knowledge on 'stock investments' the gap between the male score (60%) and the female score (40%) is quite big. In the meantime, areas as 'bank accounts' (82% male, 80% female) and 'payments' (74% male, 72% female) seem to show no substantial differences related with genders. Results from other areas show a very good knowledge about 'inflation' (79%) and good scores on 'retirement and insurance' (63%), 'debts' (57%), 'interest rates' (57%), and 'mortgages' (56%).

The chance that financial literacy can change between different age groups has been addressed referring to ten age groups (Figure 8.2).

The distribution of financial literacy across ages is quite flat. The age group 46–50 is the one with the best score (72.5%), and the two closest groups show high performances too (41–45 year-olds 64.4%, 51–55 year-olds 64%). The 25–30 years-old group scored at 66.6%, which represents the second best performance.

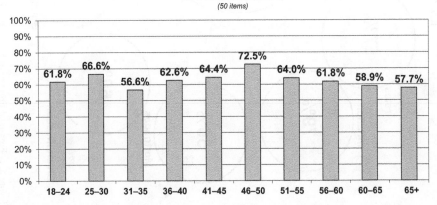

Figure 8.2 Overall score of financial literacy in Spain: break down by age

Source: Author analysis of CFRC data (2015)

The good performance of the 25–30 years-old group is confirmed in the analysis of financial literacy that takes into account knowledge about 'interest rates' (Figure 8.3).

Having correct answers in 72% of cases is quite above the average (57%) and is 7 percentage points higher than the second best score, achieved by those older than 65 (65%). The fact that the oldest groups scored pretty well (60–65 year-olds 61.8%, 65+ 65%) and that the 18–24 year-old respondents showed the lowest average score (47.5%) can be the related with the low interest rates scenario of European countries in the last decade. While the young generation never experienced a scenario with high interest rates, the elderly can have developed a better knowledge by having memories of past experiences. This hypothesis is coherent with the positive trend of financial literacy scores by age groups, with the only exception of the 25–30 years-old group.

Knowledge about 'inflation' (Figure 8.4) seems to be quite familiar to the respondents. The 25–30 year-olds are still the best performing age group (90%), followed by the 60–65 (85.5%) and the 41–45 (84.2%). The fact that even the lowest group (65+) scored around 70% proposes a flat distribution of the financial literacy scores between age groups.

The results of financial literacy on 'mortgages' (Figure 8.5) show some differences between age groups.

The 25–30 year-olds are not anymore the most knowledgeable group (score 60%), which is represented by the 46–50 years-old group, with an average score of 75%. The fact that the 31–35 years-old group, which represents the least knowledgeable, scored 47% highlights big differences (28 percentage points)

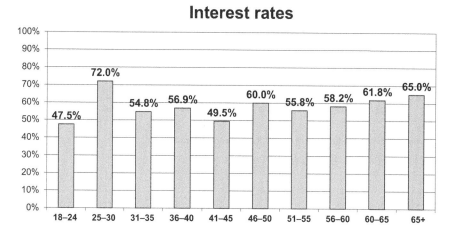

Figure 8.3 Financial literacy in Spain: knowledge on interest rates

Source: Author analysis of CFRC data (2015)

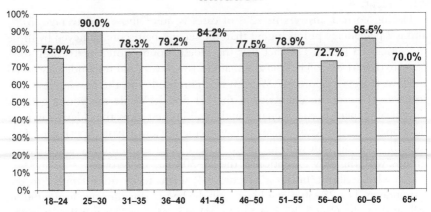

Figure 8.4 Financial literacy in Spain: knowledge on inflation

Source: Author analysis of CFRC data (2015)

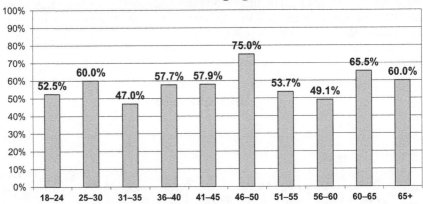

Figure 8.5 Financial literacy in Spain: knowledge on mortgages

Source: Author analysis of CFRC data (2015)

between age groups. Even in this case, there is not a clear trend between the age groups.

The financial literacy score on 'diversification' confirms the 46–50 years-old group as one of the most knowledgeable (Figure 8.6).

However, the difference of score values with other groups, as with the 51–55s (67.4%) and the 25–30s (66%), is pretty small. The less knowledgeable about

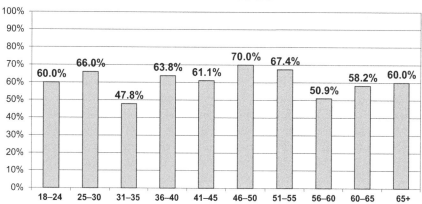

Figure 8.6 Financial literacy in Spain: knowledge on diversification

Source: Author analysis of CFRC data (2015)

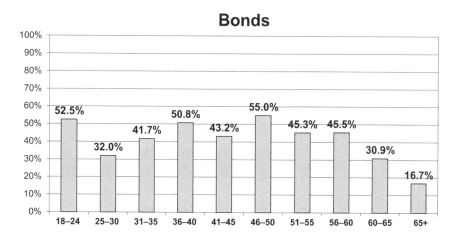

Figure 8.7 Financial literacy in Spain: knowledge on bonds

Source: Author analysis of CFRC data (2015)

'diversification' seem to be the 31–35s (47.8%) and the 56–60s (50.9%), and there is not a clear trend by ages.

The 46–50 years-old group is the most knowledgeable also when financial literacy is measured on 'bonds' (Figure 8.7).

Its average score, equal to 55% of correct answers, means that there is almost a wrong answer for each correct answer. The fact that bonds and, generally speaking, the investment decision related topics are the most complicated for financial consumers is not a shocking result, but the number of correct answers drops in some cases below one correct answer of three (e.g. 32% for 25–30 years-old group, 30.9% for the 60–65s), and arrives at a minimum of 16.7% for those older than 65.

Results on knowledge of 'stock investments' (Figure 8.8) confirm the positive correlation between investment related topics (e.g. diversification, stock investments, etc.) that have been already found in other countries.

The 46–50s (70%) and the 25–30s (68%) are the most knowledgeable groups. With respect to the results on 'stock investments' it seems that the financial knowledge of the last groups (56–60s score 54.5%, 60–65s score 30.9%, and 65+ score 45%) is less than that of the younger groups (18–24s score 62.5%, and 25–30s score 68%). If a clear downward trend does not exist, data from single age groups show two of the top three scores in the first two (young) groups.

Results on financial literacy about 'bank accounts' are extraordinarily positive (Figure 8.9).

If the fact that people tend to know bank accounts better than other financial products is quite usual, the average score of 81% of correct answers is not. Those older than 65 achieved the best average score in the age group comparison, with 88.3% of correct answers. At the same time, the functioning of bank accounts seems to be quite well known also by the 18–24s (85%), the 25–30s (84%), the 31–35s (81.7%), the 41–45s (85.3%), and the 46–50s (87.5%), who all scored above the threshold of four correct answers of five questions, equal to 80% of correct answers.

Very good performances are reported also in the case of 'payments' (Figure 8.10), where an outstanding 92.5% of correct answers was achieved by the 46–50 years-old group.

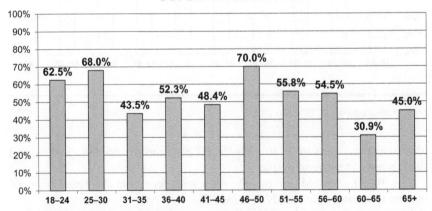

Figure 8.8 Financial literacy in Spain: knowledge on stock investments

Source: Author analysis of CFRC data (2015)

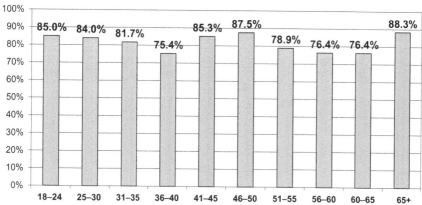

Figure 8.9 Financial literacy in Spain: knowledge on bank accounts

Source: Author analysis of CFRC data (2015)

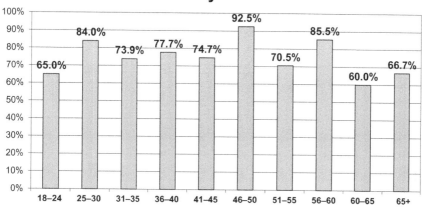

Figure 8.10 Financial literacy in Spain: knowledge on payments

Source: Author analysis of CFRC data (2015)

Compared with the financial literacy scores on 'bank accounts', the ones on 'payments' are less homogeneous, with a gap between the top score (92.5%) and the bottom score (60%) larger than 30 percentage points.

The analysis of financial literacy between age groups, when financial literacy is referred to 'loans and debts', shows results that confirm the previous cases (Figure 8.11). The 25–30s and the 41–45s are the most financially literate

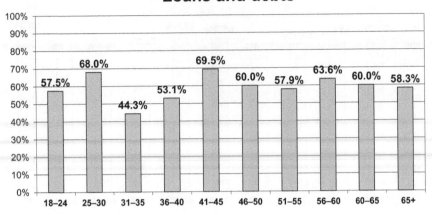

Figure 8.11 Financial literacy in Spain: knowledge on loans and debts

Source: Author analysis of CFRC data (2015)

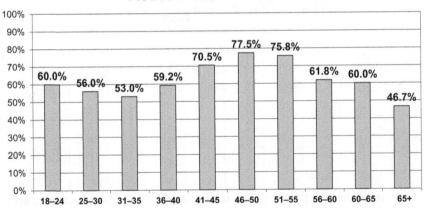

Figure 8.12 Financial literacy in Spain: knowledge on retirement and insurance

Source: Author analysis of CFRC data (2015)

groups. However, in this case the last (older) groups seem to be more skilled overall about indebtedness than the younger groups.

The case of financial literacy on 'retirement and insurance' (Figure 8.12) is probably the only one with a clear age group difference, represented by a hump shape.

With the only exception of the first two age groups (18–24s 60%, 25–30s 56%) the others show an increasing (average) score up to the 46–50 years-old group, and a declining (average) score for the last groups. The fact that the elderly are less knowledgeable about retirement and insurance related topics can be explained by the fact that these groups are already in retirement age or are pretty close to going on retirement, so they are not called to "plan for their future" because they should have already done so. In addition, the fact that the older groups belong to generations that received the benefit of more generous welfare systems (compared with the new generations) can explain why they are less knowledgeable about pension planning. The reduction of coverage provided by the public pillars of the pension systems requires people to be more active in planning their retirement decisions, so they have more incentive to learn about these topics.

The differences between the financial literacy scores based on single topics suggest to analyze the correlation between these scores. The results of the correlation analysis are reported in Table 8.1.

The correlation of single topic scores with the overall score is biassed by definition by the fact that the five questions of each topic-based score are included in the 50 questions of the overall score. However, even bearing this in mind, the topic-based scores are highly correlated with the overall score. In most of the cases the correlation is above 0.60, with a peak of 0.84 (financial literacy score on 'stock investments') and other values above 0.70 ('loans and debts' 0.79, 'retirement and insurance' 0.75, 'diversification' 0.73).

Table 8.1 Correlation between financial literacy scores (overall score, and the ten scores on single areas of knowledge)

	FL_OVERALL	FL_Interest rates	FL_Inflation	FL_Mortgages	FL_Diversification	FL_Bonds	FL_Bank accounts	FL_Payments	FL_Stock investments	FL_Loans and debts	FL_Retirement and insurance
FL_OVERALL	1										
FL_Interest rates	0.57	1									
FL_Inflation	0.69	0.35	1								
FL_Mortgages	0.60	0.41	0.44	1							
FL_Diversification	0.73	0.43	0.56	0.42	1						
FL_Bonds	0.64	0.13	0.30	0.22	0.44	1					
FL_Bank accounts	0.59	0.28	0.36	0.27	0.23	0.24	1				
FL_Payments	0.60	0.29	0.28	0.28	0.18	0.34	0.46	1			
FL_Stock investments	0.84	0.40	0.52	0.39	0.57	0.56	0.43	0.54	1		
FL_Loans and debts	0.79	0.36	0.53	0.49	0.47	0.45	0.46	0.46	0.62	1	
FL_Retirement and insurance	0.75	0.36	0.46	0.27	0.60	0.40	0.47	0.35	0.61	0.58	1

Source: Author analysis of CFRC data (2015)

Looking at the correlations between single topic scores, the scores between 'stock investments' and 'loans and debts', 'stock investments' and 'retirement and insurance', and 'loans and debts' and 'retirement and insurance' show the highest correlations (0.62, 0.61, 0.58). The fact that all of them involve a long-term perspective can be a possible explanation. In other cases, the correlation between scores is not so high. The financial literacy scores on 'bonds' is strongly correlated only with 'stock investments' (0.56) and 'retirement and insurance' (0.40), while the correlation is pretty low with 'interest rates' (0.13), 'mortgages' (0.22), and 'bank accounts' (0.24). These results seem to confirm the hypothesis that the financial literacy of individuals tends to be different when different areas of knowledge are taken into account, and they are coherent with the assumption that people develop financial literacy according to their needs and their personal financial experiences.

8.3 The determinants of financial literacy in Spain

To test the hypothesis that financial literacy is developed by people according to their need of knowledge and so can differ from individual to individual when assessed on different financial topics, a set of regression models has been used. Both the overall financial literacy score and each of the ten topic-based scores were included as dependent variables in different regression models.[3] The main socio-demographic characteristics of the individuals (age, gender, education, and income) were used as explanatory variables. Some descriptive statistics of the sample variables are reported in Table 8.2, while the results of the empirical analysis are included in Table 8.3.

Table 8.2 Descriptive statistics of the Spanish sample

	#	%
Age		
18–24	8	5.4%
25–30	10	6.8%
31–35	23	15.6%
36–40	26	17.7%
41–45	19	12.9%
46–50	8	5.4%
51–55	19	12.9%
56–60	11	7.5%
60–65	11	7.5%
65+	12	8.2%
Gender		
Male	85	57.4%
Female	62	41.9%
n.a.	1	0.7%

	#	%
Education		
Primary school or less	4	2.7%
Middle school	5	3.4%
High school	14	9.5%
Some college	11	7.4%
University degree	72	48.6%
Post-graduate degree	41	27.7%
n.a.	1	0.7%
Income		
Less than 500€ a month	14	9.5%
500€–749€ a month	4	1.4%
750€–1,000€ a month	9	3.0%
1,000€–1,499€ a month	29	9.8%
1,500€–1,999€ a month	29	9.8%
2,000€–2,999€ a month	35	11.8%
3,000€–3,999€ a month	16	5.4%
More than 4,000€ a month	4	1.4%
n.a.	8	2.7%
Total	**148**	**100%**

Source: Author analysis of CFRC data (2015)

The analysis of the **age** of respondents in explaining the financial literacy in the Spanish sample provides different results. **The effect of age on the overall score is null**. None of the age groups seems to differ from the reference 18–24 years-old reference group. The same result comes from analysis of the topic-based financial literacy scores in the cases of 'interest rates', 'investments', 'bonds', 'stock investments', 'loans and debts', and 'retirement and insurance'. At the same time, there are some cases where the differences between the financial literacy scores of different age groups are statistically significant. In the case of 'inflation' almost all the age groups differ from the 18–24 years-old reference group. The analysis of the coefficients reports that the 31–35 years-old group is the one that differs more (coef. 3.83) from the 18–24 group. In the case of 'mortgages' there are some age groups that differ substantially from the reference group, but in this case the biggest differences are between the 18–24 (reference group) and the 60–65 years-old groups (coef. 3.55), and with the 46–50 group (coef. 3.19). There are no differences between the reference group (18–24) and the 25–30s, 31–35s, and 36–40s. The case of 'payments' confirms the differences between the 18–24 group and those older than 45. As in the cases of 'inflation' and 'mortgages' in the case of 'payments' the 46–50 (coef. 3.86), the 51–55 (coef. 2.10), and the 56–60 (coef. 2.36) groups are the ones that differ from the reference group and that know on average more about these areas of knowledge.

Table 8.3 Results from regression models on financial literacy scores

	Total (50 items)		Interest rates (1|2|3|4|5)		Inflation (1|2|3|4|5)		Mortgages (1|2|3|4|5)		Investments (1|2|3|4|5)		Bonds (1|2|3|4|5)		Bank accounts (1|2|3|4|5)		Payments (1|2|3|4|5)		Stock investments (1|2|3|4|5)		Loans and debts (1|2|3|4|5)		Retirement and insurance (1|2|3|4|5)	
	Coef.	p-value	Coef.	p-value	Coef.	p-value	Coef.	p-value	Coef.	p-value	Coef.	p-value	Coef.	p-value	Coef.	p-value	Coef.	p-value	Coef.	p-value	Coef.	p-value
Age (years)																						
18–24	(Ref. group)		(Ref. group)		(Ref. group)		(Ref. group)		(Ref. group)		(Ref. group)		(Ref. group)		(Ref. group)		(Ref. group)		(Ref. group)		(Ref. group)	
25–30	2.58	0.589	0.15	0.896	3.67	**0.005****	0.60	0.591	0.14	0.919	−0.47	0.702		.	0.22	0.853	0.82	0.567	−0.11	0.929	−0.18	0.888
31–35	1.52	0.733	−0.56	0.611	3.83	**0.002****	1.03	0.333	−0.61	0.640	0.01	0.992		.	1.46	0.213	−0.65	0.619	−0.10	0.936	−1.36	0.244
36–40	−1.21	0.786	−1.24	0.261	3.06	**0.011***	1.23	0.251	−0.20	0.878	−0.02	0.985		.	1.50	0.201	−1.02	0.432	−0.58	0.633	−1.64	0.166
41–45	2.71	0.551	−1.36	0.214	3.57	**0.004****	1.93	**0.077***	−0.32	0.806	−0.35	0.772		.	1.23	0.293	−0.85	0.506	1.88	0.130	−0.07	0.955
46–50	6.58	0.180	−0.89	0.468	2.88	**0.027****	3.19	**0.007****	0.96	0.488	0.34	0.796		.	3.86	**0.006****	1.44	0.312	0.55	0.678	1.12	0.418
51–55	1.28	0.784	−0.66	0.566	2.44	**0.055***	1.88	**0.098***	−0.05	0.970	−0.34	0.800		.	2.10	**0.090***	0.08	0.950	0.40	0.758	0.14	0.909
56–60	−0.47	0.923	−1.34	0.276	1.36	0.279	1.08	0.367	−1.22	0.363	−0.21	0.872		.	2.36	**0.062***	−0.81	0.550	0.53	0.682	−1.10	0.390
60–65	3.92	0.375	0.33	0.755	3.33	**0.006****	3.55	**0.002****	0.42	0.721	−0.60	0.614		.	0.74	0.506	−1.17	0.336	1.56	0.195	−0.05	0.963
65+	−0.32	0.948	−0.21	0.860	1.59	0.203	2.16	**0.067***	−0.34	0.799	−2.01	0.124		.	0.48	0.700	−0.54	0.689	1.04	0.421	−2.60	**0.042****
Gender																						
Female	(Ref. group)		(Ref. group)		(Ref. group)		(Ref. group)		(Ref. group)		(Ref. group)		(Ref. group)		(Ref. group)		(Ref. group)		(Ref. group)		(Ref. group)	
Male	9.32	**0.000*****	1.08	**0.005****	2.03	**0.000*****	1.92	**0.000*****	2.33	**0.000*****	1.28	**0.001****		.	1.36	**0.001****	1.57	**0.000*****	2.23	**0.000*****	1.81	**0.000*****
Education																						
Primary school or less	(Ref. group)		(Ref. group)		(Ref. group)		(Ref. group)		(Ref. group)		(Ref. group)		(Ref. group)		(Ref. group)		(Ref. group)		(Ref. group)		(Ref. group)	
Middle school	8.19	0.170	2.65	**0.064***	2.06	0.166	2.22	0.118	0.81	0.564	0.23	0.870		.	8.60	**0.000*****	2.10	0.126	0.26	0.853	−1.90	0.241

	(1)	(2)	(3)	(4)	(5)	(6)	(7)	(8)	(9)	(10)	(11)
High school	7.26 / 0.144	1.86 / 0.123	4.20 / 0.001**	2.17 / 0.082*	-0.03 / 0.978	-0.59 / 0.629	(Ref. group)	5.76 / 0.000***	2.61 / 0.028**	2.13 / 0.081*	-3.70 / 0.012**
Some college	1.76 / 0.725	2.80 / 0.023**	1.73 / 0.170	1.07 / 0.368	-0.75 / 0.540	-1.34 / 0.267	.	3.46 / 0.005**	1.91 / 0.102	0.48 / 0.681	-2.78 / 0.061*
University degree	6.38 / 0.155	2.14 / 0.044**	2.22 / 0.042**	2.49 / 0.017**	0.01 / 0.994	-0.12 / 0.903	.	6.03 / 0.000***	2.74 / 0.009**	1.06 / 0.316	-3.37 / 0.012**
Post-graduate degree	10.86 / 0.025**	2.70 / 0.020**	2.69 / 0.024**	3.77 / 0.001**	0.02 / 0.988	0.25 / 0.820	.	6.30 / 0.000***	3.40 / 0.003**	2.56 / 0.027**	-2.16 / 0.127
Income											
Less than 500€											
500€ to < 750€	(Ref. group)	(Ref. group)	(Ref. group)	(Ref. group)	(Ref. group)	(Ref. group)	(Ref. group)	(Ref. group)	(Ref. group)	(Ref. group)	(Ref. group)
750€ to < 1,000€	3.33 / 0.546	-2.15 / 0.105	3.53 / 0.023**	0.86 / 0.495	-1.25 / 0.336	0.16 / 0.904	.	5.62 / 0.001**	1.73 / 0.258	2.09 / 0.123	-1.92 / 0.181
1,000€ to < 1,500€	0.470 / -0.66	0.420 / -0.80	0.170 / 0.77	0.761 / -0.21	0.429 / 0.80	0.175 / -0.91	.	3.23 / 0.002**	1.77 / 0.087*	0.50 / 0.599	0.59 / 0.562
1,500€ to < 2,000€	0.822 / 2.14	0.309 / 0.35	0.258 / -1.08	0.771 / 0.71	0.303 / -0.76	0.220 / -0.72	.	0.85 / 0.265	0.18 / 0.819	1.26 / 0.408	0.10 / 0.894
2,000€ to < 3,000€	0.471 / 5.37	0.666 / 1.41	0.190 / 0.12	0.319 / 0.89	0.319 / 0.89	0.320 / 0.14	.	1.68 / 0.265	0.38 / 0.819	1.06 / 0.109	0.73 / 0.894
3,000€ to < 4,000€	0.077* / 8.28	0.084* / 0.90	0.887 / 0.77	0.454 / -0.39	0.261 / 2.23	0.849 / 0.71	.	0.040** / 1.22	0.636 / 1.37	0.109 / 1.06	0.344 / 1.76
4,000€+	0.013** / 9.15	0.005** / 3.40	0.423 / 2.12	0.620 / -1.25	0.010** / 0.66	0.400 / -0.10	.	0.131 / 1.59	0.089* / 2.21	0.182 / 2.38	0.021** / 2.24
	0.057*	2.12	0.887	0.454				0.076** / 1.93	0.013** / 3.05	0.010** / 3.11	0.009** / 2.24
Constant	14.23 / 0.032**	0.009** / 3.40	0.154 / 2.12	0.255 / -1.25	0.574 / 0.66	0.937 / -0.10	.	0.131 / 1.93	0.024** / 3.05	0.010** / 3.11	0.462 / 0.92
Obs.	138	138	138	138	138	138	138	138	138	138	138
Adj. R-squared	0.3452	0.1234	0.1786	0.1158	0.1458	0.0911	0.1249	0.2054	0.1587	0.1965	0.1643

* = p-value < .10; ** = p-value < .05; *** = p-value < 0.001

Source: Author analysis of CFRC data (2015)

The analysis of **gender** in Spain not only provides additional evidence that there is a gender gap in favour of males (who are able on average to provide correct answers more frequently than females), but represents a case where this gap is quite big. Looking at the case of the overall score, the coefficient for 'male' is 9.32. The gender effect is confirmed for all of the regression models that analyzed financial literacy using items on specific topics.

The role of **education** in explaining financial literacy requires us to stress some differences. The analysis of the overall score reports that only individuals with a post-graduate degree (coef. 10.86) differ from the reference group (primary school) in a statistically significant manner, while results for other educational groups are not significant. But if we analyze financial literacy referring to 'interest rates' or 'payments', the difference with the reference group (primary school) becomes relevant for all the other educational groups.[4] What is interesting is that the values of the coefficients are not always increasing from low to high education level. A quite clear role of education in explaining financial literacy comes out also in the case of 'inflation', 'mortgages', 'stock investments', and 'loans and debts', while none of the education related variables are relevant in explaining financial literacy on 'investments' and 'bonds'.

Results about the **income** level are quite interesting. While in other countries the household income was not relevant in most of the cases, in the Spanish sample it seems to be a different scenario. The overall score is positively related with all the income groups beyond 2,000€ a month. The 2,000€–3,000€ (coef. 5.37), 3,000€–4,000€ (coef. 8.28), and 4,000€+ (coef. 9.15) groups are all significant in explaining the financial literacy of individuals. When financial literacy is assessed with topic-based questions, the explanatory power of income still remains in the case of 'interest rates', 'stock investments', 'loans and debts', and 'retirement and insurance'. Moreover, in the case of 'payments' the level of income not only is relevant for the highest income ranges, but some differences exist even between the reference group (less than 500€) and other low income groups (500€–750€ coef. 5.62, 750€–1,000€ coef. 3.23). In all cases the relationship between income and financial literacy is positive.

8.4 Conclusions

The presence of different potential biases in the sample[5] does not allow us to arrive at general conclusions that can be extended beyond the sample and suggests that we need to treat carefully results from empirical analysis, although the analysis of the data confirms several results found in other countries. A **gender gap** is evident, with males scoring much better than females. This result is consistent for all the financial literacy measures, with the only exception of scores related to 'bonds' and 'stock investments', where males still perform better than females in the financial knowledge tests, but with a difference between average scores that is pretty small.

At the same time, the evidence that **'bonds' and 'stock investments' are the most critical areas of knowledge** for individuals comes out from the

Spanish sample as it did from other countries. The fact that **financial knowledge on 'bank accounts' and 'payments' involves the two most well known areas** is another similarity between Spain and the other countries analyzed in the study. The analysis of correlation contributes to support the idea that individuals develop financial literacy according to their need of knowledge. The low correlation between financial knowledge in different areas is coherent with the results of the statistical analysis of the data (regression models) that change consistently when different areas of knowledge are used to assess financial literacy.

Notes

1 The Instituto de Estudios Financieros (Institute for Financial Studies) is a financial education institute on banking and finance. Established in 1990, during the development project of the Barcelona Stock Exchange (Bolsa de Barcelona) and the creation of the Spanish derivative market (Mercado de Futuros Financieros – MEEF), the IEF has the mission to provide financial education and support the financial literacy of both the local community (Catalonia) and the whole Spanish country. For further information: www.iefweb.org.
2 Of the respondents 75% have a university degree.
3 In the case of the overall score (whose range of values is from zero to 50) an OLS model has been used. For the topic-based score, the fact that these scores go from zero to five recommended the use of an ordered logistic regression model.
4 The only exception is for the educational group "some college" in the case of "interest rates", where the p-value is above .10.
5 The main potential source of concern regards the sample size, the overrepresentation of respondents from a specific geographical area of the country, and the big percentage of high-educated respondents.

Reference

CFRC- Consumer Finance Research Center (2015). Survey on Consumers' Financial Literacy in Spain. www.consumer-finance.org/

9 Financial literacy in Sweden

9.1 Introduction

This chapter analyzes financial literacy in Sweden. Data come from a survey of the Consumer Finance Research Center (CFRC) administrated in 2015 to a sample of Swedish adults (18+ years old). The structure and the contents of the questionnaire are the same as those of other national surveys of the CFRC, described in §4.2 of this study. Even the sample size (636 observations) is comparable with that of the other surveys.

In the first part of the chapter some descriptive statistics will be presented, taking into account differences across genders and age groups. The second part will show the results of regression analysis used to stress the role of the socio-demographic profile of the Swedish in explaining their financial literacy.

9.2 The characteristics of financial literacy in Sweden

The assessment of financial literacy in Sweden starts from an overview about the average financial literacy scores in the whole sample, based on the sum of correct answers to the 50 questions included in the sample, and from the use of ten topic-based scores that count the number of correct answers to a set of five questions each. Results from this overview are reported in Figure 9.1.

The average percentage of correct answers to the full set of 50 financial literacy questions is 39%. With regard to males vs. females, some differences come out, with males (46%) scoring 12 percentage points better than females (34%). This gender gap is quite big and is bigger than the ones highlighted in Germany (11 points), Italy (nine points), the UK (seven points), and France (six points). However, as in previous cases, the overall score risks being misleading in explaining the financial literacy of the sample, and an analysis of financial literacy referring to single topics is recommended to realize how knowledgeable the Swedish are about finance.

The average score about 'interest rates' is 23%. That means one correct answer for every four questions. As in the overall score, the gender gap is strong with males scoring 29% and females 20%. This gap arrives, in the case of 'inflation', at 21 percentage points. While males are able to give a correct answer two times

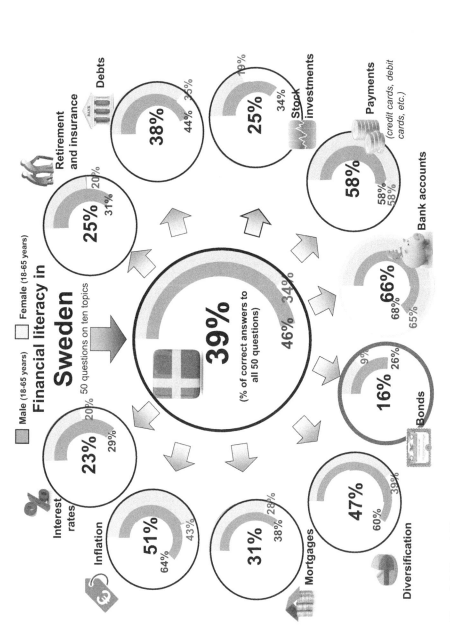

Figure 9.1 Financial literacy in Sweden: break down and gender analysis

Source: Author analysis of CFRC data (2015)

of three (score 64%), females are below the threshold of one (correct answers) of two (score 43%). At the same time, the financial literacy score on 'inflation' shows a big difference as compared with the one on 'interest rates', supporting the need to measure financial literacy on different topics and stressing the risk of biassed conclusions about how much individuals are financially literate when a summary measure is preferred. Financial literacy about 'mortgages' is different from either the score on 'Interest rates' (23%) or the score on 'Inflation' (51%), with an average score of 31%. The gender gap is clear even in this case, with males scoring 38% and females 28%, but it is the analysis of financial literacy about 'diversification' that shows the biggest distance between the male average score (60%) and the female score (39%). The average score of 47% is other evidence that the Swedish sample shows a lot of volatility in the topic-based financial literacy scores. In the case of 'bonds' the average response rate is only 16%. This score is evidence of a lack of knowledge that sees males answer only one question of four (financial literacy score 26%), while females' score on 'bonds' does not reach 10% (score 9%). Switching from 'bonds' to 'bank accounts' there is a difference of 50 percentage points, with an average financial literacy score equal to 66%. This result is interesting not just because it is quite far from the previous one, but also because the gender gap seems to disappear with males and females achieving almost the same scores (68% for males, 65% for females). This is even more true in the case of 'payments', where the 58% average score matches with the average scores for males (58%) and females (58%). However, when financial literacy is assessed by items related with 'stock investments' the percentage of correct answers falls to 25%, and the gender gap is quite relevant (15 percentage points) with males scoring better than females. These results are quite similar with financial literacy scores on 'retirement and insurance', where an average score of 25% is between the males' score of 31% and the females' score of 20%. Finally financial literacy about 'debts' is pretty close to the overall average score (39%), with an average percentage of correct answers equal to 38% and a gender gap of 9 percentage points (males 44%, females 35%).

The analysis of the financial literacy scores of **age groups** allows us to better understand the differences between youths, adults, and the elderly, and to test the hypothesis that financial literacy changes across the different stages of life of individuals according to their financial needs and their experiences with finance.

The overall score, based on the 50 items of the questionnaire, shows a reverse U-shape (Figure 9.2), with the younger age groups (less than 36) scoring less than the adults, and the last age groups (more than 55) scoring better than the youths but worse than the adults, with the only exception being the 60–65 years-old group, which is the group with the best performance (47%). The gap between the worst group (18–24 years old) and the best one (60–65 years old) is around 17 percentage points. In absolute terms, the younger gave a correct answer to less than one of three questions, while the best group is close to a one of two correct answer rate. The increase of financial literacy with age in the first part of the age group distribution, with a smooth decrease for the last age groups, confirms results on financial literacy from previous studies.

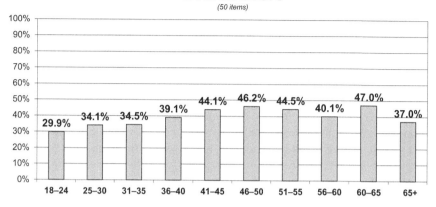

Figure 9.2 Overall score of financial literacy in Sweden: break down by age

Source: Author analysis of CFRC data (2015)

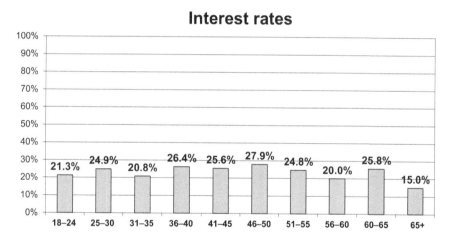

Figure 9.3 Financial literacy in Sweden: knowledge on interest rates

Source: Author analysis of CFRC data (2015)

The break down of the overall score in the ten topic-based scores shows how the conclusions about financial literacy of the Swedish adults considerably change when different areas of knowledge are taken into account. The 'interest rates' financial literacy score (Figure 9.3), based on five questions with different rates of difficulty, is on average 23%, which is quite different from the overall score of 39%. Looking at these scores for different age groups the big picture is an almost flat trend across ages, with just a small hump shape. The age groups of adults are still the best performing ones, but the differences between them and youths are pretty small. Those older than 65 are the only group that seems to show a gap with the other groups, with a score of 15%. The evidence that only one question of four has been answered right highlights a lack of knowledge across all the age groups.

Compared with the scores on 'interest rates', the results about financial literacy on 'inflation' are quite different (Figure 9.4).

If the 60–65 years-old group is the one with the best response rate (71.6% of correct answers), the other cases seem to be distributed according to a pyramidal shape. From the bottom age group (18–24 years old), which is also the worst performing group (34%), the percentage of correct answers about inflation increases to 41.4% (25–30 years-old group), then to 45.6% (30–35 years-old group) up to the 41–45 years-old group with a 67.5% of correct answers. The financial literacy of the older groups decreases systematically to 64.7% (46–50), 62.3% (51–55), 55.3% (56–60), and 45% (65+), with the only exception of the aforementioned 60–65 years-old group.

The flat trend across ages, found in the case of 'inflation', is a feature of the financial literacy scores distribution in the case of 'mortgages' (Figure 9.5).

The average (correct) response rate equal to 31% is quite representative of all the age groups. The youths tend to know less than the other groups, but the differences between ages are less evident than in other cases. The distance between the top performance (41.4%, 51–55 years-old group) and the bottom of the rank (24.2%, 25–30 years-old group) is around 17 percentage points.

Differences between age groups are quite evident when financial literacy is measured on 'diversification' of investments (Figure 9.6). Those older than 65, who were the age group with the worst performance in the case of 'interest rates', are clearly the most knowledgeable group when the diversification effect is the topic used to assess financial literacy. The 70% score is 8 percentage points

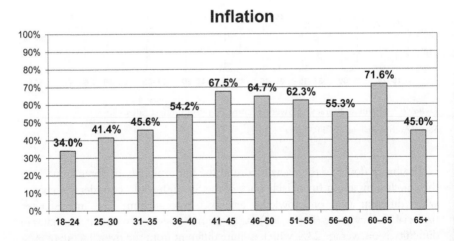

Figure 9.4 Financial literacy in Sweden: knowledge on inflation

Source: Author analysis of CFRC data (2015)

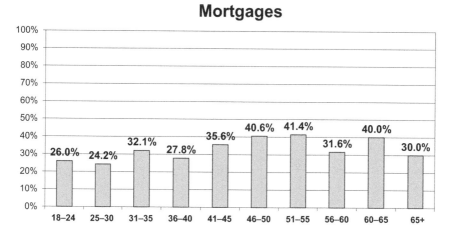

Figure 9.5 Financial literacy in Sweden: knowledge on mortgages

Source: Author analysis of CFRC data (2015)

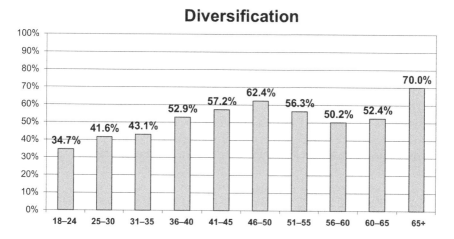

Figure 9.6 Financial literacy in Sweden: knowledge on diversification

Source: Author analysis of CFRC data (2015)

higher than the second best age group (the 46–50 years-old group), which scored 62.4%. The upward trend of the financial literacy scores in the first age groups of the distribution and the negative slope in the second part are similar to the case of financial literacy on 'inflation'.

Knowledge about 'bonds' is confirmed as the most critical area of knowledge for individuals (Figure 9.7).

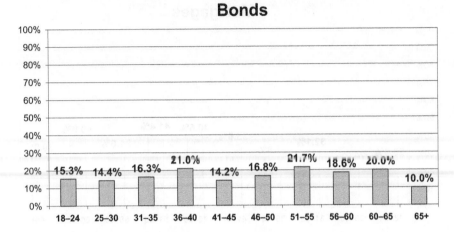

Figure 9.7 Financial literacy in Sweden: knowledge on bonds

Source: Author analysis of CFRC data (2015)

As in other countries (see the chapters on financial literacy in Italy and in the UK), in Sweden people struggle to understand the functioning of bonds and bond pricing. The mean score of 16% is the average of the percentages of right answers to the five questions, which is 10% for those older than 65, and is around only 20% (one question of five) for the best performing groups (36–40, 51–55, and 60–65 years-old groups).

The scenario is a bit more positive when financial literacy is assessed on 'stock investments' knowledge. Even if bonds and stocks are two areas of knowledge that belong to the same macro-area of saving and investment decisions, the scores related with stocks are better than the ones on bonds (Figure 9.8).

The outstanding results of the 25–30 years-old group, which scored on average at 52.5%, increase the average response rate on this topic to 25%. The big picture of financial literacy on stock investments by age groups is coherent with the hypothesis of financial literacy developed by experience, because – ignoring the 25–30 years-old group – there is a positive trend on the financial literacy scores, with the 60+ groups (60–65s and those older than 65) showing the best scores. The fact that even for these top performers the number of correct answers is just a bit more than one of three questions is a source of worry about the financial skills of the Swedish with regard to investment decisions.

The negative feeling about the preparedness of the Swedish about bonds and stocks is not confirmed by the financial literacy scores on 'bank accounts' (Figure 9.9).

An average score of 66% of right answers and the response rate distribution across age groups show how the functioning of bank accounts is quite

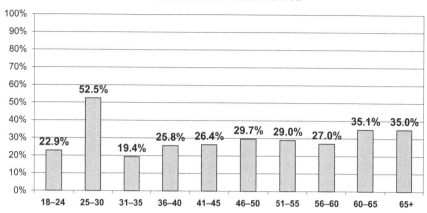

Figure 9.8 Financial literacy in Sweden: knowledge on stock investments

Source: Author analysis of CFRC data (2015)

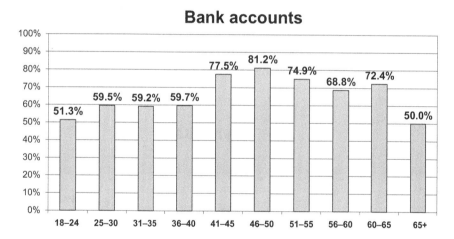

Figure 9.9 Financial literacy in Sweden: knowledge on bank accounts

Source: Author analysis of CFRC data (2015)

well known by the respondents. The 46–50 years-old group scored on average above 80%, which represents four correct answers of five questions. Even other groups scored pretty well, like the 41–50s (77.5%), the 51–55s (74.9%), and the 60–65s (72.4%). The 18–24s confirm their lack of knowledge compared with other groups, even if their score (51.3%) is better than the ones achieved in other cases.

The similarities between the financial literacy scores on 'bank accounts' and the scores on 'payments' (Figure 9.10) confirm the results of other countries.

The average score of 58% is a bit lower than the one on bank accounts, but still represents a positive result, especially when it is compared with other areas of knowledge. The volatility of the age group scores in the case of 'payments' is lower than the ones on 'bank accounts' with a top-to-bottom performance distance that is around 25 percentage points (44.2% for the 18–24 years-old group vs. 69.3% for the 60–65 years-old group), while the same value for the financial literacy scores on 'bank accounts' was above 31 percentage points (50.0% for those older than 65 vs. 81.2% for 46–50s).

Financial literacy on 'loans and debts' (Figure 9.11) shows an average score of 38%, pretty close to the average overall score (39%). The distribution of age group scores tends to confirm some of the previous results, with an upward trend in the first part, followed by a decrease in the second.

Knowledge about 'retirement and insurance' seems to be pretty low (Figure 9.12). On average the percentage of correct answers was 25%, like the score on 'stock investments' and just better than the score on 'bonds' (16%), which represent the most critical areas of knowledge in the sample. Another similarity that the scores on 'retirement and insurance' have with bond and stock scores is the flat distribution of scores of the age groups. As opposed to other cases, where age seems to make a difference, knowledge on retirement and planning seems to be equally distributed across age groups, with those older than 65 and those younger than 25 scoring lower than the others (10% for those older than 65, 18.7% for the 18–24s).

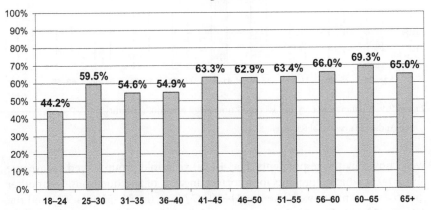

Payments

Figure 9.10 Financial literacy in Sweden: knowledge on payments

Source: Author analysis of CFRC data (2015)

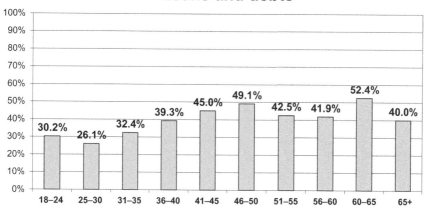

Figure 9.11 Financial literacy in Sweden: knowledge on loans and debts

Source: Author analysis of CFRC data (2015)

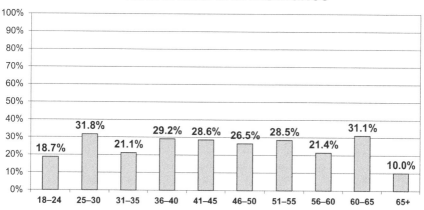

Figure 9.12 Financial literacy in Sweden: knowledge on retirement and insurance

Source: Author analysis of CFRC data (2015)

The differences that came out from the analysis of financial literacy scores based on different topics and the differences between age groups recommend an analysis of correlation between scores (Table 9.1).

The correlations between the topic-based scores and the overall score show how, on average, there is a high correlation between knowledge on single topics

Table 9.1 Correlation between financial literacy scores (overall score, and the ten scores on single areas of knowledge)

	FL_OVERALL	FL_Interest rates	FL_Inflation	FL_Mortgages	FL_Diversification	FL_Bonds	FL_Bank accounts	FL_Payments	FL_Stock investments	FL_Loans and debts	FL_Retirement and insurance
FL_OVERALL	1										
FL_Interest rates	0.54	1									
FL_Inflation	0.80	0.37	1								
FL_Mortgages	0.71	0.27	0.58	1							
FL_Diversification	0.81	0.42	0.63	0.51	1						
FL_Bonds	0.57	0.27	0.35	0.35	0.41	1					
FL_Bank accounts	0.74	0.33	0.51	0.45	0.53	0.23	1				
FL_Payments	0.71	0.31	0.50	0.42	0.50	0.28	0.68	1			
FL_Stock investments	0.75	0.34	0.51	0.45	0.59	0.50	0.45	0.43	1		
FL_Loans and debts	0.79	0.35	0.60	0.55	0.56	0.43	0.58	0.53	0.59	1	
FL_Retirement and insurance	0.69	0.35	0.49	0.47	0.50	0.38	0.43	0.40	0.55	0.51	1

Source: Author analysis of CFRC data (2015)

and the overall scores. In two cases – 'interest rates' and 'bonds' – the correlation with the overall score is below the average, even if in both cases it remains above 0.50 (0.54 for 'interest rates', 0.57 for 'bonds'). The correlations between scores based on single topics are still quite positive, even if some combinations have values of the correlation index below 0.30. The highest correlation is the one between 'payments' and 'bank accounts' (0.68). This result is not surprising, due to the close connection between the use of bank accounts and the use of payment tools (e.g. debit cards, credit cards, cheques, etc.). There is a good correlation also between 'diversification' and 'stock investments' (0.59), 'diversification' and 'inflation' (.63), and 'stock investments' and 'retirement and insurance' (0.55). The fact that these topics concern long-term investment decisions can be a possible explanation of these results.

9.3 The determinants of financial literacy in Sweden

In order to figure out how much financial literacy changes when assessed by using different topics and test the hypothesis that different groups of the population tend to develop more financial literacy in some areas of knowledge than others (according to their financial needs and their financial experiences) different regression analyses have been done. The 11 financial literacy measures (the overall score, plus each of the ten topic-based scores) have been used as dependent

variables, while a set of variables representing the socio-demographic characteristics of the respondents have been included as explanatory variables. These independent variables are (1) age, (2) gender, (3) education, and (4) income. If these
variables cannot completely explain the financial literacy of individuals, they can
shed light on the possible similarities between groups and test the hypothesis
that the degree of financial knowledge of individuals depends on the topics that
are included in the financial literacy assessment. A brief summary of the socio-
demographics of the Swedish sample is reported in Table 9.2.

Table 9.2 Descriptive statistics of the Swedish sample

	#	%
Age		
18–24	90	14.8%
25–30	85	14.0%
31–35	71	11.7%
36–40	59	9.7%
41–45	72	11.8%
46–50	68	11.2%
51–55	71	11.7%
56–60	43	7.1%
60–65	45	7.4%
65+	4	0.7%
Gender		
Male	269	44.2%
Female	305	50.1%
n.a.	35	5.7%
Education		
Primary school or less	3	0.5%
Middle school	60	9.4%
High school	276	43.4%
Some college	85	13.4%
University degree	175	27.5%
n.a.	37	5.8%
Income*		
Less than 8.000 SEK	89	14.0%
Between 8,000 and 15,000 SEK	68	10.7%
Between 8,000 and 15,000 SEK	42	6.6%
Between 15,000 and 22,000 SEK	83	13.1%
Between 22,000 and 30,000 SEK	131	20.6%
Between 30,000 and 38,000 SEK	84	13.2%
Between 38,000 and 45,000 SEK	19	3.0%
Between 45,000 and 55,000 SEK	15	2.4%
More than 55,000 SEK	10	1.6%
n.a.	95	14.9%
Total	**636**	**100%**

* 1 SEK ("Swedish Krona") = 0.104876€ (10,000 SEK = 1,048.76€)

Source: www.x-rates.com (exchange rate on Friday, October 6, 2017). Author analysis of CFRC data
(2015)

The different ranges of values of the overall score and the topic-based scores suggested the application of different regression models. The overall score is made by the number of correct answers to the 50 financial literacy questions. It follows that it represents an integer value that ranges between zero and 50. According to this, a linear regression model has been applied. The ten topic-based financial literacy scores count the number of correct answers to five questions, and their range is between zero and five. In these cases an ordered logistic regression model was considered more suitable to these variables. Results of these statistical analyses are summarized in Table 9.3.[1]

The statistical analysis provides interesting results.[1] Looking at **the overall score** and the explanatory power of age on this comprehensive financial literacy measure, it seems that there is a **gap between the 35+ and the younger groups**. Using the 18–24 years-old group as a reference point, the analysis shows that there are not statistically significant differences between this group and the other groups of those younger than 35 (25–30, 31–35). On the contrary, every group above that threshold shows significant differences in the level of financial literacy. The gap between the 18–24 years-old group and those older than 35 achieves its peak for the 46–50 years-old group (coef. 6.68). Values of coefficients for the 35+ groups tend to increase in the first groups (36–40 coef. 3.42, 41–45 coef. 3.92) and decrease after the 46–50 group (51–55 coef. 6.04, 56–60 coef. 6.00, 60–65 coef. 5.91), proposing a humped shape for the financial literacy score distribution across age groups. Only the 65+ years-old group seems to be not very different from the 18–24 reference group. This age effect is clear even in two other regression models – the one on 'bank accounts' and the one on 'loans and debts' – while in the case of 'mortgages' there is a gap of knowledge that is evident only for three age groups (46–50, 51–55, and 60–65). This age effect almost fades when financial literacy is measured on 'interest' and 'bonds'.

The typical **gender effect** of financial literacy studies is confirmed also in the case of Sweden. The overall score analysis shows a significant difference between males and females, with the latter providing fewer correct answers than males for the 50 questions on financial literacy of the questionnaire. This **gender effect is persistent** when financial literacy is assessed by questions on the same topic, with the only exception of knowledge on 'bank accounts'.

Results about the role of **education** in explaining financial literacy require some distinctions. When financial literacy is assessed using all 50 items (overall score), the attendance of some college (even without earning a degree) increases a lot the average financial literacy score (coef. 14.46) as does the achievement of a university degree (coef. 13.27). Lower levels of education do not seem to make a difference with respect to the reference group (primary school). What is interesting about education is that the positive effect of education on the financial literacy scores is even stronger and clearer when financial literacy is assessed by questions on 'interest rates' or questions on 'bank accounts'. On the other hand, the influence of education is not confirmed at all in the cases about 'mortgages', 'bonds', 'stock investments', 'loans and debts', and 'retirement and insurance'.

Table 9.3 Results from regression models on financial literacy scores

	Total (50 items)		Interest rates (1|2|3|4|5)		Inflation (1|2|3|4|5)		Mortgages (1|2|3|4|5)		Investments (1|2|3|4|5)		Bonds (1|2|3|4|5)		Bank accounts (1|2|3|4|5)		Payments (1|2|3|4|5)		Stock investments (1|2|3|4|5)		Loans and debts (1|2|3|4|5)		Retirement and insurance (1|2|3|4|5)	
	Coef.	p-value	Coef.	p-value	Coef.	p-value	Coef.	p-value	Coef.	p-value	Coef.	p-value	Coef.	p-value	Coef.	p-value	Coef.	p-value	Coef.	p-value	Coef.	p-value
Age (years)																						
18–24	(Ref. group)	.	(Ref. group)	.	(Ref. group)	.	(Ref. group)	.	(Ref. group)	.	(Ref. group)	.	(Ref. group)	.	(Ref. group)	.	(Ref. group)	.	(Ref. group)	.	(Ref. group)	.
25–30	-0.66	0.663	0.03	0.923	.	.	-0.40	0.218	.	.	-0.57	0.127	-0.02	0.950	.	.	-0.18	0.565	-0.09	0.777	0.14	0.665
31–35	0.12	0.942	-0.17	0.626	.	.	0.25	0.468	.	.	-0.19	0.618	0.00	0.994	.	.	**-0.58**	**0.097***	0.08	0.824	-0.16	0.655
36–40	**3.42**	**0.046****	0.45	0.230	.	.	-0.12	0.736	.	.	0.33	0.399	0.22	0.546	.	.	0.17	0.639	**0.80**	**0.028****	**0.73**	**0.046****
41–45	**3.92**	**0.016****	0.11	0.740	.	.	0.28	0.422	.	.	**-0.68**	**0.089***	**1.21**	**0.001****	.	.	-0.09	0.795	**0.92**	**0.008****	0.42	0.222
46–50	**6.68**	**0.000*****	**0.63**	**0.070***	.	.	**0.84**	**0.014****	.	.	-0.04	0.925	**1.58**	**0.000*****	.	.	0.44	0.195	**1.41**	**0.000*****	0.44	0.209
51–55	**6.04**	**0.000*****	0.30	0.399	.	.	**0.98**	**0.005****	.	.	0.32	0.411	**1.00**	**0.004****	.	.	0.37	0.286	**1.05**	**0.002****	**0.66**	**0.061***
56–60	**6.00**	**0.001****	0.28	0.485	.	.	0.37	0.346	.	.	0.53	0.223	**0.83**	**0.033****	.	.	**0.73**	**0.066***	**1.15**	**0.003****	0.27	0.503
60–65	**5.91**	**0.001****	0.21	0.592	.	.	**0.73**	**0.057***	.	.	-0.11	0.794	**0.83**	**0.033****	.	.	0.57	0.136	**1.69**	**0.000*****	0.64	0.100
65+	3.70	0.411	-0.28	0.747	.	.	0.34	0.706	.	.	-0.09	0.926	-0.42	0.640	.	.	0.95	0.316	1.05	0.330	-0.85	0.381
Gender																						
Female	(Ref. group)	.	(Ref. group)	.	(Ref. group)	.	(Ref. group)	.	(Ref. group)	.	(Ref. group)	.	(Ref. group)	.	(Ref. group)	.	(Ref. group)	.	(Ref. group)	.	(Ref. group)	.
Male	**5.46**	**0.000*****	**0.72**	**0.000*****	.	.	**0.58**	**0.000*****	.	.	**1.47**	**0.000*****	0.20	0.227	.	.	**1.20**	**0.000*****	**0.51**	**0.002****	**0.88**	**0.000*****

(Continued)

Table 9.3 (Continued)

	Total (50 items)		Interest rates (1|2|3|4|5)		Inflation (1|2|3|4|5)		Mortgages (1|2|3|4|5)		Investments (1|2|3|4|5)		Bonds (1|2|3|4|5)		Bank accounts (1|2|3|4|5)		Payments (1|2|3|4|5)		Stock investments (1|2|3|4|5)		Loans and debts (1|2|3|4|5)		Retirement and insurance (1|2|3|4|5)	
	Coef.	p-value	Coef.	p-value	Coef.	p-value	Coef.	p-value	Coef.	p-value	Coef.	p-value	Coef.	p-value	Coef.	p-value	Coef.	p-value	Coef.	p-value	Coef.	p-value
Education																						
Primary school or less	(Ref. group)		(Ref. group)		(Ref. group)		(Ref. group)		(Ref. group)		(Ref. group)		(Ref. group)		(Ref. group)		(Ref. group)		(Ref. group)		(Ref. group)	
Middle school	8.53	0.173	3.59	0.003**		.	0.41	0.765		.	-0.22	0.876	1.67	0.118		.	0.96	0.505	-0.29	0.895	0.72	0.606
High school	8.97	0.147	3.43	0.004**		.	0.55	0.685		.	-0.37	0.787	1.78	0.088*		.	0.91	0.521	0.00	1.000	0.45	0.744
Some college	14.46	0.021**	2.68	0.026**		.	1.08	0.433		.	0.30	0.826	2.51	0.018**		.	1.73	0.227	0.74	0.732	1.25	0.365
University degree	13.27	0.033**	2.84	0.018**		.	0.87	0.525		.	0.29	0.831	2.32	0.029**		.	1.96	0.170	0.41	0.851	1.13	0.413
Income																						
< 8,000 SEK	(Ref. group)		(Ref. group)		(Ref. group)		(Ref. group)		(Ref. group)		(Ref. group)		(Ref. group)		(Ref. group)		(Ref. group)		(Ref. group)		(Ref. group)	
8,000 to < 15,000 SEK	-1.23	0.473	-0.13	0.728		.	0.08	0.828		.	0.43	0.290	-0.19	0.594		.	-0.33	0.365	-0.30	0.426	-0.13	0.732
15,000 to < 22,000 SEK	-0.89	0.534	0.79	0.010**		.	-0.01	0.968		.	0.23	0.516	-0.02	0.953		.	-0.44	0.143	-0.49	0.110	-0.41	0.191
22,000 to < 30,000 SEK	-2.23	0.102	0.25	0.380		.	-0.14	0.638		.	0.01	0.965	-0.03	0.910		.	-0.65	0.026**	-0.67	0.020**	-0.18	0.544

	(1)	(2)	(3)	(4)	(5)	(6)	(7)	(8)	(9)	(10)	(11)
30,000 <38,000 SEK	-0.44	0.33	.	0.02	.	0.10	-0.04	.	-0.51	-0.44	0.04
38,000 to <45,000 SEK	*0.775* / 3.79	*0.311* / **1.13**	.	*0.942* / **1.41**	.	*0.798* / 0.84	*0.900* / 0.70	.	*0.114* / -0.01	*0.177* / 0.04	*0.909* / 0.83
45,000 to <55,000 SEK	*0.118* / -2.14	***0.034**** / 0.14	.	***0.005**** / -0.18	.	*0.111* / 0.20	*0.199* / -0.49	.	*0.985* / -0.12	*0.930* / **-1.42**	*0.104* / -0.13
55,000+ SEK	*0.399* / 3.67	*0.784* / 0.48	.	*0.716* / 0.58	.	*0.727* / **1.58**	*0.352* / 0.31	.	*0.809* / 0.92	***0.007***** / 0.13	*0.805* / 0.22
Constant	0.238 / 4.87 / *0.429*	*0.452*	.	*0.354*	.	***0.026*****	*0.671*	.	*0.162*	*0.841*	*0.730*
Obs.	533	533	533	533	533	533	533	533	533	533	533
Adj. R-squared	8.5744 / 0.0441	0.0441	0.0745	0.039	0.0644	0.0698	0.0472	0.0355	0.0625	0.0469	0.0474

* = *p-value* < .10; ** = *p-value* < .05; *** = *p-value* < 0.001

Source: Author analysis of CFRC data (2015)

The analysis of **income** is quite clear. Whatever the financial literacy measure is, the level of income in explaining the Swedish financial knowledge is **almost meaningless**. None of the income levels are significant when financial literacy is measured by the overall score, and the same result comes out from regression models based on financial literacy measures on 'bank accounts' and 'retirement and insurance'. In other cases, only a few of the income levels seem to be useful to predict the financial knowledge of individuals. These results confirm the ones from other studies, where household income was not considered a relevant variable in explaining financial literacy of individuals.

9.4 Conclusions

The average score in the financial literacy measures that take into account all 50 available items in Sweden is 39%. This result is quite low and represents the lowest result (with France) in the countries analyzed in the present study (Germany 49%, Italy 47%, the UK 43%, France 39%). The investment related areas of knowledge are also in Sweden the ones that show the worst performance in the financial literacy test. In the case of 'bonds' the average score was 16%; in the case of 'stock investments' it was 25%. There was also a very low score on 'interest rates' (23%), which in other countries did not represent a critical lack of knowledge. On the other hand, results on 'bank accounts' (66%) and 'payments' (58%) confirm that these are the areas of knowledge where individuals tend to score at their best.

The gender gap in Sweden exists – as in other countries – and seems to be wide. Looking at the overall score the gap between males (46%) and females (34%) is 12 percentage points, representing the largest distance between genders in all the countries of this study. What is interesting is that this huge gap of knowledge between genders almost disappears in the case of financial literacy on 'bank accounts' (male 68%, female 65%) and disappears altogether in the case of 'payments' (58% for both male and female).

The break down of financial literacy by age groups shows an almost flat trend in the case of the overall score, with just a small "hump" in the middle age groups. The distribution of financial literacy across age groups shows a small humped shape also in the case of 'inflation', 'diversification', 'bank accounts', and 'debts and loans', while no difference between age groups seems to exist in the case of financial knowledge on 'interest rates', 'mortgages', 'bonds', 'stock investments', and 'retirement and Insurance', which show a flat trend. Financial literacy about 'payments' is the only area with a positive trend, which suggests an increasing level of knowledge from the younger age group to the older.

The correlation between topic-based scores is high, especially between areas of knowledge that share some logical connections, such as the financial literacy measures based on 'diversification', 'stock investments', and 'inflation' – which are all topics related to the financial investment area.

The regression analysis, which tried to explain financial literacy using the socio-demographic characteristics of the Swedish respondents, confirms the intuitions from the descriptive statistics, with a clear gender gap (both in the overall score and in the single topic-based scores), a positive relationship between financial literacy and age (especially for those older than 35), and a marginal role for education (which shows a positive relationship with financial literacy only in the case of 'bank accounts' and 'inflation'). The fact that income is almost meaningless in explaining financial literacy confirms the evidence from other countries.

Note

1 The analysis of the Swedish data did not provide results in the case of 'inflation', 'investments', and 'payments', where the statistical model did not achieve a convergence.

Reference

CFRC- Consumer Finance Research Center (2015). Survey on Consumers' Financial Literacy in Sweden. www.consumer-finance.org/

Conclusions

The results from previous studies and the evidence from empirical analysis on several European countries gave the chance to test several hypotheses and increase knowledge about financial literacy. The first part of the study analyzed the concept of financial literacy and its contents, paying attention to the available methodologies to assess financial literacy. The chance that individuals with good knowledge about financial products and services, and who are aware about the main financial principles, might not be able to use that knowledge in order to make a financial decision reminds us how financial literacy is a concept that includes the ability to use financial knowledge, and highlights that financial knowledge itself is not enough to consider an individual as financially literate. At the same time **financial knowledge represents the core and fundamental component of financial literacy**. Individuals who are knowledgeable about finance might not be able to apply this knowledge, but individuals with a lack of knowledge on basic financial principles and unaware about the functioning of standard financial products should be considered as financially illiterate by definition, due to the fact that without financial knowledge any analysis of financial skills and attitudes in the application of financial knowledge is meaningless. Keeping in mind that financial knowledge represents the key element of financial literacy and represents a big part of the story this study tried to shed light on the assessment of financial literacy showing how **the analysis of different areas of financial knowledge, related to different financial topics, helps to assess the financial literacy of individuals** much more in detail than in previous studies (based on only a few items) and making some relevant distinctions about how ready people are to make financial decisions, being aware about the possible consequences of their actions.

A first conclusion of the study is that **financial literacy is a multidimensional concept**. Individuals can be knowledgeable and skilled in a certain domain and show a deep lack of knowledge in others. As with any kind of human capital, people tend to develop their knowledge and their abilities investing time and other resources when they perceive a clear utility from such investment. It follows that individuals with different financial status who have different financial needs will develop different financial literacy. People called to invest their savings will be motivated to learn about investment, while those who need to borrow will try to better understand the functioning of debt and loans. The results from the analysis of the data from the European countries are coherent with the idea that financial literacy is developed according to the different utility that individuals perceive about different financial topics. When financial literacy is assessed using answers to questions related to different financial topics the results about how financially literate people are dramatically change. So **financial literacy should be measured and assessed keeping in mind which financial decisions or financial behaviors represent the real aim of the study.** If financial knowledge on bonds and stocks can help to explain investment behaviors, the same knowledge should not be related to borrowing decisions because the degree of knowledge in the two areas for a certain individual can be quite different. This result paves the way to another conclusion about the number of items needed to assess the financial literacy of a target or a population. Assessing financial literacy by using a small number of items makes sense when financial literacy is used in studies that analyze general financial behaviors (e.g. risk attitude, planning for the future, etc.) but not in the case of a specific financial decision (e.g. participating in the stock market, borrowing by using credit cards, etc.). The risk of using a few items – especially when they are related to different financial topics – to assess the role of financial literacy in explaining the decision to take a specific action is to use a weak measure that jeopardizes the reliability of the results. A measure of financial literacy based on questions about both investment and borrowing will not work as a good measure in the case of either investment decisions or borrowing decisions. In both cases only some of the items are potentially useful to make the decision. The scenario is even worse if none of the questions investigate financial literacy on investment or borrowing. Studies with the aim to verify the role of financial literacy in making a financial decision should rely on "targeted measures" of financial literacy, where the logical connection between financial literacy and financial behavior is clear. People can be experts in a certain domain (e.g. investments) and not be knowledgeable in another (e.g. borrowing) due to the fact that they had to tackle only some financial issues and not others (e.g. they had a need to invest and no need to borrow). The presence or not of a certain financial need has to be taken into account in the assessment of the financial literacy of a specific individual. The risk in using a wide range of topics in the assessment of the financial literacy of a group is to underestimate the financial literacy of the individuals. They could be knowledgeable only on a subset of financial topics (each one could have developed knowledge in a different area of expertise), but they might not be considered as financially illiterate or be considered at risk of making wrong decisions if they are skilled in the financial areas they need to make a financial decision. A measure of financial literacy that relies on several different topics is based on the assumption that individuals should be prepared to make any financial decision, even if people with the need to be active in all the sectors of a financial system (e.g. investments, borrowing, insurance, etc.) are quite rare. At the same time, **A measure of financial literacy that would take into account different**

topics should be based on a reasonable number of items, to avoid the financial literacy on a certain topic being based on the answer to a single question, with the risk of treating an individual as an expert or as ignorant without any shade of judgement.

This conceptual framework was used in the empirical analysis of data from six European countries whose results were presented in part two of the study. What is clear is that when we assess financial literacy on a wide range of topics the conclusion is that **financial literacy in Europe is low**. The overall score, which summarizes the correct response rate to a set of 50 questions on ten different financial topics, shows that **Germany is the country with the best knowledge**, but this score reflects an average percentage of correct answers to the 50 questions of the survey equal only to 49%. A similar result is from Italy (47%), while the results in other countries are even lower. The average overall score in the UK was 43%, while in France and Sweden it was 39%. However, there is the need to analyze the results on financial literacy looking at the percentage of correct answers to the subsets of questions related to single financial topics. The areas of knowledge in the data were 'interest rates', 'inflation', 'mortgages', 'loans and debts', 'diversification', 'bonds', 'stock investments', 'bank accounts', 'payments', and 'retirement and insurance'. Looking at **financial literacy on 'bank accounts' and 'payments' the average scores are quite a bit more positive than the overall scores**. These two financial topics are the ones where (in all the countries) the respondents of the surveys scored at their best. The highest scores are from Germany ('bank accounts' 72%, 'payments' 67%), Italy (74% and 62%), and the UK (64% and 69%), followed by Sweden (66% and 58%) and France (66% and 52%). If these scores suggest the need to still work in order to improve the financial knowledge of local citizens, they can be considered as a positive result. On the contrary there are areas of knowledge where the average scores highlight a very critical scenario. The two areas with the **worst scores were the ones related with investment decisions** and knowledge about 'bonds' and 'stock investments'. If these two areas are the ones with the lowest scores in every country of the study, in the case of France the average score for financial literacy is particularly low with an average percentage of correct answers about 'bonds' equal to 19%, and an average score on 'stock investments' equal to 20%. These results can be translated in an average number of correct answers to the questions related to each topic barely equal to one correct answer of five questions. The results in the UK are almost the same with financial literacy on 'bonds' and 'stocks' respectively equal to 19% and 24%. The results from Sweden are not different, with a (average) percentage of correct answers equal to 16% for 'bonds' and 25% for 'stocks'. Results for Germany (24% 'bonds', 34% 'stocks') and Italy (26% 'bonds', 36% 'stocks') are more encouraging, even if they are still related to a very low performance, with response rates equal to one of four or one of three. The great distance between the best scores and the worst scores in every country confirms the need to measure financial literacy taking into account a specific topic and to not rely on summary measures that risk being too wide to effectively assess financial literacy with respect to a specific financial behavior.

The similarities between countries are not limited to the financial topics people know at their best and the ones people struggle the most to answer, but include **clear evidence of a gender gap**, with males performing better than females in almost all the financial literacy measures (the overall score and the topic-based scores). The presence of a gender gap has been found in almost all the previous studies on financial literacy, regardless of the country or the target of the population (e.g. youth, adults, elderly, etc.). Referring to the differences in the overall score – based on 50 items – the country with the biggest gender gap is Sweden, where the difference between the average male and female score is about 12 percentage points. However, the gap is quite large in Germany (11%) and Italy (9%) too, while the distance between males and females is smaller in the UK (7%) and France (6%). These results are not always so evident when single areas of knowledge (single financial topics) are used to assess financial literacy. For instance, the gender gap in the case of knowledge about 'payments' is not significant in the UK, Germany, France, and Italy. At the same time financial literacy on 'bank accounts' seems not to be affected by gender issues in Germany and Sweden, while in France a gender gap exists about 'bank accounts' but is (surprisingly) in favour of female respondents, who scored (on average) 10 percentage points better than males (average scores for male 61%, for female 71%).

The similarities between European countries include the relationship between financial literacy and education. Results suggest that there is a **positive relationship between financial literacy and people's education**, but this relationship is significant only between very low- and very high-educated individuals, with the attendance of university as a significant threshold. At the same time, some differences between countries exist, with a more relevant role of education in financial literacy in France compared to others, and with no evidence in Italy about any connection between education and financial literacy. What seems to be a common result in every European country in this study is that **income is not related with financial literacy**. With few exceptions for the very high income groups, on average people with different income are not showing (ceteris paribus) differences in their financial literacy. On the contrary **age has some relationship with financial literacy**. The common result shows a positive linear trend between financial literacy and the age of the individuals, even if this result is not consistent when different measures of financial literacy are used and when different countries are taken into account. The positive trend sometimes disappears, becoming a flat trend between age groups, suggesting that there are no differences across age groups. This flat trend was particularly evident in France. A more persistent result across financial topics and across countries is that the young age groups (those younger than 30) tend to be systematically less knowledgeable than those older than 50. If this result can be explained by the chance to learn by experience, it represents news if compared with previous studies – especially the ones from the US – where a "reverse U-shape" trend was typically found. A humped shape of the financial literacy distribution across age groups has been found only in Sweden, and only when financial literacy was assessed by the overall score.

Another interesting result concerns the **correlation between financial literacy measures** based on questions related to different topics. The hypothesis that people develop financial literacy according to their (perceived) financial needs is coherent with the results from the correlation matrix where each of the ten financial topic-based scores is related with the others. **Correlations are positive**, so knowledge on a certain financial topic is somehow related with the development of knowledge in other areas. This correlation is coherent with the assumption that some core competences in financial literacy exist (e.g. basic principles) and that – once you have developed these competences in a certain context – they can be applied to several other financial decisions. However, **the values of the correlation across financial knowledge scores on different financial topics can be quite different**, and there are **some areas that seem to be more correlated than others**, as there are also some countries where the distance between correlations across topic-based scores is wider. The country with the biggest gap between the highest and lowest values of correlation is the UK. The maximum correlation index across the financial literacy topic-based scores is 0.69 (correlation between knowledge on 'bank accounts' and 'payments'), and the minimum is 0.12 ('bonds' vs. 'interest rates'). The distance between these extreme values (0.57) is quite big and stresses how some areas of knowledge are more related to each other than others. This difference between extreme values of the correlation matrix is 0.51 in Germany (max. 0.53 'stock investments' vs. 'diversification'; min. 0.02 'bonds' vs. 'payments'), 0.49 in Spain (max. 0.62 'stocks' vs. 'loans and debts'; min. 0.13 'bonds' vs. 'interest rates'), 0.49 in France (max. 0.42 'inflation' vs. 'interest rates'; min. −0.07 'bonds' vs. 'bank accounts'), 0.45 in Sweden (max. 0.68 'bank accounts' vs. 'payments'; min. 0.23 'bonds' vs. 'bank accounts'), and 0.37 in Italy (max. 0.52 'bank accounts' vs. 'loans and debts'; min. 0.15 'bonds' vs. 'bank accounts').

Beyond these extreme values it is interesting how in the UK most of the correlations are below the 0.50 threshold (the aforementioned highest value of 0.69 is the only exception), and how in France seven of the 36 values of the correlation matrix were below 0.10, showing an almost uncorrelated scenario between financial literacy on different topics. On the contrary, in Sweden the correlation across financial literacy on single topics is quite high, with 16 of the 36 values of the correlation matrix above 0.50.

The differences across financial literacy measures based on different topics have been analyzed by regression models, whose results have been discussed in detail in the chapters of the second part of this work. The results from this empirical analysis confirm the differences in the assessment of financial literacy and the key role of the financial topics used in this process. At the same time, this analysis stresses the differences across countries and, at the same time, the presence of similarities in the financial literacy of the six European countries analyzed.

If the main aims of this study were (1) to improve knowledge about the assessment of financial literacy by comparing the results from the use of different measures of financial literacy based on different financial topics, and (2) to measure financial literacy in Europe by data on six countries, the will is to go forward in the study of financial literacy in Europe by an analysis of the connection between financial literacy and financial behaviors. The financial literacy measures developed in this study can help to better understand the role of financial literacy in the financial decision making process of individuals by testing the explanatory power of different measures on different financial behaviors. The motivation behind the present and future studies is based on the belief that a better understanding about the degree of the financial knowledge of European citizens can improve knowledge in the field of consumer finance and support regulators, policy makers, and consumer protection bureaus with regard to their duties by giving them a better understanding of financial consumers.

Appendix
Financial literacy items

In this section the 50 items used to assess financial literacy in the six European countries that were part of this study are listed. The items in this list are the ones from the UK. Some marginal changes in the questions or in the available options for the answers have been made when the survey in a different country was planned in order to make the questions best fit with the national context (e.g. currencies, legal framework, available products, etc.). The structure of the questions, the number of available options, the contents of the questions, and their difficulty remained unchanged in all the national surveys.

The financial literacy items represent the second of the three parts of the full questionnaire used by the Consumer Finance Research Center (CFRC) in its surveys. The other two parts regard the socio-demographic characteristics of the respondents (part I) and their financial behaviors and attitudes (part III). The decision to not include these parts in this section is motivated by the fact that the questions on the socio-demographic variables follow the standard structure of consumer finance surveys (age, gender, income, etc.) and the questions about financial behaviors were not discussed in this study.

The financial literacy questions are presented in the same sequence used during the data collection, and are organized by topics.

The questionnaire

Part I – Socio-demographic questions (questions 1–15) (omitted)

Part II – Financial literacy questions (questions 16–65)

Interest rates

16 Suppose you had £100 in a savings account and the interest rate was 2% per year. After 5 years, how much do you think you would have in the account if you left the money to grow?

- More than £102
- Exactly £102
- Less than £102

  - *Do not know*
  - *Prefer not to say*

17 Suppose you borrow £200 for two years from a bank that asks you to pay interest at 2% a year. After 2 years, how much do you think you would have to pay to settle your debt?

- More than £204
- Exactly £204
- Less than £204

  - *Do not know*
  - *Prefer not to say*

18 Suppose you had £100 in a savings account and the interest rate was 2% per year. After 5 years, how much do you think you would have in the account if you left the money to grow?

- More than £110
- Exactly £110
- Less than £110

  - *Do not know*
  - *Prefer not to say*

19 Suppose you had £100 in a savings account and the interest rate was 10% per year. After 2 years, how much do you think you would have in the account if you left the money to grow?

- £110
- £120
- £121

  - *Do not know*
  - *Prefer not to say*

20 What is the interest rate (the APR – annual percentage rate) of a loan where a lender gives you £100 and you have to pay back £110 after one month?

- 10%
- Around 120%
- More than 200%

  - *Do not know*
  - *Prefer not to say*

Inflation

21 Imagine that the interest rate on your savings account was 1% per year and inflation was 2% per year. After 1 year, how much would you be able to buy with the money in this account?

- More than today
- Exactly the same amount as today
- Less than today

    - *Do not know*
    - *Prefer not to say*

22 Imagine that the interest rate on your savings account was 4% per year and inflation was 4% per year. After 1 year, how much would you be able to buy with the money in this account?

- More than today
- Exactly the same amount as today
- Less than today

    - *Do not know*
    - *Prefer not to say*

23 Imagine you deposit £100 in your savings account. If after one year the balance on your account (including the interest) is £104 and the inflation rate during the last year was 5%, how rich do you think you are compared to one year before?

- More rich
- Exactly as rich as one year before
- Less rich than one year before

    - *Do not know*
    - *Prefer not to say*

24 If your bank will pay 4% a year on the £100 balance in your savings account, how much inflation would you expect if you think that you will maintain your purchasing power after 2 years?

- 0% a year
- No more than 4% per year
- No more than 8% per year

    - *Do not know*
    - *Prefer not to say*

25 In the last year the inflation rate was 20%. If today the price of a London Underground ticket is £2.40, how much was the price one year ago?

- £1.92
- £2.00

- £0.48
    - *Do not know*
    - *Prefer not to say*

Mortgages

26 A 15-year mortgage typically requires higher monthly payments than a 30-year mortgage, but the total interest paid over the life of the loan will be less.

- True
- False
    - *Do not know*
    - *Prefer not to say*

27 Compared to a 15-year mortgage, if you want to reduce the total interest paid over the life of a loan, which of the following mortgages would you have to prefer?

- A 30-year mortgage
- A 20-year mortgage
- A 10-year mortgage
    - *Do not know*
    - *Prefer not to say*

28 For a 15-year mortgage which of the following options will minimize the total interest paid over the life of the loan?

- Annual payments
- Semi-annual payments
- Monthly payments
    - *Do not know*
    - *Prefer not to say*

29 Consider a 15-year mortgage where you can choose between monthly payments and six-month payments. If after 5 years you would like to close the mortgage in advance, which one would result in the lowest final payment?

- Monthly payment mortgage
- Six-month payment mortgage
- Both of them would make people pay the same amount
    - *Do not know*
    - *Prefer not to say*

30 To reduce the payments (instalments) of a 15-year mortgage with six-month payments, which of the following is a good option?

- • Reduce the maturity of the loan, switching to a 10-year mortgage
- • Increase the frequency of the payments switching to monthly payments
- • Reduce the collateral

    - • *Do not know*
    - • *Prefer not to say*

Investments (diversification)

31 Buying a single company's stock usually provides a safer return than a stock mutual fund.

- • True
- • False

    - • *Do not know*
    - • *Prefer not to say*

32 Compared with an investment in stocks, the risk of investing in stock mutual funds is . . .

- • . . . equal
- • . . . greater
- • . . . smaller

    - • *Do not know*
    - • *Prefer not to say*

33 In a stock mutual fund, when the number of stocks issued by different companies increases, what happens to the investor's risk?

- • Increase
- • Decrease
- • Nothing: it is the same

    - • *Do not know*
    - • *Prefer not to say*

34 Which of the following investment options fits well for investors that want to double their money in a very short term?

- • Money market mutual fund
- • Stock mutual fund
- • Single stock investment

    - • *Do not know*
    - • *Prefer not to say*

35 Suppose you invested £1,000 one year ago in a well diversified stock mutual fund. If the performance of the stock market index (in which the

fund invested its money) during the same period has been +5%, what return do you expect from your investment?

- Less than £5
- More than £500
- Around £50

  - *Do not know*
  - *Prefer not to say*

Bonds

36 If interest rates rise, what will typically happen to bond prices?

- They will rise
- They will fall
- They will stay the same
- There is no relationship between bond prices and the interest rates

  - *Do not know*
  - *Prefer not to say*

37 Is there a relationship between interest rates and bond prices?

- Yes, when interest rates fall bond prices fall
- Yes, when interest rates fall bond prices rise

  - No, there is no relationship
  - *Do not know*
  - *Prefer not to say*

38 If you expect a drop in the interest rate what is a good investment strategy?

- Buy a bond
- Sell a bond
- Hold a bond

  - *Do not know*
  - *Prefer not to say*

39 Buying a bond is a good strategy if you think that...

- ...stock indices will rise
- ...interest rates will fall
- ...inflation will rise

  - *Do not know*
  - *Prefer not to say*

40 If you expect a rise in the interest rate what is the worst investment strategy?

- Buy gilts that mature in less than a year (new issue)
- Buy gilts with two to ten year maturities (new issue)

- Buy gilts that mature between 10 and 30 years in the future (new issue)

  - *Do not know*
  - *Prefer not to say*

Bank accounts

41 You have an "overdraft" on your bank account if...

- ...you use more money than you have in your account
- ...you receive interest on your deposit from the bank
- ...you pay by cheques

  - *Do not know*
  - *Prefer not to say*

42 What do you NOT need to access your bank account in the case of e-banking (or "Internet banking")?

- A user ID (or Username) and a password
- A device connected to Internet (computer, tablet, etc.)
- Your passport

  - *Do not know*
  - *Prefer not to say*

43 If the balance of your bank account is zero and you issue a cheque...

- ...your account will be automatically closed by the bank
- ...the cheque will be paid only if you have an overdraft facility
- ...your credit score will drop for sure

  - *Do not know*
  - *Prefer not to say*

44 Which of the following scenarios does NOT apply to e-banking (or "Internet banking")?

- Access to bank services and information 24 hours a day
- Large use of cash transaction (withdrawals and deposits)
- Access to bank services from abroad

  - *Do not know*
  - *Prefer not to say*

45 If the balance of your account over a full year has been zero, your bank ...

- ...cannot charge you any fee
- ...will close your account

- ... will send you a bank statement anyway

  - *Do not know*
  - *Prefer not to say*

Payments

46 What kind of card lets you buy something now and pay for it in the future?

- Debit card
- Credit card
- Pre-paid card

  - *Do not know*
  - *Prefer not to say*

47 If you have no money in your bank account and you cannot have an overdraft, which of the following payment options do you have to buy something in a shop?

- Cheques (without any cheque guarantee card option)
- Debit card
- Pre-paid card

  - *Do not know*
  - *Prefer not to say*

48 Which of the following payment options will affect the balance of your bank account?

- Cash
- Pre-paid card
- Debit card

  - *Do not know*
  - *Prefer not to say*

49 If you pay the balance of your credit card in full at the end of the month, do you have to pay interest?

- Yes
- No
- Only if you used your credit card abroad

  - *Do not know*
  - *Prefer not to say*

50 Do you think it is possible to use a credit card to withdraw cash from an ATM?

- No, you can do it with a debit card, but not with a credit card
- Yes, but you will be charged

- Yes, and it will be free of charge

  - *Do not know*
  - *Prefer not to say*

Savings and (stock) investments

51 Ignoring the case of the issuer defaulting, which of the following investment products guarantees the reimbursement of invested capital?

- Stocks
- Bonds
- Stock mutual funds

  - *Do not know*
  - *Prefer not to say*

52 Using cash for saving, which of the following risks do you avoid?

- Risk of inflation
- Risk of theft
- Risk of liquidity

  - *Do not know*
  - *Prefer not to say*

53 Which is the standard measure of the default risk of a bond issuer?

- Rating
- APR
- Benchmark

  - *Do not know*
  - *Prefer not to say*

54 If the same company issues short-term and long-term bonds, typically the
interest rate of the long-term bond is . . .

- . . . higher
- . . . the same
- . . . lower

  - *Do not know*
  - *Prefer not to say*

55 You can invest £100 in stock A or in stock B. The value of stock A is £50,
the value of stock B is £1. Comparing the risk of buying two £50 A-shares
with the risk of buying one hundred £1 B-shares we can say that. . .

- . . . the risks are the same
- . . . the two £50 A-shares investment is riskier

- •   . . . the one hundred £1 B-share investment is riskier

  - • *Do not know*
  - • *Prefer not to say*

Loans and debts

56 Typically, if you buy things (mobile-phones, TVs, etc.) using credit you will pay . . .

- •   . . . more than paying cash
- •   . . . the same amount of paying cash
- •   . . . less than paying cash

  - • *Do not know*
  - • *Prefer not to say*

57 Everything else being equal, if the maturity of a mortgage is longer, the instalments will be . . .

- •   . . . the same
- •   . . . smaller
- •   . . . bigger

  - • *Do not know*
  - • *Prefer not to say*

58 Suppose you need to borrow £100. Bank "A" allows you to repay £10 a month for twelve months. Bank "B" allows you to repay £120 after twelve months. Which is the loan with the higher APR?

- •   Bank "A"
- •   Bank "B"
- •   The APRs of the two loans are the same

  - • *Do not know*
  - • *Prefer not to say*

59 With a mortgage, if the value of the collateral is higher. . .

  . . . the interest rate is lower
  . . . the interest rate is higher
  . . . the interest rate does not change

  Do not know
  Prefer not to say

60 Which of the following pay back options for a £100 debt has the highest APR?

- •   £102 after one week
- •   £105 after one month

- £110 after two months

  - *Do not know*
  - *Prefer not to say*

Retirement and planning (insurance)

61 Compared with a non-smoker, the premium for the healthcare insurance plan of a regular smoker ...

- ... is higher
- ... is lower
- ... is the same

  - *Do not know*
  - *Prefer not to say*

62 Taxation on pension fund income is ...

- ... higher than taxes on earned income
- ... equal to taxes on earned income
- ... lower than taxes on earned income

  - *Do not know*
  - *Prefer not to say*

63 Do you think that the performance of financial markets can affect the performance of a pension fund?

- No, they have no relationship
- Yes, they are positively related (when the market goes up the value of pension funds goes up too)
- Yes, they are negatively related (when the market goes up the value of pension funds goes down)

  - *Do not know*
  - *Prefer not to say*

64 Feeding a pension fund with £10,000 a year for 10 years is equal to feeding it £5,000 a year for 20 years.

- True
- False, to feed a pension fund with £10,000 a year for 10 years is better
- False, to feed a pension fund with £5,000 a year for 20 years is better

  - *Do not know*
  - *Prefer not to say*

65 Which of the following sentences on retirement investment products is wrong?

- They benefit from a tax-shield
- The money in these products can be distrained on by creditors

- Even a small withdrawal for any reason is prohibited by the law until the retirement of the worker

  - *Do not know*
  - *Prefer not to say*

Part III – Financial behaviors and attitudes questions (questions 66–101)
(*omitted*)

Index